Praise for *The Local Economy Solution*

"Michael Shuman is the world's most knowledgeable cheerleader and observer of efforts to promote local economies, and each of his books offers essential, practical information to advance the cause. In *The Local Economy Solution*, he shines light on new models of local economic development that are self-financing—an all-important innovation, given that many localist efforts currently depend on subsidies and grants. If you have any interest in furthering your region's economic resilience, this brilliant, clear book should be at the very top of your reading list."
—**Richard Heinberg**, senior fellow, Post Carbon Institute

"Michael Shuman, long a pioneer in the local-economy movement, has pushed the conversation forward once again, showcasing new tools for localists, new business models for entrepreneurs, and new development strategies for economic planners. A terrific resource for cash-strapped communities building wealth and resilience from the ground up."
—**Judy Wicks**, author of *Good Morning, Beautiful Business*, cofounder of BALLE, and founder of the White Dog Café

"I have been impressed by Michael Shuman for a long time, but *The Local Economy Solution* sent my admiration soaring. He shows the genuine myopia and 'legal corruption' of the prevailing model of state and local economic development, then he explains the new localist model taking hold in many enlightened communities; and, best of all, he brings his engaging writing skills to describe the real people and enterprises that are bringing this model to life. His book is both an inspiration and a handbook for doing real development."
—**James Gustave Speth**, author of *America the Possible: Manifesto for a New Economy* and *Angels by the River: A Memoir*

"First rate! Cutting-edge strategies for community-sustaining business development without bribing big corporations—by one of the nation's leading and most creative localists!"
—**Gar Alperovitz**, author of *What Then Must We Do?: Straight Talk About the Next American Revolution*

"Michael Shuman has done it again. In *The Local Economy Solution*, he shreds the conventional wisdom about economic development and local business initiatives that rely on grants. His Rx: self-financing 'pollinator' businesses. This one is sure to make some waves!"

—**Amy Cortese**, author of *Locavesting: The Revolution in Local Investing and How to Profit from It*

"Michael Shuman's first book showed us a vision of community economics and empowerment; his latest book, *The Local Economy Solution*, examines some of the best examples of community-based enterprise as he teaches us how to bring vision to reality. An excellent and welcome addition to my library that builds on Michael's extraordinary expertise and insights."

—**Jed Emerson**, coauthor of *The Impact Investor: Lessons in Leadership and Strategy for Collaborative Capitalism*

"The emerging localization movement owes a huge debt of gratitude to Michael Shuman. A visionary thinker with decades of hard-won, grass-roots experience, he offers not only a clear picture of a very different economic landscape but the steps we need to take—as individuals and as communities—to move from here to there."

—**Helena Norberg-Hodge**, founder and director of Local Futures and producer and codirector of *The Economics of Happiness*

"Shuman's book is critically important to anyone who cares about genuine economic development. Neither left nor right politically, it's positive and encouraging, while confronting head-on the challenges of the approach he has advocated for years. Unlike many economic-development books that can be tedious, this one is engaging, even fun to read, like a good story told over a beer—but a practical story that will help communities reach a resilient future."

—**Michael Kinsley**, manager, Rocky Mountain Institute

"Michael Shuman is a pioneering voice for an economic development model that is sustainable and truly democratic. I've read all his books, and this is the best one yet. Do yourself a favor and absorb his brilliance."

—**Kevin Danaher**, cofounder of Global Exchange, Green Festivals, and Fair Trade USA

THE LOCAL ECONOMY SOLUTION

ALSO BY MICHAEL H. SHUMAN

Local Dollars, Local Sense
How to Shift Your Money from Wall Street
to Main Street and Achieve Real Prosperity

The Small Mart Revolution
How Local Businesses Are Beating the Global Competition

Going Local
Creating Self-Reliant Communities in a Global Age

Towards a Global Village
International Community Development Initiatives

Security without War (co-written with Hal Harvey)
A Post-Cold War Foreign Policy

Citizen Diplomats (co-written with Gale Warner)
Pathfinders in Soviet-American Relations

THE LOCAL ECONOMY SOLUTION

How Innovative, Self-Financing
"Pollinator" Enterprises
Can Grow Jobs and Prosperity

— MICHAEL H. SHUMAN —

CHELSEA GREEN PUBLISHING
WHITE RIVER JUNCTION, VERMONT

Editor: Joni Praded
Project Manager: Bill Bokermann
Copy Editor: Deborah Heimann
Proofreader: Helen Walden
Indexer: Peggy Holloway
Designer: Melissa Jacobson

Printed in the United States of America.
First printing May, 2015.
10 9 8 7 6 5 4 3 2 1   15 16 17 18

Chelsea Green Publishing is committed to preserving
ancient forests and natural resources. We elected to print
this title on 100-percent postconsumer recycled paper,
processed chlorine-free. As a result, for this printing, we
have saved:

63 Trees (40' tall and 6-8" diameter)
28 Million BTUs of Total Energy
5,470 Pounds of Greenhouse Gases
29,668 Gallons of Wastewater
1,986 Pounds of Solid Waste

Chelsea Green Publishing made this paper choice because
we and our printer, Thomson-Shore, Inc., are members
of the Green Press Initiative, a nonprofit program dedicated to supporting authors, publishers, and suppliers
in their efforts to reduce their use of fiber obtained
from endangered forests. For more information, visit:
www.greenpressinitiative.org.

Environmental impact estimates were made using the Environmental Defense Paper Calculator.
For more information visit: www.papercalculator.org.

Our Commitment to Green Publishing

Chelsea Green sees publishing as a tool for cultural change and ecological stewardship. We strive to align our book manufacturing practices with our editorial mission and to reduce the impact of our business enterprise in the environment. We print our books and catalogs on chlorine-free recycled paper, using vegetable-based inks whenever possible. This book may cost slightly more because it was printed on paper that contains recycled fiber, and we hope you'll agree that it's worth it. Chelsea Green is a member of the Green Press Initiative (www.greenpressinitiative.org), a nonprofit coalition of publishers, manufacturers, and authors working to protect the world's endangered forests and conserve natural resources. *The Local Economy Solution* was printed on paper supplied by Thomson-Shore that contains 100% postconsumer recycled fiber.

Library of Congress Cataloging-in-Publication Data
Shuman, Michael.
The local economy solution : how innovative, self-financing
"pollinator" enterprises can grow jobs and prosperity / Michael H. Shuman.
     pages cm
 ISBN 978-1-60358-575-0 (paperback) -- ISBN 978-1-60358-576-7 (ebook)
1. Economic development. 2. Community development. 3. Communities. 4.
Small business. 5. Economic development--United States. I. Title.

HD82.S4983 2015
338.6'420973--dc23

                              2015003853

Chelsea Green Publishing
85 North Main Street, Suite 120
White River Junction, VT 05001
(802) 295-6300
www.chelseagreen.com

To mom, in honor of her ninety-third year of life,
who taught me how to speak truth to power—with good humor.

Contents

Acknowledgments

T his is my fourth book on local economies, and the arguments that follow inside necessarily build on the previous three. That means thanking again the several hundred people I acknowledged in the earlier books—thinkers, advocates, practitioners, businesspeople, investors, civil servants, teachers, and journalists who collectively call themselves "the local economy movement." Their names, once ridiculously few, are now way too many to repeat, so let me just say to all of you who have played any role in this movement, large or small, a heartfelt thank you. This book is for you.

Most of the material here comes from interviews I conducted with the entrepreneurs leading three dozen "pollinators" (self-financing businesses with an economic-development mission of supporting other local businesses) between January and December of 2014. I'm extremely grateful for their making time for our conversations, sharing important documents, and reading drafts for accuracy. There's no need to name them here; you will meet them all inside these pages.

Kate Poole, who so ably assisted me with *Local Dollars, Local Sense*, took charge of about a third of these interviews, and delivered fine work under tremendous time pressure. Anthony Price also provided valuable research assistance.

Joni Praded at Chelsea Green helped me frame the book and provided great feedback at every stage. I'm especially grateful that she laughed when I said I would write this book in three months, and showed mercy when it wound up taking twelve. She also helped me coin the term "pollinators."

Several sections of the book were drawn from earlier works and then revised. Many thanks to the Business Alliance for Local Living Economies (BALLE) for allowing me to republish a profile I did of Kimber Lanning and Local First Arizona, and to the Wallace Center for Sustainable Agriculture for allowing me to republish a profile I wrote of Fundación Paraguaya that originally appeared in our study of *Community Food Enterprise* (with research contributed by Sarita Role Schaeffer).

Thanks to Rick Foster, Ricardo Salvador, and the Kellogg Foundation for funding the study of state subsidies summarized in chapter 1.

I am grateful to Reyn Anderson, Scott Campbell, Amy Cortese, Michael Gordon, Kate Poole, Judy Wicks, Claudia Viek, and Kristin York for reading drafts and saving me from many potential embarrassments. All the remaining errors are my own responsibility.

Stephanie Miller served as a guardian angel throughout this process: encouraging me to write the book when common sense counseled against; continually reading critically my umpteenth drafts; and pampering me silly along the way. And the original worldview of my children, Adam and Rachel, continues to inspire my thinking, as does my mom, to whom I've dedicated this book.

Introduction

"The road to power," explains Frank Underwood, "is paved with hypocrisy—and casualties." Underwood, the lead character of the hit Netflix series *House of Cards*, is a wily South Carolina representative who in the first and second seasons, as House Whip, connives, lies, backstabs, and even commits murder to become president of the United States. His self-serving reflections on American politics could also describe another all-American obsession that's the subject of this book—economic development. Indeed, it could have been Underwood himself who showed up at a local wine bar in Annapolis, Maryland, to shake down recalcitrant state lawmakers for millions in additional subsidies to pay for the show's third season. But, no, it was Kevin Spacey, the actor playing Underwood.

In mid-March 2014 the Maryland Senate had just voted to increase the state's annual coffers to lure movie and television production companies from $7.5 million to $18.5 million.[1] The principal beneficiary was Media Rights Capital (MRC), the production company for *House of Cards*, which had received $26 million to film the first two seasons in Maryland. But the Assembly, the lower state house, was waffling. "This just keeps getting bigger and bigger," complained Delegate Eric G. Luedtke, who had previously supported the tax credits. "When does it stop?"

With political instincts that Frank Underwood surely would have admired, MRC deployed both carrots and sticks to get wobbly state legislators in line. Gerard Evans, the chief lobbyist for the show, encouraged state politicians to come and sip free cocktails with Spacey. To dispel any fears that the actor, reportedly worth $100 million, might be animated by self-interest, Evans assured reporters. "He loves Maryland. He's got a house here."[2]

MRC sent a letter to Governor Martin O'Malley, variations of which went to other key state politicians.[3] "MRC and *House of Cards* had a wonderful experience over the past two seasons and we want to stay in Maryland. We are ready to assist in any way possible to help the passage of the bill. . . . In the event sufficient incentives do not become available, we will have to break down our stage, sets and offices and set up in another state."

The threat was not idle. Just south of Maryland, Virginia was considering whether to increase its tax credits for film projects and gearing up to woo MRC. Indeed, according to the National Conference of State Legislatures, thirty-nine states and Puerto Rico provide film production incentives.[4] These payouts in 2012 were $1.5 billion—a 750-fold increase over film subsidies a decade earlier and so common that seven of the nine 2014 Oscar nominees for Best Picture received at least one state subsidy.[5]

Assembly Delegate Mark N. Fisher probably spoke for most of his colleagues when he said, "We're almost being held for ransom."[6]

Laying the groundwork for this grand act of extortion, like the consigliere for the Godfather, were the state's economic developers. At strategic moments Maryland's Department of Business and Economic Development trotted out data designed to impress wavering legislators.[7] Season 1, they pointed out, led to production expenditures of $63.6 million in the state, and 2,200 Maryland residents were hired as cast, crew, or extras. Season 2's expenditures were $55.5 million, and 3,700 people were employed. Armed with computer models of the economy that project jobs and other benefits to several decimal points—and that almost no one in the general public really understands—they argued that the total "economic impact" in the state was $138 million for the first season and $120.5 million for the second. And beyond these direct benefits was the great public relations boost Maryland would get in prestige from millions of Americans watching *House of Cards*. They could point to another television show, *Breaking Bad*, which had been supported by New Mexico's subsidies and spawned a whole new local tourism industry for Albuquerque, where visitors now are bussed to key spots to see where the main characters cooked methamphetamine. Who could tell how many Frank Underwood wannabes might consider moving their businesses to Maryland. And the price tag for all these goodies was a measly $11 million!

MRC's gambit worked brilliantly. The Maryland Assembly caved, the ransom was duly approved, Season 3 proceeded as planned, and everyone pretended to be happy. No one even noticed the casualties.

Moving Away from Legalized Bribery

Welcome to the world of conventional twenty-first-century economic development, one of the most counterproductive and corrupting enterprises of our time. If done correctly, economic development might bring a community more jobs, more wealth, a larger tax base, and greater prosperity. Consumers might enjoy more and better goods and services. More businesses might get started and become more profitable. Residents might enjoy better schools and better funded public services. Yet the actual practice of economic development and its dismal results are poorly understood, in part because its activities are often conducted in secrecy. Were the public really to understand what's being done on its supposed behalf, there might be rioting in the streets.

This book is about how economic development can and should be done differently. If we were to focus the field on growing locally owned business, we could increase the effectiveness of economic development and reduce its price tag. In fact, if we replicated the two dozen models described in the chapters ahead, economic development ultimately could be done by the private sector and at virtually zero cost to the public. A growing number of small, private businesses are now beginning to carry out the most important functions of economic development. They are facilitating local planning and placemaking, nurturing local entrepreneurs, helping local consumers buy local and local investors finance local business. And most remarkably, by charging clients reasonable fees for their services, they are able to cover their costs. These successes, however, and the opportunities they present to states, counties, cities, and towns everywhere, are practically unknown. They are crowded out of the headlines by the farcical antics of economic development as actually practiced today.

Several years ago Ira Glass, the great storyteller on National Public Radio, dedicated a segment of his popular show, *This American Life*, to the annual convention of the International Economic Development Council. Reporter Adam Davidson astutely observed: "Yeah, that's what they call it, business attraction. I came up with a different word. I call it stealing. They're trying to steal jobs from each other. After a few hours, I was thinking this conference is like a convention of incredibly collegial pickpockets."[8] By offering incentives worth millions of dollars—grants, low-interest loans, tax breaks, new highways and rail lines, you name it—economic developers trawl conventions like this one for corporate captains who might be convinced to abandon their hometowns.

It's understandable why a smart company or desperate community would play this game. Corporations mindful of the bottom line for shareholders are naturally looking for ways to lower costs. And if a locale can make just the right pitch, it could mean hundreds or thousands of new jobs. If a community has to put a little public money on the hook to reel in a big fish, who could possibly complain?

Let's immediately point out two flaws in this narrative. First, these practices are doing absolutely nothing for the national economy. Any reasonable definition of the term "economic development" would aim to create new jobs, new factories, new companies, and new opportunities. Yet except for the relatively rare case of a community attracting a foreign company (which itself carries special risks[9]), *economic development today is creating almost no new jobs whatsoever.*[10] In fact, as companies crisscross the country, all the turmoil and upheaval that economists blithely call "transaction costs"—moving expenses, mothballing old factories, constructing new ones, putting laid off workers on unemployment, hiring new ones—constitute a net drag on the economy.

Second, from the local perspective, the winners are almost always losers. Cut through the hype, the half-baked studies, the well-orchestrated champagne-opening ceremonies, and the silly political boasts and one soon realizes that almost all the promised benefits are illusory—indeed, a proverbial house of cards. Moreover, with thousands of communities chasing a handful of companies and with the brokers in the corporate relocation industry working for these companies, the game is rigged against communities.

Back to the math. Maryland paid MRC $26 million for 5,900 jobs, which works out to about $4,400 per job. Given that some economic incentive programs pay tens of thousands per job, sometimes even hundreds of thousands or millions, this price tag is not unreasonable. But does the state really benefit? Researcher Robert Tannenwald of the Center on Budget and Policy Priorities answered this question in his definitive study of film subsidies: "Jobs for in-state residents tend to be spotty, part-time, and relatively low-paying work—hair dressing, security, carpentry, sanitation, moving, storage, and catering—that [are] unlikely to build the foundations of strong economic development in the long term."[11] The *House of Cards* incentives, in fact, created no lasting jobs for Maryland whatsoever. Once the set is broken up for Season 3, all the jobs vanish.

More importantly, there are what economists blithely call "opportunity costs." How else could the state have used that money besides enriching an outside company like MRC? Might other local companies have been able to deliver more jobs for each public dollar? Suppose that Maryland had held an auction, allocating its economic-development budget to businesses that provided the most, and best, jobs for the least cost. Surely in a state with half a million companies, several thousand might have been willing to provide more permanent jobs than MRC did for less than $4,400 each. Some might have asked just $1,000 per job, $500, or even $100. The point is—who knows? Unless and until incentives are put to a market test like this, claims by economic developers, that paying millions in corporate incentives is the only strategy for creating jobs, have no basis.

Another opportunity cost is this: What else could have been accomplished had the money taxed for the boondoggle just stayed in the hands of taxpayers? Is the state government really in a better position to choose "winners and losers" than its resident consumers and investors? This, again, is rarely studied by economic developers. One of the perversities of economic development is that its practitioners laud the free market, harangue about taxes and regulations, and then happily dole out subsides that violate the free market and constitute a textbook example of government overreach.

The case for Maryland's film subsidies falls short in other ways too. The claim by Maryland's economic developers that the first two seasons of shooting *House of Cards* generated more than $100 million in "economic impact" assumes that all the dollars spent by the film company stayed in the state. In fact, according to Tannenwald's study, much of the spending ultimately occurs outside the states doling out the incentives, which means the consequent economic benefits are largely enjoyed elsewhere: "The film industry and some state film offices have undertaken or commissioned biased studies concluding that film subsidies are highly cost-effective drivers of economic activity. The most careful, objective studies find just the opposite."[12]

One way to measure whether a government program is cost-effective is to estimate how much income the subsidizing state earns in the form of taxes for each public dollar dispensed. Almost all studies on the point—except those sponsored by the beneficiaries of film subsidies—have found that tax-revenue returns range from 7 to 28 cents on the dollar.[13] In 2010, for example, according to the BaxStarr Consulting Group, Louisiana spent $196.8 million on film tax credits but only generated $27 million in tax receipts for the state and $17.3 million for local governments.[14] Film subsidies, in other words, are financial losers for the state taxpayers who foot the bill.

Perhaps the nonmonetary benefits of *House of Cards* being filmed in Maryland make the loss worthwhile, an argument often made by the owners of sports franchises who are looking for hundreds of millions of dollars to pay for their teams and stadiums. But if Maryland's politicians buy this line, argues commentator Liz Malm, they haven't paid very close attention to the actual story of the series:

> For all those that watch House of Cards, *you'll notice that Season 2 wasn't kind to Maryland (with the exception of a shout-out to the Baltimore Orioles). The production company disguises [Maryland landmarks] to look like [Washington] D.C. . . . For example, the* Washington Herald *building is actually the* Baltimore Sun *building, just altered. In the opening episode of Season 2, a fake Washington, D.C., metro station was created using an existing Baltimore metro station. They even make fun of Joppa, Maryland. . . .*
>
> States often hope being featured in a movie or television show will drive tourism to the state—but that won't be the case with House of

Cards. *I wouldn't doubt that the show drives visitors to our nation's capital, but it's unlikely that any will make a stop in Maryland.*

A few states have begun to understand that they've been conned. Michigan's Republican Governor Rick Snyder, for example, drastically reduced the state's film subsidy program in 2011 (though the state legislature has since insisted on reviving it). A half dozen other states also have dumped film incentives, and pressures are mounting in others to follow suit. But the film industry can rest easy. As Frank Underwood observes, "Proximity to power deludes some into thinking they can wield it."

The Deeper Problems

If you think film subsidies are just an isolated instance of good economic development gone bad, think again. As we explore in the first chapter of this book, a growing body of evidence shows that the lion's share of economic development manifests in "attraction" incentives like these, and almost all such economic incentives are losers. Politicians and economic developers scoff at this evidence, and too many don't care about the evidence at all because in the end their mission is not about developing their economies. It's about generating headlines and protecting Number One's job. The economic developer who brings a new company to town with a thousand jobs is treated as a local hero, and the politician who underwrites the effort has a solid pitch for reelection. By the time a community realizes that the deal under-delivered and public dollars were wasted, those responsible have happily moved into other private-sector jobs or retired.

Perhaps I'm too cynical. Perhaps I should credit those economic developers who sincerely believe that their projects can be those one in a million that will beat the odds and enrich their community. Maybe they'll focus their subsidies exclusively on high-wage manufacturers. Maybe they'll impose tough "clawbacks" of the subsidies if the companies don't deliver on their promises. Maybe their community will be the first ever with a perfect corporate-attraction track record. Yet none of these so-called "reforms" can possibly fix three deep problems with the incentives game.

First, incentives focus exclusively on nonlocal businesses, which are the ones least likely to deliver real benefits to a community. Here's a simple and amusing exercise to try the next time you chat with an economic developer. Count the number of times he or she utters the phrase "attract and retain." My experience is that it trips off the tongue at least once per minute. What's strange and revealing about this lexicon is that it demonstrates that economic developers are paying no attention to locally owned business. You cannot attract a local business from somewhere else—that would be an oxymoron. And if the only way you can retain a local business is by paying it some kind of special bribe unavailable to other local businesses, then how deep are its roots in the community anyway?

The oversight is not trivial. If you look at the US economy by jobs, about half are in large firms with more than five hundred employees and the rest are in small and medium-sized firms. We know that about 99.9 percent of all small and medium-sized firms are locally owned. If you add the twenty-six million Americans who are self-employed, it's clear that economic developers are consistently ignoring most of the economy.

Worse, as we explore in chapter 1, economic developers consistently ignore the most important part of the economy. Locally owned businesses are by far the most significant contributors to a community's jobs, social equality, sustainability, and a dozen other important indicators of success. Indeed, given that one consequence of economic incentives is to make it harder for unsubsidized local businesses to compete fairly against subsidized nonlocal ones, economic development is effectively undermining precisely those businesses it should be most supporting. Put positively, a smarter approach to economic development is to focus on local businesses because they generate the greatest benefits.

A second inherent problem with the existing practice of economic development is the clear and present danger of corruption. Today, as I write, former Virginia Governor Bob McDonnell and his wife are heading to prison because of the gifts, favors, and money they accepted from a slick businessman trying to extract government support for his magical elixir synthesized from tobacco plants. Public commentators universally denounced the McDonnells for accepting Rolex watches and a $10,000 wedding gift for their daughter, without noticing that the pattern of misbehavior—granting public rewards to politicians' favorite private companies—is the essence of almost all economic development today. The goal of economic development should be to minimize public subsidies, and to find the lowest-cost ways of activating and spreading private-sector businesses.

Economic development now does exactly the opposite. Its lavish incentives and other programs depend on regular infusions of grants and gifts from government agencies, foundations, and wealthy individuals. That those ostensibly committed to promoting free-market entrepreneurship are, themselves, among the least entrepreneurial members of our society is another central contradiction of economic development—and its third inherent problem.[15] If a sign-wielding beggar had better hygiene, more stylish clothing, a clearer mission, and the guts for a bigger ask, he would fit right in with the local economic-development office.

Does it really matter that those promoting the free market depend on government subsidies? I believe it does. When you don't or won't "walk the talk," your credibility and ability to exert a healthy influence on others is impaired. Call me priggish, but I'm skeptical when a preachy vegetarian wears leather boots or a chronic adulterer drones on about family values. If your ostensible goal is to promote an entrepreneurial culture, then you strengthen your message if you can show your capability to meet the rigors of the marketplace as an entrepreneur yourself.

Moreover, charity, whether public or private, is terribly unreliable, and economic-development programs that rely on it are condemned to being equally unreliable. Regions tend to go through their own business cycles, with leaders expanding government programs in good times and cutting them in lean ones (like the years after the financial crisis of 2008). Governments also go through political cycles, with more progressive administrations creating or expanding programs and more conservative ones cutting them. The same seesawing occurs with foundation grants. Most foundations support a noble cause for a few years and then expect the beneficiary to develop new sources of grants. Wild budget oscillations necessarily follow that make serious program planning exceptionally difficult.

Even the best beggars face the risk of donor fatigue. There's only so much government and charitable money available for economic development. Yet the challenges inherent in helping every individual and family within one's region find well-paying jobs, with rewarding work, through environmentally and socially beneficial business—what the real goals of economic development should be—are almost limitless. The only way economic development can possibly begin to fulfill this mission is if it is reshaped to do more with less.

My concerns are not confined to the practitioners of "attract and retain." I'm equally concerned about the dependence on outside cash in the various networks embracing local businesses. While charitable dollars helped many of these organizations get on their feet, the eventual goal should be self-sufficiency. Yet dependence on government and charitable funding defines those economic developers practicing Economic Gardening, a movement launched in Littleton, Colorado, which nurtures small, young, local, fast-growing "gazelle" businesses. It infuses the practitioners of Main Street projects and downtown revivals across the country. And it continues to beset the nearly two hundred local business alliances that are affiliated with the Business Alliance for Local Living Economies (BALLE) and the American Independent Business Alliance (AMIBA)—a shortcoming for which I must take some personal responsibility.

BALLE was founded in 2001 by a small group of entrepreneurs, led by Laury Hammel and Judy Wicks, who believed in the power of local business and creating local business networks. I sat on the board until 2008 when I stepped off to become a staff person for several years. Throughout my tenure, I became convinced that, to achieve their full potential, the affiliated networks (of which there are now more than eighty) needed more diversified revenue streams. We needed strategies for our networks to self-finance their work—like the coupon books, local debit cards, local commercial development companies, and local investment funds that you'll read about in the pages ahead. But our priority was to raise money from foundations and wealthy individuals who were excited about financing our work. Fiduciary responsibility demanded, above all, that we make payroll next month. That said, what might have happened if we spent more of our organizational resources on testing these ideas? What if we were more entrepreneurial ourselves and were able to wean ourselves off grants and gifts altogether?

My worry is that overreliance on dues and philanthropy led many once-strong local business networks, in Portland (OR) and Santa Fe (NM), for example, to shut down their operations. Others struggle to raise enough money to support just one full-time staff person. How long can even the most dedicated organizer donate time to a good cause before his or her personal needs (a house, education for the kids, retirement) kick in and the looming prospect of burnout compels calling it quits? One motivation for writing this book is to help my colleagues in BALLE, AMIBA, Main Street projects, and Economic Gardening, as well as their counterparts worldwide affiliated with groups like Transition Towns, rethink their organizational designs, become more entrepreneurial, create more economically stable models, and ultimately grow bigger.

Country Roads

To imagine what a more entrepreneurial and cost-effective practice of economic development could look like, I'd like to introduce you to a remarkable innovator who has toiled largely in obscurity in the Upper Ohio Valley. I first met Lou Stein when I spoke in Wetzel County, West Virginia, in 2011. Like much of West Virginia and Appalachia, this region has had a long history of wretched poverty, exacerbated in recent years by the departure of steel companies overseas and by what the locals call the federal government's "war on coal." This was also an area with rock deposits rich with natural gas where the recent rise of fracking technology has been creating overnight millionaires.

After my talk, in which I spoke about eye-popping economic-development incentives that were now paying upwards of $1 million per job, an avuncular gentlemen with the gift of gab—the only person in the room in a suit and tie—came up to chat. He confided that he was producing jobs for about $500 each. The previous year his nonprofit, Valley Ventures, with an annual budget of about $150,000, had generated between three hundred and five hundred jobs. My jaw dropped.

To put Stein's record in perspective, consider that when Christina Romer, the first head of the Obama administration's Council on Economic

Advisers, was wrapping up her brief tenure in 2010, she boasted that the stimulus package that she had helped design created or saved three million jobs.[16] This means that the stimulus package that Congress approved in the 2008–2010 period, which cost about $775 billion, created each new job for $258,000. *Had the Administration decided instead to implement its stimulus through people like Lou Stein rather than through thousands of Congress-sponsored white elephant projects, the United States would have been back to full employment in a year at one hundredth the cost.*[17]

What accounts for Stein's stunning success? It's simple. He focuses laser-like on local business. He organizes meetings of entrepreneurs. He visits existing small businesses. He finds out exactly what they need to succeed, and then methodically delivers carefully tailored assistance to them. "I can't tell you," he fumes, "how many economic developers never go to existing businesses and ask 'how can I help?'"

While Stein is not beyond pitching occasionally for a company to move to West Virginia, he concedes that this strategy alone is difficult at best. Most communities will never attract more than a couple of businesses per year, and the handful of jobs they bring have little impact. Besides, the incentives game has gotten so competitive, with some communities willing to give away taxes, land, buildings, you name it for free, that a fiscally sober jurisdiction can't possibly win. And even if you do prevail, Stein warns, "be careful what you wish for. Those larger businesses are skilled at taking advantage of you." When your incentives expire, they will happily move elsewhere, because they have no roots in the community.

Stein explains that big businesses are no longer the significant job creators in the United States. In fact, once these businesses become publicly traded on Wall Street, they are rewarded by investors when they cut jobs in the name of increasing efficiency. The main sources of job creation, from his perspective, are start-ups and existing small and medium-scale businesses.

National statistics back up Stein's view. If you've got a computer, log into a terrific website called YourEconomy.org, which presents one of the richest and most nuanced sources of data on the relative impact of locally owned versus nonlocal businesses.[18] Look at job growth in the United States between 2008 and 2013, and you will find that all jobs in the country grew by a paltry 0.8 percent. Locally owned businesses increased jobs during this period by 1.2 percent. Nonlocal businesses actually reduced their jobs by 4.3 percent.

One of the fastest growing segments of the labor market is Americans choosing self-employment.[19] Those twenty-six million Americans run 88 percent of the nation's businesses. Moreover, start-up firms are getting smaller—from 7.6 employees in the 1990s to 4.7 employees in 2011. According to Heidi Pickman and Claudia Viek, two leaders in the US microenterprise movement, "With less than 3 percent of outside investment, microbusinesses employ 260 percent more people than venture capital–backed firms and generate about 77 percent of the [gross domestic product] that venture capital–backed firms do."[20]

The only way a community will ever have successful large businesses, Stein argues, is to create many start-ups. Most won't survive after a few years. But those that do can become the job-producing anchors for a local economic renaissance.

Moreover, more mature small businesses need help, too. The people running these businesses are extraordinarily creative, but often don't have the time or the bandwidth for thinking about the future. They have to do everything themselves. They have to be their own lawyer, sweep their own floors, do whatever it takes to succeed. Most haven't a clue how to get the capital they need to grow.

Stein set up Valley Ventures with a two-year grant from the Pittsburgh-based Benedum Foundation. He used some of the money to create a microloan fund for start-ups and a larger fund for existing businesses, and the rest he used to pay for his staff of two—himself and an assistant. Originally, the target region was just three counties in West Virginia, but as word of Stein's success spread, other counties wanted in. The program expanded to encompass two more counties in West Virginia and then one county in neighboring Ohio. Stein himself lived in the geographic center of this area, and was never more than an hour's drive to any of his clients.

To assist start-ups, according to Stein, "I'd go to a city. I'd place an ad for a free business seminar. I'd attract sixty to one hundred people. No one does this, especially in small towns. I'd bring three to four success stories from nearby counties. And I'd tell people: Here's how it works. If you have an idea, don't worry about the money—let me worry about it. I will meet with you personally for an hour. I'll come to you or you come to me and we will discuss your business idea. There are no dumb ideas here."

Stein assured every start-up client that he would help every step of the way—assist in writing a business plan, recruit partners, teach basic business and accounting skills, solve a specific problem. He would then introduce them to a personally vetted network of about fifty service providers like lawyers, accountants, graphic artists, and software writers. He did everything possible to help them succeed. What he asked in return was that the client come up with 10–20 percent of the start-up funds for the proposed enterprise from friends, family, credit cards, or savings. He would then add money from his microloan fund, typically $500–$5,000 per client, go to one of several local banks with which he had a good relationship, plunk down 25 percent, and ask the bank to finance the rest.

According to Stein, two-thirds of the clients he met with followed through. And once they received their loans, they were diligent about paying back their low-interest microloans over thirty to forty months, usually at the rate of a few hundred dollars per month. "I had people that would sooner cut off their right arm than miss a payment."

For existing businesses, Stein deployed a similar strategy of gauging their needs and devising specialized packages of assistance. But because their capital needs were substantially greater than those of start-ups, he created a larger fund to support them. Ultimately the goal was to bring vetted expansion plans to bankers who trusted Stein's judgment. The bankers, in turn, appreciated getting new clients, because they then started using the bank's other services.

Stein reckons that he was creating thirty-five to fifty new small businesses per year, each of which had an average of four or five full-time employees by the end of a year. He also was facilitating about twenty-five to thirty-five expansions a year, each yielding between three and five new employees. This is how he came up with his three hundred to five hundred new jobs estimate. And if you think these numbers are implausible, consider that microenterprise networks in California and Oregon also have calculated that they are creating jobs for about $1,000–$2,000 each.

A consummate entrepreneur, Stein was mindful that Valley Ventures couldn't and shouldn't rely on foundation money forever. He gradually asked clients to pay finder's fees for each bank loan that he successfully brokered. His own loan funds started to earn interest income. And he periodically entered bigger contracts with communities for more ambitious job-creating projects. After about five years, the nonprofit was more than halfway toward financing its own operations, and Stein reckons that complete self-financing was not far away.

Unfortunately that point was never reached. The Valley Ventures board did not follow through with their promise to assist in fundraising for the organization, and Stein concluded that he could not carry out on-the-ground work in six counties and assume the board's fundraising role too. He made the decision after five years to move on to another position as chief fundraiser for the Jefferson Behavioral Health System in Steubenville, Ohio. But he still continues to work with entrepreneurs outside his day job. He's still helping them find technical assistance and capital. He's still creating jobs for his region. And he's still engaging in low-budget, high-impact economic development, because "it's what I love to do."

Pollinator Businesses

A small but growing cadre of Lou Steins around the country is attempting to redefine economic development, end financially reckless incentive practices, and develop more prudent, self-financing alternatives. This is exactly what happened with public officials a generation ago, thanks in part to a book that celebrated these new approaches for state and local government called *Reinventing Government*. Authors David Osborne and Ted Gaebler provided dozens of innovative examples of how state and local governments were becoming more enterprising and thereby able to stretch precious taxpayer dollars to deliver more public services. That pioneering book provided a framework for a new Vice President, Al Gore, to create self-financing centers within the federal government as well.

In many ways, *The Local Economy Solution* pays homage to Osborne and Gaebler's seminal work. My central argument is that ending today's wasteful incentives requires reinventing economic development through private businesses that carry out the important functions of economic development—businesses that can and should be self-financing. They should be designed to achieve a level of cash flow so that their economic-development activities can continue, grow, and flourish. And by being self-reliant, these initiatives will no longer be subject to the mercurial and often foolish decisions of politicians and philanthropists and no longer carry the poisonous seeds of public corruption.

The message of this book is that it's high time for economic developers to get back to business. Like other businesses, economic-development businesses should provide a valuable good or service for some form of payment—a fee, a license, a royalty, or a share of ownership. Over time their revenues should exceed their expenses. To achieve these goals, management must carefully orchestrate human, financial, and other forms of capital. Unlike most other businesses, however, economic-development businesses should focus on nurturing locally owned businesses.

I call this new generation of self-financing, economic-development businesses *pollinators*. In nature pollinators like bees, butterflies, or bats carry pollen from plant to plant, and they instinctively know that the intermixing of these pollens nourishes the entire ecosystem. Pollinator businesses similarly carry the best elements of one local business to another, thereby fertilizing all local businesses and creating a healthy entrepreneurial ecosystem.

To extend the analogy a bit, economic development today is the opposite of pollination. It brings into communities invasive species, with little consideration about how these corporations might systematically destroy the local ecosystem. These invasive species thrive with subsidies that weaken the competitiveness of existing, unsubsidized local business. And even when the invasive species ultimately move on or die out, it can take many decades before any semblance of ecological balance returns.

Arguably, many kinds of businesses today serve this pollination function. A corporate law firm helps local businesses address specific legal problems on a fee-for-service basis. Accountants, insurers, bankers, investors, Internet providers, advertisers, and myriad other professionals assist local businesses in a thousand important ways. But these mainstream businesses are not what this book is about. What distinguishes pollinator businesses is their acute sense of mission—to not only strengthen a particular local business for private profit but also strengthen the entire local business community. This intention, this dedication to strengthening the whole ecosystem, is so innate that, like bees, pollinator businesses may not even be aware of it.

A pollinator business will measure success not only by its own rate of return—though that matters—but also by its answers to questions like these:

- Have I increased the community's percentage of jobs in locally owned business?
- Have I expanded the percentage of residents, particularly smart young adults, prepared to start new businesses?
- Have I pushed up the three-, five-, and ten-year survival rate of local business start-ups?
- Have I multiplied the number of local businesses consciously benchmarking, measuring, and improving their social performance with respect to workers, stakeholders, and the environment?

Skeptics may wonder what I mean by *local* business. I address this question at length in an earlier book, *The Small-Mart Revolution*,[21] but let me offer a brief recap here: Locally owned businesses are those with a majority of owners living in the same geographic community where the business is based. That community can be a town, city, metro area, county, or region. It usually means less than 50 miles away. Local ownership can come in many forms, including local corporations, nonprofits, and co-ops. Most local businesses are small, which the US Small Business Administration defines as having five hundred or fewer employees. But some large businesses are locally owned too. Regional chains can be local, but national chains cannot. Franchises that allow the owner lots of latitude over an outlet's design and supplies could be considered local (say certain gas stations), but those with encyclopedic top-down requirements (such as McDonald's) would not. Whatever the uncertainty that remains in this definition, one distinction is absolutely clear: Public companies traded on the NASDAQ or New York Stock Exchanges cannot be considered local—period.

The concept of pollinators can also be understood by contrasting two similar concepts some readers may be familiar with: *socially responsible businesses* and *social enterprises*. The universe of socially responsible businesses, which can be found in an expanding number of screened, socially respon-sible investment portfolios, usually includes well-behaved publicly traded companies. Pollinators, in contrast, mindfully ignore all nonlocal compa-nies. Why waste time on companies least likely to result in meaningful economic development (even if they are otherwise good public citizens)? Social enterprises are typically self-financing nonprofits, such as Housing Works, which provides services and advocacy for homeless people with HIV/AIDS in New York City financed through a bookstore, a café, thrift shops, and rental companies. Pollinator businesses, in contrast, can be nonprofit or for-profit and target their efforts exclusively on strengthening other local businesses.

In earlier books, I elaborated that local economic development should embrace six concepts beginning with the letter *P*: planning, purchasing, people, partners, purse, and public policy. For the attentive local economic developer, each *P* poses an important question that must be answered:

Planning. What are the most plausible opportunities for new or expanded local businesses to meet local needs? (Planning here means both the "spacial" planning undertaken by urban planners and the "business" planning undertaken by consultants.)

Purchasing. How can the community help these businesses, once estab-lished, flourish with concerted buy-local efforts involving nearby consumers, businesses, and government agencies?

People. How can a new generation of entrepreneurs and employees be trained for these new local business opportunities?

Partnership. How can local businesses improve their competitiveness by working together as a team?

Purse. How can local capital be mobilized to finance these new or expand-ing local businesses?

Public Policy. How can laws, regulations, and practices at all levels of government—local, state, national, and global—be recalibrated to eliminate the current advantages nonlocal businesses enjoy?

This book tells the stories of pollinators who are answering the first five questions and performing successful economic-development activities with little or no public money. (Public policy, the sixth *P*, does not fit in the domain of private initiatives, though, as we will explore in the final chapter, public policymakers have an indispensable role to play in nurturing pollinators.) So five of the following chapters focus on different types of pollinators—or, if you prefer, different species. Planning pollinators help local businesses plan improvements of their performance, including improvements that flow from their relationship to a place. Purchasing pollinators pump up local businesses through more foot traffic, more orders, and more contracts. People pollinators improve the performance of entrepreneurs and local economic developers themselves. Partnership pollinators enable local businesses to become more profitable by working together. And purse pollinators make it easier, cheaper, and more lucrative for local investors to finance local business. A smart economic developer will seek to have all five types of pollinators buzzing away in his or her community.

The first chapter, however, elaborates why economic-development today is failing. It opens in NASCAR country in North Carolina, where local leaders, disappointed with the results of their Economic Development Council, decided to start moving their money away from corporate attraction incentives and into nurturing local business. I then share the latest research on why policies of "attract and retain" fail, and lay out eight myths that continue to propel economic development in the wrong direction.

Chapter 2 looks at "planning pollinators" who give meaningful direction for economic development. I describe my own efforts to develop a low-cost tool for communities to measure economic "leakage." We then meet Eric Koester, whose new company, Main Street Genome, provides local businesses with data that helps them identify and get competitive prices for their inputs. In Grand Rapids (MI), Guy Bazzani uses green architecture to help redesign the local economy. Halfway around the world in Australia, Gilbert Rochecouste has brought the alleys of Melbourne back to life through creative design and grassroots engagement.

Chapter 3 focuses on pollinator business models for local purchasing, often branded around "Buy Local," "Think Local First," or "10% Shift" campaigns. We will see a successful coupon book in Bellingham (WA), the spread of *Edible* magazine—which promotes local food—across North

America, ShopCity web platforms that originated in a small community in Ontario, a local debit card in a neighborhood in San Francisco (CA), a local gift card in Edmonton (AB), and a local loyalty card in Portland (OR).

Chapter 4 looks at people pollinators—that is, businesses that support entrepreneurship. The chapter begins with one of the godfathers of the modern local economy movement, Ernesto Sirolli, who helps communities master the art of "enterprise facilitation." In Vancouver (BC), Simon Fraser University has a self-financing program for teaching local economic development and social entrepreneurship. In Paraguay, a high school teaches students how to run local food businesses through school-based enterprises that also pay the bills for the entire school. In Ann Arbor (MI), a delicatessen called Zingerman's has launched a series of self-financing entrepreneurship support programs for employees and outsiders. Finally, we look at a business "accelerator" in Seattle (WA) called Fledge, which gives promising companies a more intense injection of assistance and capital, and gets repaid through royalties.

Chapter 5 reviews pollinator businesses that facilitate partnerships and help groups of local businesses achieve competitive advantages that they could never achieve on their own. We examine how two BALLE networks, in Arizona and in Calgary (AB), have come close to financing themselves. We look at Tucson Originals, a network of local food businesses that collectively buys supplies to bring down prices. In Vancouver, a company called Small Potatoes Urban Delivery has rebuilt local distribution capacity for foodstuffs from the region's local farmers. We then look at how local food businesses collaborate through public markets in Seattle and Philadelphia.

Chapter 6 focuses on purse pollinators committed to moving more capital into local businesses. We begin by examining the credit union movement and one of its most successful examples in North America, Vancity, based in Vancouver. We then turn to the "equity" side of finance and the emerging world of local stocks and stock exchanges being promoted by Mission Markets in New York and Cutting Edge Capital in Oakland. In Nova Scotia, a community economic-development investment fund act has unleashed sixty small-scale funds, primarily supporting family farms and small food businesses. In California a capital-raising site called Credibles mobilizes finance through preselling.

Chapter 7 concludes with final thoughts about implementation: What's necessary to shift the failed approaches of economic development today to new pollinator models? What kinds of public policies might support pollinator innovation and accelerate their replication? How might these approaches have relevance for the international development community? Some answers to these questions are suggested by public banking initiatives in Phoenix and Tucson in Arizona, and by an effort to rebuild an entire college town in northeastern Ohio.

Caution Ahead

In just the past year while I've been writing this book, I've learned about nearly a hundred other pollinators that have great stories to tell. The field is expanding rapidly, and I ultimately concluded that this book could only include a representative sampling. If you are running a pollinator that I didn't discuss, or you know one, let me underscore that my choices were made, not because your model is unworthy, but just because I felt duty bound to bring this book to completion.

Another caveat is that the five categories in which I place the pollinators are mine, not theirs. In fact, most of the pollinators depicted here would claim they were performing many kinds of support for local businesses. A purchasing pollinator also sees itself as strengthening the planning capacities of its clients and as putting them together in partnerships. The important thing to remember is that the more of these functions that are happening in your community—whatever the label—the stronger your economic-development capacity will be.

However inspiring you find the stories that I did include, be aware that nearly all the pollinator businesses I describe are works in progress. Even the best pollinators are only a few years old and have yet to withstand the tests of cash flow crises, product failures, and managerial shortcomings that beset young businesses. Many of the pollinators have not broken even yet, let alone generated a significant profit. Some will fail. But as Thomas Edison noted, it took ten thousand failed attempts to make a lightbulb to find one idea that worked. Even colossal failures, if properly understood, can help the next generation of pollinators succeed. My hope is that readers will be inspired to conceive and deploy new kinds of pollinators that no one has ever thought of.

I encourage would-be local economic developers to be cautious in one final respect. Place matters. And what works in Edmonton might not work in Providence. There are no cookbook formulas for success here. A pollinator must be created like any other business, with careful attention to the local market, meticulous business planning, adequate capital, shrewd management, and just a little bit of luck.

This book presents a compass that points to true North. It's up to you, the readers, to draw up the maps and set sail.

CHAPTER I

Principles

Moving Beyond "Attract and Retain"

*I*t was a sunny, brisk morning in North Carolina, in early December 2010, when John Day, then county manager of Cabarrus County, insisted on taking me out to a big southern breakfast of grits and eggs. Accompanying him was Liz Poole, a local entrepreneurship teacher and the chair of the board of five elected commissioners responsible for governing the county. They explained that the local unemployment rate was hovering around 10 percent, well above the national average, with eight thousand residents out of work. Could I help?

Cabarrus County, I quickly learned, is a crazy quilt of fascinating contrasts. Many of its 175,000 inhabitants consider themselves residents of greater Charlotte, a metropolitan area with more than two million. But Cabarrus County also can be described as a loose network of six small towns, the most familiar being Concord, Kannapolis, and Harrisburg. The remaining towns resemble the fictional Mayberry in *The Andy Griffith Show*. The biggest defining force on the popular culture, which imbues how everyone thinks about Cabarrus County (and also is responsible for several spin-off industries), is the NASCAR race track in Concord. The county is also dotted with suburban enclaves, connected by main drags with a seemingly endless array of chain stores. Two congressional districts run through the county, one held by a Democrat, one by a Republican.

By any standard, the Cabarrus economy in 2010 was struggling. Like much of North Carolina, this region once had thriving textile manufacturers like Pillowtex, but they fled to Mexico when the United States signed the North American Free Trade Agreement in the 1990s.[22] Other once dominant Cabarrus businesses were also in sharp decline. The cigarette manufacturer Philip Morris, for example, recently shuttered a big plant. The ghosts of these corporate giants continued to haunt the imaginations of the county's Economic Development Council (EDC), a public–private partnership that historically received more than $200,000 each year from the county coffers.

The director of the EDC, John Cox, had big plans for bringing great new businesses to the county, so grandiose that his Twitter handle was @CzarCEO. He regularly distributed brag sheets that his recruitment initiatives between 2004 and 2011 had snagged 2,711 jobs. While super-ficially impressive, this job-creation rate actually would not roll back unemployment in Cabarrus for another twenty-five years. John Day and Liz Poole were convinced that his single-barreled approach was insuffi-cient, and they were ready to try something different. I signed on to spend the next year creating a framework for economic development rooted in local business. But I barely knew what I was in for.

Why *Local* Economic Development

Over the past two decades, I've performed "local economy studies" of several dozen communities, counties, regions, and states. While these reports differ from place to place, two features are fairly standard. First, I show the importance of locally owned businesses to the overall health of the economy. Second, I use a computer model to demonstrate how a modest shift in purchasing by resident consumers, businesses, and government agencies, away from distant sources and toward local goods and services, can expand local business, stimulate the economy, and create jobs.

Cabarrus County, like most places I've studied, turns out to have an economy predominantly made up of local businesses. According to the 2009 edition of *County Business Patterns*, all but 6 of the 3,958 business "establishments" in the county have fewer than 500 employees and there-fore officially qualify as small businesses. This is misleading, however, because not all small establishments are locally owned. In the nomenclature of federal statistics, establishments include franchises or subsidiaries of larger firms. Another business database from Dun and Bradstreet (available for public use on the website mentioned in the Introduction, YourEconomy.org) showed that 13,644 residents, or about 18 percent of the private workforce, were employed by nonresident companies. The Cabarrus County economy includes more than private sector employees, though these other categories are local too. Some residents work for themselves, and the most recent data on self-employment showed that 11,553 Cabarrus residents had their own businesses, most of them home-based. The public workforce is also rooted locally. About 8,000 residents work in the public schools, and 3,500 in state and local government.

The bottom line was that six in seven working Cabarrus residents were employed by a local business or institution. And my immediate observation was that any economic-development policy that neglects the kinds of business responsible for 85 percent of the current jobs is clearly misdirected.

I contrasted the composition of the Cabarrus economy with that of the United States. Cabarrus County has relatively more of its workforce deployed in construction, retail, real estate, entertainment, personal services, and local schools. These categories reflect the implicit choices the county has made to serve as a bedroom community for commuters working in Charlotte, and to connect to the outside world largely through NASCAR and related tourism businesses. In every other sector of the economy, including manufacturing and finance, the county has a smaller proportion of jobs than the national average. Unfortunately these under-represented sectors typically pay higher wages and create more local economic benefits.

Next, I performed an economic leakage analysis. The term *leakage* refers to the outflow of dollars that occurs when residents unnecessarily purchase goods and services from nonlocal producers or sellers. Every lost local transaction means lost jobs, lost taxes, and lost spending. Using IMPLAN, the Minnesota input–output model used extensively by economic-development agencies across the country, I can see the potential outcome of adding more local purchasing to the existing economy, and trace the consequent expansion of local businesses (direct effects), their purchases from other local businesses (indirect effects), and their employees' purchases from local businesses (induced effects). I found that a shift of 25 percent of residents' nonlocal purchases toward local businesses could create 9,492 new jobs: 5,208 directly, 2,157 indirectly, and 2,127 induced. IMPLAN predicted, moreover, that these new jobs would lead to $397 million more in wages each year, $676 million in additional annual value-added production (the regional equivalent of gross domestic product), and $59 million more in business taxes.

So the choice facing Cabarrus County was pretty stark: It could continue economic development as usual through corporate attraction and, if it was lucky, continue to create several hundred new jobs a year to fix an eight-thousand-job deficit. Or it could help shift purchasing toward greater self-reliance and create thousands of new jobs.

Supplementing this empirical research were several dozen interviews I conducted with Shannon Johnson, the county's paid organizer of "local first" initiatives. We spoke to policymakers and economic developers in the six towns, along with many entrepreneurs, all of whom confirmed the enormous degree to which local business had been neglected by the EDC.

As I prepared my findings for the five county commissioners, I originally planned not to criticize the EDC directly, and just point out how much more could be accomplished with a new strategy. But behind the scenes, a small war was brewing. The two Johns steering economic development in Cabarrus County—John Day and John Cox—were once good friends, but repeated clashes over policy and direction had frayed their relationship to the breaking point. Prior to my being hired, Day had rallied the county commissioners to cut $50,000 from the EDC's budget and redirect that money toward local economy work. Cox was livid. And he now was quietly mobilizing his political supporters to form a new advocacy group called Cabarrus Jobs Now not only to restore the $50,000 to the EDC but also to add more county money to his budget. And these new cheerleaders for more business attraction were gearing up to discredit anyone who stood in the way.

For Cabarrus Jobs Now, it was an axiom of almost religious faith that incentives were the only way to undertake economic development. And the principal heretic who needed to be burned at the stake before he could win converts was that damn outsider who "stole our money"—namely me. Worse, about halfway through my contract, John Day unexpectedly retired early (his new passion was the nonprofit 7th Street Public Market in Charlotte), which left a huge power vacuum. Cabarrus Jobs Now was newly emboldened to undo all of this silly stuff on localization.

I resolved to wrap up my work quickly before the pitchforks and torches came through my hotel window. I added several pages to my final report that might help the commissioners, then all still largely sympathetic to localization, to hold the EDC more accountable. Specifically, I asked the commissioners to put eight tough questions to the EDC about its claim that it had attracted 2,711 jobs between 2004 and 2011:

Significance. How does the number of new jobs attracted compare to the overall "churn" of jobs within the economy? In other words, what might have happened in Cabarrus County had there been no EDC and no attraction initiatives whatsoever? According to the Kauffmann Foundation, the nation's leading philanthropic supporter of entrepreneurship, a typical jurisdiction in the US economy generally can be expected to gain 18 percent more jobs in a typical year and lose 16 percent of its existing jobs. In 2004 Cabarrus County had a labor force of about 77,000. Over the next eight years, therefore, the economy naturally created 119,000 new jobs. *At most, therefore, the EDC increased the natural rate of job expansion by about 2 percent.* Might the EDC have done better simply by focusing its resources on improving the overall business environment in which all existing businesses were creating jobs?

Causality. When you look at the corporations that did move to Cabarrus County, how decisive were the EDC's initiatives in their decision-making? Are you sure? How? Most researchers have concluded that incentive packages are such a small fraction of a corporation's bottom line that they actually have very little impact on siting decisions. Far more important are the proximity of qualified workers, local input suppliers, available land, target markets, and even good schools. In other words, companies chose their favorite site and *then* run the competition for incentives to lower costs.

Job Retention. Were the jobs that the EDC attracted for the long-term or temporary? This, recall, was the central problem with the film subsidies described in the Introduction. And did the promised jobs actually materialize? One EDC project, for example, tried to bring a bunch of major biotech companies to a new research campus—effectively a glorified industrial development park—in Kannapolis, yet that initiative had yet to produce more than a tiny fraction of the jobs envisioned.

Living Wages. Were the jobs that the EDC attracted paying high wages? If not, every new low-wage job created could actually drive down average labor costs in the region and reduce family incomes—the exact opposite of what John Cox claimed to be accomplishing. In Cabarrus, about 20 percent of the jobs the EDC said it attracted came from Great Wolf Lodge, a popular indoor water-park resort with many minimum wage jobs. Had the EDC calculated the detrimental impact on regional per capita income? The poverty rate in Cabarrus County has doubled since the year 2000, underscoring the importance of this question.

Resident Employment. To what extent did the EDC create jobs for unemployed residents of Cabarrus County? Various national studies suggest that about 80 percent of the jobs attracted are taken by workers who hear about a new project elsewhere and move to that community for the job.[23] In other words, corporate attractions—especially of big companies—do very little to bring down local unemployment. How many of the EDC's new jobs went to existing residents?

Subsidy Costs. Could the EDC estimate what it actually cost Cabarrus County, in foregone taxes and infrastructure costs, to finance each attraction? Besides the million dollars it had given the EDC between 2004 and 2011, the county had helped underwrite EDC attractions by awarding local tax breaks and paying for infrastructure improvements that undoubtedly cost millions more, all in ways largely hidden from public scrutiny. In the absence of a comprehensive analysis of these costs and a careful weighing against the benefits, how could the EDC possibly know whether they were helping or hindering the economic well-being of the county?

Opportunity Costs. Could Cabarrus County have created more jobs by skipping the attraction game and just supporting local business? A newspaper study of corporate attractions in Lane County, Oregon, found that the cost of attracting a job from an outside business was more than thirty times more expensive than the cost of incentivizing a local firm to hire one more worker.[24]

Over the next few months the county commissioners did start to ask these questions, and radical changes were set in motion. Tea Party Republicans seized control of county government, and proceeded to cut every program in sight, including the EDC. Ironically, Cabarrus Jobs Now suddenly became the voice of moderation, and successfully pushed for a modest revival of the EDC with a greater balance between old-style attraction and support for existing local business. And what became of John Cox? He fled south to become president of the Greater Naples Chamber of Commerce in Florida.

A Discredited Profession

Every year I typically speak in thirty to forty US cities, and everywhere I go I run into empire-builders like John Cox. They are usually men, usually charismatic. Their self-promoting, testosterone-rich story line is always the same. Big claims of jobs "created" through attraction. Indifference and condescension toward local business. Secret meetings that disburse millions of public money. Little accountability in the years that follow. Zero analysis of what was lost by not putting the same money into local business.

No matter how many of these stories I share, some of you will still insist that your economic developers are doing a better job than that. If my local EDC can spend a little money to catch a big company that will bring five, ten, twenty thousand new jobs, if they can convince that company to guarantee that the jobs pay well and hire existing residents, if they can get the state or someone else to pick up the bill for the incentives, then surely this type of economic development is worth it. Okay, you may be right. I shouldn't claim that every single corporate attraction is a loser. But the probability of getting all these factors right is exceedingly small. It's like winning the lottery. Sure, it can happen. But no one should mistake purchasing Lotto tickets for a serious personal financial strategy.

For a 30,000-foot look at the economic-development field, there's no better person to turn to than Ann Markusen, director of the Project on Regional and Industrial Economics at the Humphrey Institute of Public Affairs, based at the University of Minnesota. Several years ago, she assembled the best thinkers in the field of economic development to explore the validity of the attract-and-retain approach and to offer reforms. The experts had diverse views: some believed corporate attraction deals were ultimately beneficial, some didn't, and some withheld judgment. The resulting book of essays, *Reining in the Competition for Capital*, is perhaps the best assessment of the academic literature on incentives to date.[25] In the opening essay, Markusen and Katherine Ness, of the University of Illinois at Urbana-Champaign, lay out their conclusion: "Incentive competition is on the rise. It is costly, generally inefficient, and often ineffective for the winning regions."[26]

Markusen and her colleagues reviewed a number of troubling problems with corporate attraction practices. Among the biggest concerns:

- Companies attracted usually don't stay very long and under-deliver the jobs they promise.
- The jobs created pay poorly and have few benefits.
- Many of the costs that a community promises to subsidize—of capital improvements, for example—are often much greater than originally projected.
- The structure of site-selection representatives' compensation, mostly finders' fees, gives them an incentive to represent community interests poorly—that is, to overstate the benefits, understate the costs, and exaggerate the packages other communities are putting on the table.
- The secrecy surrounding much of the deal-making increases the risk of communities making ill-informed decisions and short-circuits the normal benefits of democratic accountability.
- The details of these deals are so embarrassing to the politicians who approve them that they fight to keep them secret. For example, in his waning days as governor of New Mexico, Bill Richardson worked around the clock to kill legislation that would have required immediate publication of the details of his own corporate attractions.

• Most communities engaged in global attraction wind up losing any given bid, which means they are draining precious civic time, money, and goodwill—and, at a minimum, these costs need to be weighed against the purported benefits of the occasionally won deal.

The case against corporate attraction has become so powerful that it's exceedingly difficult to find any serious economist not on the payroll of the attraction industry prepared to defend the practice. Almost every scholarly article on the topic either questions the value of incentives or disapproves of them altogether. The few exceptions are hardly worth the paper they are written on. Let me give you just one example.

One much-discussed article for the National Bureau of Economic Research, written by Michael Greenstone and Enrico Moretti in 2003,[27] claimed that communities winning bidding wars experienced greater wage growth and greater increases in local property values than did losing communities. As Peter Fisher of the University of Iowa points out, however, it would be surprising if this result did not take place, at least in the short term.[28] The basic tenet of Keynesian economics is that when the economy is petering out because of insufficient demand, a sudden infusion of government money can help reverse course and create jobs, expand payrolls, and inflate the value of assets. But that doesn't justify the government handing out big bags of cash to a few pet businesses, especially if far greater benefits are possible if the same spending were spread over many local businesses.

Fisher identifies several additional flaws in the study. One is that Greenstone and Moretti undercount actual costs by only tallying subsidies given by the responsible local government. Most big deals, however, also contain a state contribution that's at least as large. The authors overcount the benefits by only looking at effects over a five-year period. Many economy-wrecking corporate departures, however, happen to occur after five years. Finally, the authors offer no compelling evidence that any of the subsidy packages were ultimately decisive for the deal undertaken. As noted, a number of studies have shown that firms decide in advance where they would like to place a plant, and use the bidding process to manipulate gullible local officials to shave costs.[29]

For me, the biggest flaw in the Greenstone and Moretti study—one that we've already introduced and one that is ubiquitous in the field—is its silence on opportunity costs. What weren't these communities able to do in the name of economic development because they wasted all their dollars on outside attraction? What local businesses were not grown? What local entrepreneurs felt abandoned and moved elsewhere? What tax dollars from these jilted businesses never made it into the local government coffers? What benefits might have manifest had those subsidy dollars stayed in residents' pockets?

Markusen and Ness mention the opportunity-cost problem at the outset of *Reining in the Competition for Capital*. They admit that "[b]idding wars divert decision-makers' attention from a broader portfolio of economic tools and options,"[30] and that "even for bid-winning localities whose jobs and tax base expand, economic-development outcomes might have been positive had those resources been used differently."[31] Most of the other scholars in their volume concede the issue looms large but little research has been done on it.

Ironically, the only writer in Markusen's compendium who looks seriously at the opportunity-cost issues—and by "seriously" I mean devotes a few paragraphs to the topic—is a cautious *supporter* of incentives, Timothy Bartik, senior economist with the W.E. Upjohn Institute for Employment Research. Bartik considers the possibility that local businesses might constitute a superior alternative to outside attraction, but then dismisses this line of thinking: "Rather than competing for mobile capital, local areas could 'just say no,' eliminate incentives for mobile corporations, and rely on locally generated capital. . . . The main problem with this approach is that greater reliance on local capital and local production would significantly reduce an area's real per capita income."[32]

In subsequent correspondence with Bartik (much of whose work I admire, by the way), I asked him how he came to his conclusion. He clarified that what he meant is that an area that avoids trade would naturally become poorer. True enough. But locally owned businesses can trade as easily as absentee businesses and usually generate more income for a community (per unit trade) than do absentee businesses, because they respend more of their gains locally. And moving local capital into local businesses, on top of their existing nonlocal sources of capital, will usually increase the full universe of investment capital for businesses in the community. When I pressed Bartik if he had any evidence that an economic-development dollar was better spent on attracting nonlocal business than on nurturing local business, he conceded he had none.

Eight Myths of Economic Development

There's plenty more to criticize about the theory and practice of mainstream economic development. Let me just focus on what I regard as the eight biggest myths promulgated by the profession.

(1) The Ownership Myth

"We should focus our economic-development efforts on any businesses operating in our jurisdiction, whether or not they are locally owned."

This is perhaps the most fundamental and destructive error of mainstream economic development. It's driven by a misunderstanding of the causes and consequences of globalization. Starting in the 1980s, many of the world's biggest companies began deserting their hometowns and home countries to find "competitive advantages" elsewhere on the planet in places like Mexico, El Salvador, Thailand, and China. Communities were urged to hold onto as many of these companies as possible and to attract others by creating a "favorable business climate." Early progressive writers, like former Labor Secretary Robert Reich, argued for a high-road approach that included "skilling up" the workforce and building up local infrastructure such as highways, rail connections, airports, and high-speed Internet.[33] But most communities seemed intent on taking the low road, which meant poverty wages, busted unions, paltry benefits, low taxes, and skimpy environmental standards.

The difference between one jurisdiction's economic-development strategy and another's was really its political tilt. High-road jurisdictions were Democratic states like Massachusetts, Rhode Island, and Washington, while low-road jurisdictions were Republican states like Alabama, South Carolina, and Texas. Whatever their political differences, however, all fifty states embraced the economic-development catechism of using public incentives to win the corporate attraction auction—it was just a matter of degree. The politics of this were all the more disturbing because of the contradictions. How could progressive regions pay millions in bribes to the Fortune 500 businesses they otherwise distrusted? How could conservative regions suspend their belief in free markets and so readily embrace crony capitalism? The predominant ideology about incentives seemed to trump all other principles, following Margaret Thatcher's declaration that "there is no alternative" to the globalization of trade, investment, and money—TINA.

The underlying error economic developers made was their belief that all the companies that mattered were now globally mobile. Hardly. As discussed earlier, more than half the US economy comprises small and medium-scale businesses that are almost entirely locally owned and unlikely to move. True, not every big business is roving the planet looking for a new home, and not every small business is uninterested in moving to improve its bottom line. But no one seriously doubts that locally owned businesses are significantly less mobile than publicly traded companies are.

Economic developers have been slow to recognize that the relative immobility of local business actually confers huge benefits on a community:

- Economic-development investments in rooted local businesses are much more likely to pay long-term dividends to local residents than investments in fickle global businesses whose captains are inclined to take the money and run.

- A community that doesn't depend on global businesses will not be compelled to cut wages or weaken environmental standards to create a good "business climate." Because local businesses are more willing than their global compatriots to adapt to higher standards rather than to flee them, they provide a better foundation for high-road economic development.

- As married partners know, trust flows from longevity and reliability in relationships. The strangers in global companies who come and go, like gigolos looking for one-night stands, cannot possibly inspire much trust in the communities they aim to seduce. The local businesses that relate to community members for generations—as consumers, investors, suppliers, and workers—are more motivated to nurture their relationships.[34]

This list, by the way, just begins to elucidate the differences between local and nonlocal business. As I've documented in my previous books, there's a growing mountain of evidence that local businesses are also better at promoting jobs, income growth, entrepreneurship, smart growth, environmental responsibility, charitable giving, and political engagement.[35]

(2) The "New Money" Myth

"The key to economic development is to bring new money into the economy. When citizens buy just from local businesses, they are simply recirculating existing dollars and not producing new wealth."

Nonsense. What economic developers forget is that every local dollar spent on a local good or service can also be a dollar not spent importing an outside good or service. What's the difference between a dollar that comes into a community as income from an export and a dollar that's not lost from the community because of an import substitution? Nada, zip, nothing.

Far more important to economic development is how much of that additional dollar, whether earned or saved, continues to circulate in the local economy. Equally important is how much additional local economic activity that dollar generates through what economists call the "multiplier effect." This concept is the cornerstone of community economics. The higher the multiplier, the more income, wealth, and jobs enjoyed locally.

Economic developers rarely understand how ownership influences the power of the multiplier effect. An absentee-owned automobile assembly plant that earns an export-generated dollar, for example, is likely to spend much of that dollar outside the local economy—on managers, lawyers, and accountants in the distant home office, on outside advertising agencies, on parts and materials imported from China, and so forth. More than two dozen studies over the past decade have compared the economic impacts of locally owned businesses with their nonlocal equivalents, and they consistently show that local businesses generate two to four times the multiplier benefits.[36] That means that every dollar that moves from a nonlocal to a local business in a community generates two to four times the income boost, two to four times the jobs, two to four times the local taxes, and two to four times the charitable contributions.

(3) The Traded Sectors Myth

"Manufacturers, wholesalers, distributors, and other 'traded sectors,' are far more important to economic development than other sectors."

This is a variation of New Money Myth, with the underlying assumption, again, that a dollar earned from trade is somehow better than a dollar saved from an import replacement. But another myth is embedded here as well—that traded goods always pay better than supposedly nontraded services, and therefore offer the only "high road" to a high-wage economy.

What's foolish about prioritizing traded sectors and assuming that goods are better for economic development than services is that the concept is both over- and under-inclusive. According to the Bureau of Statistics, the average manufacturer of durable goods paid a weekly wage of $1,090 in June 2014, while the average leisure and hospitality business paid a weekly wage of $362—a threefold difference. But these data are deceptive. "Leisure and hospitality" is one of the lowest paying service sectors. The average "service" sector, in fact, pays $804 per week, while the average "goods" sector pays $1,045—a much smaller difference. And within these averages are huge variations. For example, several service sectors, including "information," "financial activities," and "professional and business services," pay more than the average "goods" sector. There are also huge regional variations. Given these wide ranges of pay, insisting that economic development be rooted in the traded sector, the goods sector, or manufacturing businesses is way too simplistic. Economic development should be rooted in good paying jobs, wherever they can be found—period.

(4) The White Knight Myth

"For communities that are especially suffering—decaying inner cities, depopulating rural communities, destitute Native American reservations— a corporate attraction strategy offers the only chance at ending poverty."

The probability of an outside company coming to the rescue of any community, fulfilling its promises of jobs and investment, and sticking around for the long-term is slim, and it makes no difference whether that community is rich or poor. The evidence suggests that the best way economically challenged communities will improve their overall economic condition is to embrace local small businesses.

A 2010 study appeared in the *Harvard Business Review* under the headline "More Small Firms Means More Jobs."[37] The authors wrote, "Our research shows that regional economic growth is highly correlated with the presence of many small, entrepreneurial employers—not a few big ones." Another paper recently published by the Federal Reserve in Atlanta performed a regression analysis of counties across the United States, and found statistically significant "evidence that local entrepreneurship matters for local economic performance . . . [T]he percent of employment provided by resident, or locally-owned, business establishments has a significant positive effect on county income and employment growth and a significant and negative effect on poverty...."[38]

Some see these results as paradoxical, because there's also evidence that smaller businesses, which are most likely to be locally owned, pay somewhat lower wages and offer fewer employee benefits than larger businesses (though the differential appears to be shrinking). How can it be that local businesses pay less, and yet local business communities prosper more? Conclusive research has yet to be done, but let me offer several theories that might reconcile these results:

- Remember Lou Stein's argument: Because successful small businesses often grow into larger businesses, an entrepreneurial community made up of many small businesses increases the probability of it ultimately having larger businesses that pay better wages. Moreover, these larger businesses that grow indigenously remain locally owned and offer a more reliable basis for economic growth than briefly attracted outsiders.
- Even when local businesses contribute less to the local economy in wages than do nonlocal outsiders, they contribute more in other ways like local taxes, local supplier purchases, and local charitable contributions, which cascade through the economy generating greater income,

wealth, and jobs. The economic multiplier "benefits" of local businesses may turn out to be more important to community prosperity than the "costs" of lower wages.

- Many of the most talented people in a community, particularly younger people, increasingly gravitate to companies that offer great opportunities rather than great wages. They are willing to take less pay, at least for a while, for independence and ownership. These "creatives," as urbanist Richard Florida calls them in *The Rise of the Creative Class*, are important generators of global competitiveness.[39]
- Another critical determinant of local prosperity is the strength of civil society through volunteer organizations, civic groups, foundations, and political groups. The state of Kerala in India, for example, has been able to achieve life expectancy and literacy rates matching Western standards without high incomes, because of its dense network of social institutions.[40] In *Bowling Alone*, Harvard's Robert Putnam has made similar arguments about the importance of strong civil society in ensuring the prosperity of American communities.[41] Local business communities, with rich intimate personal relationships, are more likely to foster this kind of social capital.

I look forward to future graduate dissertations that might prove which of these theories (if any) is right. But let's be clear: The explanation of causality may be less important than the correlation, which is now empirically solid: *Local businesses are associated with more social equality and more long-term prosperity.*

(5) The Competitiveness Myth
"Local businesses are a poor bet for economic development because their goods and services cannot compete against global companies."

More nonsense, often spouted by economic developers when they bring a Wal-Mart to town, brag about all the new jobs they've created, and deny responsibility for killing existing retail jobs. Please.

Broadly speaking, local businesses have done remarkably well at competing, despite the best efforts of economic developers to knock them down through neglect or by subsidizing their global competitors. And two basic facts underscore this conclusion:

- First, if local businesses were becoming less competitive, we would have seen jobs shift from the local half of the economy to the non-local half. In fact, when the spectacular growth of home-based businesses in the United States is properly accounted for, there has been no shift whatsoever for almost a generation. Despite receiving little government support, local businesses have steadily maintained their "market share" of employment.
- Second, if local businesses were becoming less competitive, their profit rates would be lower than those of big businesses. Yet the most recent tax data available from the Internal Revenue Service show that in 2008, sole proprietors, which most small businesses either are or start out as, generated eleven times more net revenue per sales dollar than C-Corporations. In Canada, not a wildly dissimilar nation next to the United States, the most profitable businesses have ten to twenty employees and have profit rates 63 percent higher than big businesses.[42]

These generalizations, of course, mask important exceptions. Some small businesses have had enormous difficulty competing against bigger businesses. For example, the proliferation of shopping malls and chain stores has certainly killed many small retailers over the past two decades. But retail looms especially large in our consumer consciousness, because brick-and-mortar stores are where we purchase most of our daily goods. In fact, retail itself actually only accounts for about 7 percent of the economy.

The real story of retail is much more nuanced and interesting, and helps to illuminate ways local business might compete effectively in the future. Online purchasing, for example, has probably damaged nonlocal chains as much as local businesses, because local businesses have been better able to reinvent their business models to be more responsive to local needs. In the retail niche of book purchasing, for example, Amazon destroyed Borders and is well on the way to killing Barnes & Noble, while local bookstores, many bruised from online competitors, are slowly making a comeback by repositioning themselves as community centers.

Meanwhile, Amazon itself finally may face more serious competition if the federal government eliminates its unfair advantage to sell interstate without collecting sales taxes.

It's telling that some of the same economic developers who think small business is uncompetitive have no qualms about bailing out big business. In 2008, when the global financial crisis hit, the government bailed out failing big banks, failing big insurance companies, and failing automobile companies. No similar helping hands were extended to struggling small businesses. Honestly, how can we as a society refuse to let big businesses fail and then turn around and claim that the small businesses can't compete?

(6) The Self-Financing Myth

"Hey, economic-development incentives don't cost anything,
because the growth of business ultimately pays for them."

This claim is pure alchemy. A tax break for an attracted business, we're told, really doesn't cost anything, because without the attraction, no additional taxes would have been collected anyway. This is the logic offered, for example, by the promoters of "tax increment financing" or TIFs. Originally designed to stimulate growth in low-income communities, TIFs are now being exploited by real property developers everywhere. The local government establishes a TIF district with a baseline value for an undeveloped property, and the developer must continue paying taxes on that original value. The government then ponies up public money for a project within that district, gradually increasing the assessed property valuation and gradually receiving "tax increments" until the grant is paid back. The argument is that since the government never would have collected the increased local tax without the new project, this scheme really isn't a subsidy.

If you buy that argument, then I suggest we all make the following pitch to our local governments: "Hey, I'm planning to build a $1 million addition to my house. Please give me the $1 million up front, and I'll pay it back to you in more property taxes." Or maybe: "My kids are planning to go to college. Give me the $300,000 needed for four years of tuition, room, and board, and then they'll pay you back with higher income taxes once they move back here."

If a local government let every resident do this, it would soon go broke. In all these examples, the risk of default has to be assumed somewhere. Who assumes the risk if the million dollar addition to my house—maybe I just build a shrine to Bullwinkle—turns out to be worthless? Or if my kids send a thank-you note for the college education from their new home in Paris? The capital for TIFs, tax breaks, loans, and infrastructure improvements are all coming from local taxpayers; and those taxpayers shoulder all the risk that these ventures will go bust. Why should a municipal government be investing everyone's money in a private developer's get-rich-quick scheme? If the development project falls short of its goals or fails altogether, the government loses its shirt. As long as the government is taking a risk with taxpayers' money, it's a subsidy, plain and simple.

(7) The Trade Myth

"Supporting local business means denying your community the gains from robust trade."

Recall that this was Timothy Bartik's argument, and it's a common refrain among buy-local critics. If every community increased its self-reliance through local production, global trade would collapse, and a new dystopia of global poverty and darkness would ensue. The critical assumption here is that local goods and services are always more expensive than the global alternatives. And, indeed, if people irrationally spend more money on local goods and services, they will be able to buy less and wind up making themselves poorer.

But suppose local goods and services were roughly the same price or cheaper than nonlocal alternatives. It would then impoverish local consumers *not* to buy local. Critics of local business do not even consider this possibility, even though, as noted earlier, the local businesses that make up half the US economy are clearly competitive and profitable.

Smart local economic developers will introduce resident consumers to all the great local deals they are overlooking, and alert resident investors to promising local companies seeking capital. Localization grounded in these principles is a powerful wealth-building strategy. And if every community in the world embraced this kind of localization, we all would enjoy greater wealth and greater consumer spending. Ironically, if people spent their newly acquired wealth on nonlocal goods, localization everywhere could wind up increasing the level of global trade!

Let me give you an example that makes this paradox more understandable. About a decade ago, my then wife and I decided to move our mortgage from Bank of America to a local credit union. We wound up saving several thousand dollars a year because of the lower interest rate and lower fees. What did we do with that money? Well, one thing I did was buy more of my favorite Scotch whiskey, Macallan 12. By taking advantage of an easily localized financial service, I was able to spend my savings on foreign libations that are not so easily localized.

Mainstream economic developers who insist that a community ignore the opportunities for smart localization are actually the ones who are robbing residents' pocketbooks, and thereby impairing trade and spreading poverty at home and abroad.

(8) The Equality Myth

"We support all business—local and nonlocal, big and small, anything that provides jobs."

Few economic developers admit that they are ignoring local business. They will list a dozen programs they endorse—courses, mentorships, incubators, industrial parks, angel funds—that benefit some local businesses. What they seem to be unaware of is just how trivial, in dollar terms, these programs really are. Perhaps you think I'm exaggerating?

My suspicions about the antilocal bias in economic development led me, starting about eight years ago, to raise support from the Kellogg Foundation to assess state economic-development programs across the United States. Since Kellogg had a particular interest in food systems, my colleagues and I decided to focus our study on fifteen rural states. For each state, we picked the three largest programs and inventoried all the incentives associated with each for a three-year period. We then sought to discern which recipients were locally owned and which weren't.

There were huge methodological challenges. Few states track their development investments to ensure that beneficiary companies are delivering their promises and actually improving the state's economy. To the extent that records could be found, they were often in various places (or piles), with no central repository. Even for those few states—like Maine— ostensibly committed to greater accountability, the absence of data and performance measurements for most programs made the task nearly impossible. Some states do not even try to maintain records.

Where records were not public, we filed requests under state "freedom of information acts" (where they existed). Where our requests were rebuffed or ignored, we constructed surveys for program managers, some of whom were willing to estimate the split of their subsidies between local and nonlocal businesses. While we ideally wanted to study three years of giving for the top three state programs, we had to accept that in some states only one or two programs could be studied and that for some programs only one or two years of data were available. Research that we originally projected would take one year ultimately took four.

Our methodology for counting whether a beneficiary company was locally owned was to presume that it was local unless we could establish otherwise. This ensured that our results were conservative—that is, if anything, our results would understate the nonlocal skew of subsidies. We applied two tests to each subsidy:

- First, was the beneficiary company publicly traded? (By definition, such firms are not locally owned.)
- Second, if the company was privately held, was its headquarters out of state and therefore nonlocal? (Various publicly available databases, including those from Hoover's and Dun & Bradstreet, note where the headquarters of a firm is.)

While our data were not as comprehensive as we originally had hoped, nor as consistent (we had to use different three-year periods for some states, ranging between 2003 and 2011), the study wound up demonstrating the astonishing inclination of economic developers not to support businesses in their own backyards. The findings are summarized in the following table.

Percent of Economic Development Funds Given to Local Business Nationwide

State	Program	Year 1	Year 2	Year 3	Multi-Year Average
ARIZONA	Job Training Program	26%	25%	20%	23%
	Enterprise Zones				10%
	Research & Development Income Tax Credit				10%
ARKANSAS	Consolidated Incentive Act				6%
	Economic Development Incentive Program				1%
	Economic Investment Tax Credit (Investark)				4%
KENTUCKY	Rural Economic Development Act				9%
	Jobs Development Act				7%
	Industrial Development Act				6%
LOUISIANA	Economic Dev. Award Program	34%	74%	21%	45%
	Rapid Response Fund	1%	n/a	3%	2%
	Workforce Development Program	11%	30%	3%	17%
MAINE	Employment Tax Increment Financing	36%	14%	6%	12%
	Governor's Training Initiative	44%	39%	36%	40%
	Business Equipment Tax Reimbursement	18%	12%	n/a	15%
MICHIGAN	Economic Growth Authority	8%	6%	7%	7%
	Renaissance Zones	NO DATA AVAILABLE			
	Economic Development Jobs Training Program	72%	67%	58%	66%
MISSISSIPPI	Jobs Tax Credits				0%
	Rural Economic Development				0%
	Advantage Jobs Incentive Program				20%
MONTANA	Workforce Training Grants	100%	11%	31%	27%
	Community Development Block Grants	100%	100%	28%	64%
	Big Sky Trust Fund	30%	53%	17%	29%

State	Program	Year 1	Year 2	Year 3	Multi-Year Average
NEBRASKA	Employment & Investment Growth Act	37%	55%	45%	45%
	Nebraska Advantage Act	n/a	57%	23%	32%
	Invest Nebraska Act	0%	38%	n/a	17%
NEW MEXICO	Job Training Incentive Program				25%
	Rural Jobs Tax Credit	NO DATA AVAILABLE			
	Manufacturing Investment Credit	NO DATA AVAILABLE			
NORTH CAROLINA	One North Carolina Fund	6%	9%	26%	15%
	Job Dev. Investment Grant	0%	15%	0%	10%
	Lee Tax Credits	7%	7%	6%	7%
NORTH DAKOTA	ND Development Fund	57%	80%	71%	72%
	Workforce 20/20	50%	55%	58%	55%
	Renaissance Zones	100%	100%	100%	100%
OHIO	Ohio Industrial Training Program	33%	17%	30%	30%
	Job Creation Tax Credit	38%	26%	20%	27%
	Rapid Outreach Fund	17%	66%	39%	39%
SOUTH DAKOTA	Future Fund Grant	43%	44%	60%	46%
	REDI Fund	64%	80%	64%	69%
	Workforce Development Program	54%	40%	35%	43%
WEST VIRGINIA	Capital Company Credit				23%
	Super Tax Credit				6%
	Research & Development Tax Credit				3%

The following figure presents a graphical representation of our analysis of forty-five programs. By far, the largest number of programs—twenty-six—were giving less than 25 percent of their

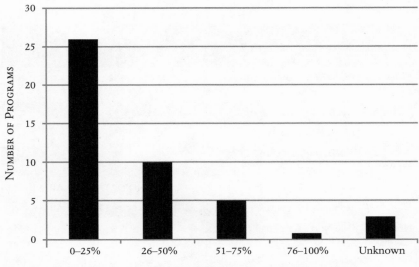

PERCENT OF PROGRAM FUNDS GIVEN TO LOCAL BUSINESS

Breakdown of 45 Programs Studied

money to local business. Of these, sixteen programs were giving 90 percent or more of their money to outside companies. Only eight of the programs were giving most of their money to local business. We were unable to pry loose information about three programs, but we suspect that the data were being withheld to hide their nonlocal character. *Adding together the first two raised columns, we can say that four out of five of the largest state economic-development programs were giving most of their money to nonlocal business.*

These data underscore that it's highly likely that your hard-earned money being taxed and spent in the name of economic development is actually going to support some other community's business rather than your own.

The Need for Reinvention

Economic development today is completely broken. Simple reforms, like community benefit agreements that compensate losers in attraction deals, are not enough. The profession and the practice need to be completely overhauled. The singular focus on attracting global corporations is not just ineffective but counterproductive, especially given the huge opportunity costs. Indeed, it's not far-fetched to suggest that the best way most communities can "develop" is by abolishing their economic-development departments altogether.

I, for one, however, am not quite that cynical. I do believe economic development can play an important and constructive role in communities. Were it to embrace the philosophy of the Lou Steins of the world, its mission might include the following initiatives:

- Nurture the start-up and growth of locally owned businesses.
- Maximize cost-effective self-reliance through import substitution, while expanding exports from local businesses.
- Identify, celebrate, and spread models of triple-bottom-line (people, planet, profit) success in local businesses.
- Accomplish as many of these goals as possible through private investment.

This last point warrants elaboration. The late Jane Jacobs argued in one of her last books, *Systems of Survival*, that when the "guardian sector," her name for the public sector, mixes with the "trading sector," "monstrous hybrids" result that are inefficient, foolish, and even criminal.[43] Jacobs believed that the public sector has many important roles to play, but it needs to be decentralized and minimal. The current structure of economic development violates all these principles. Pork-barrel support for a few businesses at the expense of all taxpayers, businesses and consumers alike, unnecessarily grows government and dangerously comingles public funds with private purposes.

To move away from corruption, economic development should be carried out through pollinator businesses, primarily funded through private capital. By holding themselves to the discipline of the marketplace, and by providing valuable services that local businesses, local consumers, and local investors pay for, economic developers can deliver better results at a lower cost. The goal should be to create an entrepreneurial ecosystem that benefits the entire local business community. This is where the six *P*s fit in—local planning, local purchasing, local people, local partners, local purse, and local public policy. The next five chapters look at the five categories where promising pollinator businesses are possible and now spreading.

CHAPTER 2

Planning

Prepping Businesses and Places for Success

The first *P* of local economic development, planning, is all about finding direction. In the twisted world of mainstream economic development, *planning* means helping a community discover its "competitive advantage" in the global economy, creating clusters of businesses around those promising trade "niches," and bringing "new" dollars into the economy through expanded exports. Once these magical clusters, niches, and exports are identified, planners then discern candidate companies to recruit, and begin to organize junkets to the far-flung locations where these firms are based. The mainstream planning process also involves conducting studies to improve the business environment, with high-road recommendations for boosting education and infrastructure, and low-road recommendations for cutting taxes and keeping wages low.

Planning for healthy local economic development requires thinking and acting differently. A local planner—or city rep or business council member or community activist or anyone else engaged in some aspect of planning—should embrace a different set of basic assumptions: Whatever your competitive global niches, celebrate them but realize that these parts of your economy are doing fine. The occupants of successful niches are the companies that *least* need help. Focus instead on your gaps, on all the businesses that should be there but aren't, on all the goods and services that should be made and consumed locally but now are imported. In other words, ignore the flashy global companies asking for millions in incentives and rechannel your scarce resources into existing and potential local businesses. This involves several sequential steps:

- Facilitate a broad community discussion about what your collective goals are, what kind of economy you want, and which businesses you need.
- Set objective indicators to measure whether your community is moving toward or away from those goals.
- Make an inventory of your community's assets—not just economic assets like labor, land, and capital, but all kinds of noneconomic assets like culture, natural resources, and civil society. Bring them to the attention of your local entrepreneurs.
- Calculate your economic leakages, which again are all the dollars that are leaving the community (and therefore doing no economic good). The reason for doing this is simple: If these demands can be localized through more local purchasing, the local economic multiplier gets pumped up. Every leakage carries the opportunity for new or expanded local business.

With a clear set of indicators offering direction and a clear sense of local assets that shape your possibilities, you can create and expand the best local businesses that plug the biggest leaks. This approach to planning, however, cannot proceed automatically, and requires the application of the other Ps—people, partners, purchasing, purse, and public policy.

Local economic-development planning confers a number of advantages over the existing practice:

- Local economic development puts your community, your vision, your market, and your entrepreneurs in the driver's seat. You're in control of your own destiny. You do not need to depend on the good will of outsiders to grow your economy—nor do you need to expose yourself to the risks of their avarice.
- Local economic development seeks to develop every business within the economy rather than reward, again and again, a handful of outside companies.

- Local economic development grows the economy from tapping local strengths, including local assets, local people, local demand, and local dreams, rather than begging for nonlocal assets to address purported local weaknesses.
- Local economic development offers the possibility of proceeding through low-cost or no-cost pollinators.

When I am asked by wide-eyed undergraduates what universities might help them become practitioners of local economic development, I'm flummoxed. My list is disappointingly short. Yes, almost every so-called Department of Planning has an oddball faculty member who teaches this material, but the vast majority of the professors and courses—many of which are required—are hopelessly stuck in the mainstream paradigm. Without teaching a coherent understanding of the critical role of local businesses in community economy work, these planning programs offer limited support for the planning ideas that follow.

Nor are most trained and certified planners equipped to become self-financing pollinators themselves. Many wind up working for state and local governments, managing transportation systems, sewers, electricity and water utilities, Internet distribution, and other forms of public infrastructure. As publicly paid civil servants, they hardly qualify as self-financing pollinators in the private sector. Some planners go into private practice and assume the role of project developers or architect-engineers. They might perform studies of business opportunities, to justify which businesses they recommend putting into their various projects—often subdivisions, shopping malls, or industrial parks. Since the mission of private planners is usually to benefit the small number of property developers that hire them, rather than all local businesses, they too are not pollinators.

But a small cadre of planners is remaking the profession, and showing how it's possible to thrive professionally while planning for the entire local economy. Some, such as Main Street Genome, are offering tools for diagnosing and improving small businesses. Others, such as Bazzani Associates in Michigan and the Village Well in Melbourne, are using their planning tools to revitalize cities through architecture and design. My appreciation for what these pioneers do has been deepened by my own efforts to walk the planning pollinator talk—and that's where I'd like to begin.

Leak Plugging 101

Two years ago my colleague Kate Poole and I published a handbook laying out, step by step, how a community can undertake local economic development.[44] The first few chapters are all about planning. We suggest a long list of critical questions a planning-minded community should answer before getting started. For example:

- If you want more local business, great: But how does your community define *local*?
- If you want low-cost indicators to measure progress with localization, which data will you follow? Employment? Income? Poverty? Infant mortality? And from which databases?
- If you want to prepare an inventory of your assets, what specifically might you place on your checklist of, say, public buildings?

All these tasks, frankly, are relatively simple, inexpensive, and even fun to carry out. But when it comes to the next phase—measuring economic leakage—grassroots groups hit a wall. To be sure, there are quick-and-dirty approaches to measuring leakage. But coming up with defensible data that can counter the fog of misinformation churned out by mainstream economic developers usually requires the use of costly and complicated econometric models, such as the one I used in Cabarrus County, North Carolina. And grassroots groups become apoplectic when faced with the prospect of understanding, let alone mastering, computer software.

That's not surprising, since economic models and those that use them inhabit an arcane world of their own. Debates over economic-development priorities are best understood as the modern equivalent of *kabuki*, the beautiful but highly stylized Japanese art of theater and dance. Just as kabuki requires the dancers to have painted, clownlike faces, and move in certain slow, rhythmic forms that no one in the audience confuses with reality, economic-development debates today call for their performers to deploy certain tools and methods that bear only a limited resemblance to reality. Consequently, about a decade ago, I taught myself how to use these models, so that I, too, could fight fire with fire, as it were, or statistics with statistics.

For nearly fifty years econometricians have sought to create workable models of economies. Different models, of course, have different objectives. The best regional and local models contain extensive data about the businesses, government institutions, consumers, and investors in their jurisdictions, both their intrinsic characteristics (like how many employees a business has) and their dynamic behavior (like how much does an average household spend each year). They tie all these factoids together in elaborate mathematical equations that reflect the modeler's best judgment about what causes what. Imagine a floor with ten thousand dominos in various lines, and predicting how one falling domino might influence the rest—that's what an economic modeler attempts to do.

When I started to develop techniques for measuring economic leakage fifteen years ago, I turned to the two models most widely used by other mainstream economic developers: RIMS II, which is sold by the US Department of Commerce; and IMPLAN, which comes from a private company called MIG. Both models provide comprehensive profiles of community economies throughout the United States, and show how a proposed change—a new stadium or a wage hike—can ripple through the economy. A skilled modeler can determine the direct effects of expanding a business, the indirect effects on what that business might purchase from other industries, and the induced effects on what the workers in these expanded industries then buy as consumers.

The first few times I used these models, I felt as if I were going cross-eyed and my head might explode. The terminology was abstract and confusing, and it bore little relationship to my own coursework in economics. The training manuals were so poorly written that I frequently had to call the help hotline—for $300 per hour—so that someone might answer my many questions. That was the first of many expenses. Every time I used a model in a given community, I had to purchase a specific database that could cost hundreds, sometimes even thousands, of dollars.

Once I mastered these models, I was able to prepare leakage analyses for various clients, in places like Spokane (WA), the Pioneer Valley (MA), greater Cleveland (OH), and Boulder County (CO). Sometimes these studies looked at leakages across the entire economy, and sometimes they zeroed in on specific sectors like food. For most of the last decade, these studies have become a significant portion of my own bread and butter. So looking back at it, I became a leakage-analysis pollinator!

But the more I used these models, the more skeptical I became about the real-world benefits I was providing clients. I began to appreciate that the three-decimal answers generated for every question—that a given construction project would generate 146.325 jobs, for example—were deceptive. If you look under the hood in the model, you realize how many gaps there are in the underlying data and how many assumptions the model makes to fill in those gaps. Most databases also have errors that are not always easy to spot. Moreover, once my clients had my results, they were perplexed by what to do next: "Okay, three-quarters of the potential sectors in our economy have no local businesses whatsoever, but how exactly do we go about creating new businesses in those sectors?" If my clients had exhausted their meager financial resources on the leakage analysis, they then had nothing left for implementation.

I could see the need for a new leakage tool that was easier and cheaper to use, so that any community could get a basic sense of the leakages within its economy and conserve most of its money for business-expanding activities. When I became research director at BALLE in 2009, one of my first assignments was to create a leakage calculator. The goal was to be able to plug in your county or zip code, press a button, and—voila!—out would pop basic information about leaks in your economy. My colleagues and I raised $50,000 for the project, and a year later the tool became available for a modest fee.

Here's how it works: Suppose I wanted to measure economic leakage in my own community. I currently live in a suburb of Washington, DC, called Silver Spring, an unincorporated area within Montgomery County, Maryland. Using the Overview Calculator, I can plug in my county and instantly see to what extent each of the 1,100 sectors is self-reliant. (The North American Industrial Classification System, or NAICS, carves up the economy into about 1,100 sectors.) If I was interested in the entertainment piece of my economy, for example, I could see that the theater sector is 125 percent self-reliant, which means that the theaters in Montgomery County are not only meeting local demand for theater goers but also selling tickets to residents of neighboring counties. I could see that there are almost no museums, zoos, or historical sites in the county (neighboring Washington, DC, a huge tourist destination, more than compensates). The calculator also shows how many new jobs would be possible if the county were self-reliant in each sector. For example, if we manufactured our own pet food, we could have 67 more jobs. If we became self-reliant in every sector, we could create 142,523 more jobs paying $6.8 billion. To put this in perspective, in July 2014, the number of unemployed Montgomery County residents was 27,483. A 20 percent shift toward self-reliance therefore could essentially eliminate unemployment!

Like a ruler, the calculators generate only measurements, and it's up to the user to apply intelligence in interpreting them. The calculators show how many jobs are *possible* through self-reliance, not how many jobs are *plausible*. And there are many reasons why a possible job might not be plausible: You can't have oil-drilling jobs, for example, if you don't have oil. You can't have theater jobs if you don't have theaters. Every region has competitive advantages, and that's why leakage analysis must proceed alongside a sober assessment of assets and business designs.

NAICS has some quirks that US government statisticians promise to fix over time, and one of the most important is that it excludes farming. So I also created a Food Calculator to provide some sense of the leakages of fresh food. Again, plug in Montgomery County, and you can see that in six major food categories—poultry and eggs, beef, pork, dairy products, fresh fruits, and fresh vegetables—less than 3 percent of what's consumed by residents is produced within the county. If Montgomery County wanted to become completely self-reliant in food, it could raise 70,000 more head of cattle, 450,000 more hogs, 27 million more chickens, 41,000 more milk cows, and 40,000 more acres of fruits and vegetables. Again, whether the county would choose to grow more of its food is another question. (It seems doubtful the McMansions of the Potomac would really want giant poultry farms next door.) But the point is to present your community with business options, and then try to prioritize them based on common sense.

A third calculator, the Finance Calculator, estimates how much money residents have squirreled away in savings. I can learn that my fellow residents in Montgomery County have $108 billion of assets—nearly all of which are being invested in nonlocal stocks, bonds, pension funds, and mutual funds. Were even one percent of those savings to be redirected, the county would have more than $1 billion for local business.

If you want to get into the weeds of the methodology, you can read various documents I've posted (see www.michaelhshuman.com) that explain where all these numbers come from and why the BALLE calculators tend to make lower estimates of the benefits of self-reliance than do those from IMPLAN. In other words, if you had more resources to perform a more thorough leakage analysis, you would probably find even more jobs and income possible.

BALLE recently sold the calculators to me, and I'm now in the process of rethinking a business model for them. If I want to become a successful planning pollinator, here are some of the questions I need to answer:

- How much will my annual budget have to be? I could probably operate the calculators, as is, for $25,000 per year. But if I want to steadily upgrade them to do more interesting analyses (like measure leakage changes over several years), I may need an annual budget of $50,000 or more.
- How much should I charge people who use the calculators? My goal is make them available for much less than the $500 to $1,000 that IMPLAN users must pay. If I charge a user $100, I'll need five hundred users per year to meet my budget. If I charge $25, I'll need two thousand users.
- How will I market the calculators to secure the breakeven number of users? Through my e-zine? Through advertising on other websites? By offering discounts to simpatico organizations?
- How much start-up capital will I need to reach my breakeven point? Even if people are willing to pay $100, it may take a while to sign up five hundred users. Should I borrow the money I need up front? Ask for a foundation grant? Crowdfund for it on Kickstarter? What structure (for-profit, nonprofit, co-op) does this imply for my work?

You can see that with a pollinator mindset, I now have to think and act like a business. I'm no longer a policy wonk telling businesses willy-nilly what to do. I'm one of them. I'm more empathetic with their struggles, and more capable of seeing their opportunities. But more importantly, I'm creating a useful service for local businesses and communities everywhere in the country that ultimately can pay for itself.

The DNA of Success

One lesson of the calculators is that yardsticks matter. When my father's mother was born in Lithuania in 1900, the average American man and woman were living to age 46 and 48, respectively. In the year my father was born, 1922, life expectancy was 58 and 61. When I was born in 1956, it was 67 and 73. Today, it's 74 and 80. One of the underappreciated explanations for this dramatic shift in life expectancy is our improved tools for diagnostics. If your cholesterol is high, you know you need to cut certain foods out of your diet and exercise more. If you have markers for colon cancer, you may need to get frequent colonoscopies and biopsies. If you weigh yourself regularly, you tend to be more mindful of the calories you're taking in with every meal. Yardsticks beget action.

If it's possible to extend our lives through smart indicators, why can't we also extend the lives of local business? According to the Small Business Administration, about half of all small business establishments fail within five years of birth and two-thirds fail within ten.[45] Skeptics of small business dwell on these statistics as if they were immutable laws of nature. But not Eric Koester, cofounder of Main Street Genome. Koester is convinced that if small businesses better understood the DNA of their discrete business models, their life expectancy could be greatly increased. Indeed, he would argue that one of the most important metrics of economic vitality is whether the survival rate of local start-ups is improving. By holding up a mirror for small businesses to see their own strengths and weaknesses more clearly, Koester is helping them with critical business planning decisions.

Koester's thinking about business began in Omaha, Nebraska—in the fourth grade. Like thousands of young entrepreneurs before him, he decided to set up a lemonade stand. Koester baked cookies, made sandwiches, and hired his little brother to take orders. The vexing marketing question was where to place the sales table. The Koester kids settled on the local golf course where they knew there was plenty of foot traffic. For several weeks business was great. Too great, however, from the golf club's perspective, because its own sales of refreshments were tanking. The club insisted that the unlicensed upstarts move elsewhere. Koester mischievously moved the table to the perimeter of the course, partially on public property, until a local marshal escorted him away and shut down the business. Ever since, it's fair to say, Koester has been trying to figure out how to help the Davids in business prevail against the Goliaths.

Koester ultimately got a law degree at George Washington University in 2006, and then worked for the Seattle office of Heller Ehrman, a prestigious corporate law firm. He spent his time helping start-ups ("you know, two guys and a dog in a garage with an interesting idea"), as well as more mature companies looking for serious capital. "My day involved a dozen different balls up in the air. The biggest guys paid the bills, but I was helping everyone fulfill their dreams." Over time, however, Koester started to feel like he was on the wrong side of the desk. "It was like working in a candy store, surrounded by delicious sweets, and told you can't have any yourself!"

One of the nonprofits Koester assisted was called Startup Weekend, which convened hackathons in which teams had fifty-four hours to put together a company from scratch. He decided to give it a whirl. "These people were my tribe." He entered the Seattle hackathon, came up with an iPhone app that would help remind you of the names of LinkedIn connections as you met them, and Koester's team won the competition. At the awards ceremony the local sponsor, Microsoft, was supposed to give them a $5,000 prize, but instead, the Microsoft reps gave the award to the second place team and abruptly left the stage. Aware of recent stories about Microsoft cofounder Steve Ballmer getting enraged and ripping an Apple iPhone out of an employee's hands, the audience immediately realized the Windows giant once again was displaying remarkably thin skin. The participants booed, denounced Microsoft, and Koester had his own fifteen minutes of fame. And about fifteen thousand new friends.

Koester stepped out of his law firm in 2010 to join a new start-up called Zaarly, an Internet company that connects consumers with top-quality handymen, housekeepers, and lawn-care specialists. "We really wanted to help sole proprietors who do what they love. For example, we made it much easier for these service providers to do reoccurring billings." Zaarly did well, but Koester ultimately felt the pull of creating something new. Plus, the ache of being apart for two years from his wife, who was then living in Washington, DC, became unbearable. It was time to head east. Georgetown's McDonough School of Business immediately snatched him up to teach entrepreneurship as an adjunct. Of course, entrepreneurs are never comfortable just teaching.

Main Street Genome became Koester's next passion. It reflected his pollinator view that the only significant way the United States can grow its economy is by strengthening its small businesses. But the traditional approach, he worried, amounts to sending every kind of entrepreneur, whether a farmer or a high-tech engineer, to the same basic, boring classes at the local Small Business Development Center. In fact, the universe of small businesses contains radically different kinds of business models, and each one needs very different types of assistance.

Koester believes that the 1,100 NAICS sectors can be reduced to maybe one hundred basic building blocks. "I say to the owner of a restaurant, 'walk me through your day,' and then I see various businesses. As he describes the kitchen, I see a food manufacturing company. The bar buys alcohol in bulk and divides it in small amounts—basically a wholesale distribution business. The to-go part of the restaurant is really an e-commerce operation. Every business is really a mash-up of basic businesses like this."

Main Street Genome helps local businesses understand each component of their unique mash-up, and then provides them with data they can use to improve performance. For each discrete building block, Koester creates a knowledge module containing data from hundreds of companies that provide benchmarks for that business's competitive performance. "Wouldn't it be great to have a 'second set of eyes' on your business— designed by owners for owners like you?"

What kinds of data? Thus far Main Street Genome has been collecting data on restaurants, wholesalers, construction companies, and doctors' and dentists' offices. The data cover a company's revenues, costs of goods sold (COGS), labor costs, marketing costs, and compliance costs. "Data mixed with deep industry knowledge," Koester argues, "can help small businesses increase their profitability, reduce risk, and eliminate unnecessary hours of work."

Right now, Main Street Genome is focusing on the purchasing patterns of restaurants in a few geographic areas. Koester explains that an estimated 60 percent of small business revenue gets spent on inputs, so this is truly the most important place to start improving the bottom line. "Independent restaurants spend $120 billion per year on stuff for their business, but they have no idea how the prices they are paying stack up against what others are paying. What's the right price for avocados? We look at their invoices, record and study the information embedded in them, and then aggregate across the network. How can all the players in a sector buy smarter? If we can improve buyer IQ, then the independents can compete more effectively against chains."

Main Street Genome's business model is not fee-for-service, but fee-for-success. Koester is currently working with three hundred restaurants in Washington, DC, and charging them nothing. In return, they agree to provide their vendor invoices in digital form and answer a survey on how well the vendors are performing. Koester then uses the data to approach vendors on clients' behalf and create a more efficient, data-driven purchasing relationship for both sides. Thus far he has been able to shave a remarkable 10–15 percent off clients' costs, and the savings are split between the restaurants, their vendors, and Main Street Genome.[46]

Sometimes, the data reveal surprisingly simple ways to cut costs. "We have one restaurant in the U Street corridor in Northwest DC that was paying a vendor on a thirty-day billing cycle. We pointed out that if the vendor were paid sooner, the restaurant's costs would be lower," says Koester. "In fact, if the business ordered on line, we might be able to convince the vendor to provide a rebate."

Main Street Genome ultimately wants to improve the competitiveness of all local businesses across America. "Look, millions of Main Street businesses are not purchasing experts. Tony, of restaurant 1905, has to oversee everything in his restaurant, and one consequence is that he's paying an unnecessary 10–20 percent premium on his food. The entire local business sector looks like the 1970s economy, with paper invoices and orders done over the phone. Technology in the rest of the economy has brought down costs, and we need to bring this technology to small business. We can help to accelerate this transition through small behavioral changes, and by working with vendors. A vendor won't make changes for one small business, but it might do so for a group of them."

Most efforts to improve input efficiency, Koester points out, aggregate the purchasing power of many small businesses with one preferred vendor to bring down costs through greater volume. This is a sensible strategy for some businesses (as we will see in our story of Tucson Originals in chapter 5). What Main Street Genome is trying to achieve is different. It's helping small businesses that share a vendor improve efficiency without switching vendors. Koester believes in reinforcing loyalty to local suppliers.

With investment from AOL founder Steve Case, Main Street Genome has grown to a staff of twenty. "We don't lack for an ambitious plan," says Koester. "We are starting with purchasing because it's a gateway to the whole ecosystem. Now we're attacking restaurant purchasing in the Mid-Atlantic. By 2015 we will expand nationwide. And then we will expand categorically, to similar businesses. Once we have a relationship with a given group of businesses, we can move beyond purchasing into other areas, like spending money wisely on technology or marketing."

Koester is especially eager to dive into the data of health-care vendors, because their prices are so opaque and high. Most doctors don't realize, or care, that some patients get charged $1,000 for the same blood test that others can buy for $10. And this is one of the reasons the US health-care system, despite its many virtues, is one of the least efficient and most expensive in the world.

While Main Street Genome's service is free for the small businesses in its target regions, communities in the rest of the country will have to wait for it—unless, perhaps, they are willing to pay a premium. Koester envisions Chambers of Commerce or cities in those regions hiring Main Street Genome to improve their businesses sector by sector. Certainly a city would be wiser to spend a few thousand dollars to make hundreds of local businesses more profitable than to pay $10 million to attract one outside factory. "Heck," says Koester, "we might be willing to set up our own incentive program. If we increase your employment by X, you pay us Y."

Performance standards for economic development? What a novel idea!

Revitalizing One Brick at a Time

No US city better embodies the destructive consequences of publicly traded manufacturers deserting their hometown than Detroit. The mighty Motor City, which once was the home to more than two million residents, now has about seven hundred thousand, with not just thousands of buildings abandoned but thousands of blocks. Flint, Ypsilanti, and dozens of other cities in Michigan have not fared much better. One exception in the state, though, is Grand Rapids, and one reason for its reversal of fortune is a local developer named Guy Bazzani who has performed about $45 million worth of renovation in the city.

Like tens of thousands of other developers in the United States, Bazzani builds things—some commercial, some residential, some civic. He conceives projects, guides the architects, raises capital, negotiates with the legal authorities for permits, carries out the construction, and then finds owners or tenants. Among his peers, Bazzani has done remarkably well. His company, Bazzani Associates, grosses about $3–6 million per year, primarily through its construction work, plus he has extensive real estate holdings in the community. But unlike his peers, Bazzani has a pollinator mindset. He enjoys being well compensated, sure, along with a fine scotch and an occasional cigar, but his mission is reflected in his company's slogan, "Building Sustainable Communities." "Community," explains Bazzani, "is really about economic and physical reconstruction."

The Bazzani Associates website shows images from twenty projects on which the company has indelibly left its mark, including office buildings, town houses, a library, the Hispanic Center of Western Michigan, and a theater. Most were redesigned to achieve high levels of water and energy efficiency. A few have "green roofs" with gardens that absorb rainwater, cool the building, improve indoor air quality, and eliminate stormwater runoff that otherwise would strain municipal infrastructure. All the visuals of the projects on the website are "after" completion. It's quite an experience to watch Bazzani's PowerPoint presentations to audiences, showing the astonishing transformation from "before" to "after." You can hear audible gasps of "Oh my God!"

Most of the buildings in Grand Rapids that Bazzani has overhauled were boarded up, basically tombstones. His strategy has been to bring these buildings back to life by opening them up. "What we've found in the restoration of neighborhoods that have been abandoned or underutilized, especially in the commercial districts, is the need for transparency on the first floor. The best neighborhoods to renovate are those with what I call a 'double loaded street,' with retail on both sides, residential above. You have more people on the street, more activity, more safety. Then it's all about orchestrating the for-profits, nonprofits, and the city to create synergy and make it all start to snowball."

When Bazzani began his makeover of Grand Rapids around 2000–2001, he discovered an obsolete city code that favored keeping residential and commercial activities far apart and contained no flexibility for green designs. "The planners didn't quite get it. Planners can be creative, but lack the power to overcome bureaucratic obstacles. So, we pushed the envelope." Regulatory changes followed, as did the thinking of public officials, and the next round of building was easier.

One of the first areas Bazzani targeted was Wealthy Street, an ironic name given that 90 percent of the buildings in the neighborhood, 1.5 miles long and half a mile wide, had been abandoned and one of the most common sounds on the street was gunfire. As if to coronate himself king of the "hood," Bazzani decided to put his castle, a dual-purpose home and office, right in the center. That building became the first in the city to achieve a LEED certification from the US Green Building Council. (LEED stands for leadership in energy and environmental design.) When he held an open house at the completion of the project, he invited 150 people. Six hundred showed up.

Over the decade since, Bazzani has developed twenty-seven buildings in the Wealthy Street neighborhood, and other developers have followed suit. Today, it's one of the strongest neighborhoods in the city, and its commercial sector is thriving. During the recession of 2008–2011, when real estate markets plummeted across the country, housing values on Wealthy Street only dropped 2 percent. A typical home there is now sold within five days.

Bazzani has moved on to conquer other challenging neighborhoods in Grand Rapids, and pushed to overhaul the entire local building industry. He revamped the 7,200-square-foot East Hill Center with a restaurant, retailers, and offices. When it was completed in 2005, it was the first building in the Midwest to have zero stormwater discharge. "I follow the practice of biomimicry rather than the widely practiced Judeo-Christian ethic of 'stewardship.' Look how our stewardship has worked so far—we have exhausted the environment. We should tread lighter on the ground, while stimulating the economy."

He's especially proud of his recent renovation of the Kingsley Building, which has one hundred thousand square feet. "We just began opening up that building, for the first time since it was boarded up in 1954. Those storefronts had been boarded up for more years than they had been open, and the building was the tallest in the area. Most buildings are two stories, but this one is five. People didn't even realize the building was there. I'd say, 'We're bringing seventeen thousand square feet of retail into the neighborhood,' and everyone would ask, 'Where is it?' I'd say it's in the five-story building in our neighborhood, and they'd reply, 'There is no five-story building in our neighborhood.' This is at the intersection of two roads where a minimum of ten thousand cars were passing per day, mind you, and no one could tell me where it was. It had been wiped out of commerce for a lack of transparency and wiped out from people's minds for more than fifty years! We opened it up and now people say, 'Wow, what a cool building!'"

Critical to Bazzani's success has been his passion for the local business community. "If you are rebuilding commercial storefronts, it's all about local businesses. A network of local businesses is a nice resource to refer other developers to and make them feel better about taking risks."

As a member of the Social Ventures Network, Bazzani attended some of the earliest organizing meetings for BALLE. He immediately saw the potential for forming a local business alliance in Grand Rapids. He asked the local Chamber of Commerce to take on a regional BALLE network, but they "poo-pooed" the idea. So Bazzani went independent. Local First Grand Rapids has since grown to seven hundred members, including some billion-dollar companies like Meijer. It has become so successful that the Chamber has since tried to copycat Local First Grand Rapids (the effort flopped).

In 2008 Local First sponsored a study from Civic Economics that compared the economic impact of local versus nonlocal banks, grocers, pharmacies, and full-service restaurants. It showed that local businesses in each sector recirculated significantly more revenue, ranging from 17 percent for groceries to 77 percent for pharmacies. Moreover, a 10 percent shift of spending in Kent County to local businesses in these sectors would create 1,600 new jobs and $50 million in new wages. These results were widely used by other BALLE and AMIBA groups across North America.

Factoids like these have made it easier for Bazzani to sell his services. He has also been able to prove that green designs save cost. Attractive buildings can increase foot traffic and business, and the addition of many local businesses on the ground floor is a bonanza for local jobs and taxes.

Bazzani concedes that some of his projects never would have happened were it not for federal tax credits for investment in buildings designated as having historical value, which motivated his first investors to take the risk of investing in dilapidated areas. "And without the loose money market of the 2000s, we wouldn't have succeeded. Timing is everything."

That was, of course, when Bazzani was relatively unknown. Now that he is celebrated as one of the best green designers in the country, clients, bankers, and partners are easier to come by. Today he's in hot demand outside Grand Rapids. He just did a $6 million renovation of the Lebowsky Theater in Owosso, Michigan, along with two other projects. In Boyne City, Michigan, he's undertaking a $9 million hotel renovation, and a $3 million housing and storefront project. Local First just landed a $400,000 state grant to spread his vision of a local business alliance to other cities in the state (though the Grand Rapids Chamber, ever behind the times, tried unsuccessfully to block the award). Through all of this, Bazzani's pollinator mission remains simple: revive boarded up downtowns, "fight the Church of the Car," and promote local living economies.

Bazzani embraces this ethos for the operations of his own company. Bazzani Associates just received a very high B-Corporation rating score for its socially responsible performance. (B-Lab is a nonprofit that runs this rating system, bases scores on a company's social performance, and awards good performance with its insignia.) "Hey, we got 147 points. Patagonia is just at 100," says Bazzani, "I had no idea we were doing this well."

As he pushes sixty, Bazzani is spending more time sailing on the Great Lakes and wonders whether it's time to retire. Or perhaps he should turn his attention to the Godzilla of all design challenges, the renovation of Detroit. Since the city declared bankruptcy in 2014, many foundations and developers have begun taking on that challenge. Parts of Detroit, such as the midtown area, are coming back, but there's a need for a lot more help. "I might need another set of balls for this one," Bazzani admits. But no one doubts he's in.

Dancing in the Streets

Melbourne, once the crown jewel of Australian cities, took a different path toward revitalization. Twenty-five years ago the city was effectively dead after 5:00 p.m. The workforce lived in low-rent suburbs that ringed the municipality like a large donut. Once the commuter traffic cleared out, nothing happened, except crime, drugs, and other social pathologies. Today, the first thing a visitor to Melbourne notices is that the alleyways are filled with thriving shops and cafes.[47] Evening foot traffic has helped make the streets safer, and people are moving back into renovated floors over the commercial spaces everywhere. Two prestigious magazines, *The Economist* and *Monocle*, each recently named Melbourne as one of the most "livable" cities in the world. While many people and initiatives are responsible for this transformation, the one pollinator who certainly deserves credit is Gilbert Rochecouste—and a friendly pod of dolphins.

Even in a country known for ebullient, wisecracking personalities, Rochecouste stands out. A typical "hello" from Gilbert might involve his tall lanky form running up to you, pouncing on you like prey, and giving you a big wet kiss like an Irish setter. He will likely be wearing one of his brightly colored suits, ties, sweaters, and hats, or perhaps a sailor suit—a fashion sensibility that says screw convention, let's have fun! If you were about to have a serious meeting to discuss municipal policy, he might whip out his bongos "just to get the energy flowing." His enthusiasm is irresistible and contagious.

Rochecouste was born in Mauritius, an island with 1.3 million inhabitants nearly 1,000 miles east of Madagascar. When he was five, his father came to Melbourne to scout out a new life for the family. He sent word that he had found a job and told the family to pack up and come. Two weeks before the move, his dad was bicycling home from his night shift and was killed by a hit-and-run driver. Gilbert's mom decided that if the family was to come to Australia to bury him, they might as well stay and make a life. That fateful choice opened doors for the young Gilbert that were unimaginable in Mauritius. After studying psychology and business planning at Monash University, he became the general manager of Chadstone Shopping Centre, then the largest shopping mall in the Southern Hemisphere. His job was not just to troubleshoot tenant problems but to create a special sense of community in the mall. In just two decades he had basically journeyed from village markets in the tropics to one of most demanding retail operations in the developed world.

The Chadstone job paid exceptionally well and Rochecouste loved the work. But he knew something was missing. He was starting to see more clearly the poverty and misery in Melbourne, and the ways in which his and other suburban malls were sucking life from the city.

In 1992 Rochecouste and several friends hired a tour company that promised "a swim with the dolphins." When they arrived, an intense electrical storm convinced the company to cancel the trip, but Rochecouste's group decided to proceed anyway on their own. Ignoring the risks of electrocution, they rented a boat and soon found about twenty dolphins. Or perhaps the dolphins found them. As the magnificent creatures circled, Gilbert and his friends jumped in the water and swam with them for two hours. The experience filled Gilbert with raw emotion, pain about how he had neglected his roots and instincts, and excitement about what opportunities lay ahead, all as he conversed with the dolphins about what he should do next with his life.

Rochecouste resigned from his shopping mall job the following day, and resolved to take on the challenges he'd been observing in Melbourne. He traveled to America, and was impressed with the emerging Main Street movement he saw for revitalizing downtowns led by the National Trust for Historic Preservation and the Project for Public Spaces. He decided to bring the lessons on "placemaking" he learned back to Australia, and start his own consulting company called the Dolphiniumm. Ultimately, Rochecouste changed the name to the Village Well to reflect the "magic and wonder" he felt as a child in the markets in Mauritius that he now wanted to bring into the streets of Melbourne.

His first client was Victoria Market, one of the largest public markets in the world. It had been operating successfully since the 1880s as a bastion of localism, with four hundred independent operators, mostly food producers, but needed a makeover. Rochecouste led a process to bring together representatives from various stakeholder groups that normally couldn't stand being in a room together: farmers, artists, politicians, shopkeepers, students, you name it. His mission was to make these strangers comfortable and engage their collective imagination to answer several questions: How could we create a market where thousands of people would want to work, live, and have fun? How could we mobilize people to get out of their houses and enjoy the public space here? How could we create public celebrations and rituals that connect people to place? How could we transform the shopping areas into play areas? And how might we do this while bringing down the use of energy, water, and other materials, and minimizing the market's carbon footprint?

The process generated not only great answers but a solid commitment from the stakeholders to implement the collective vision. The group resolved to put the public space of the market to greater use for cultural and social events, and recommended that the market be opened in the evening. The results were mind-boggling. The Victoria Market suddenly became a new hub of activity in the city, a must-see tourist destination, and a magnet for the locals day and night whose presence made the area safe. And the new cultural elements, everything from street performers to graffiti, showed residents what a truly inclusive urban culture might look like.

Next, Rochecouste convinced the City of Melbourne to hire Village Well for the activation of two deserted alleys, Flinders Lane and DeGraves Lane, into walkable and vibrant destinations. Another grassroots strategic planning process proceeded, and the group's recommendations were put into action. Carparks were removed, and traffic slowed to a snail's pace. Footpaths were widened. Trees were planted. Buildings were restored. "These alleys became places of surprise, wonder, and moments," says Rochecouste. "There was more eating late, having a glass of wine, meeting friends."

The alley project unleashed a civic revolution. Hundreds of restaurants, shops, and other local businesses opened. Young entrepreneurs and artists moved into the new apartments in the upper floors. Like a grand sorcerer and urban alchemist, Rochecouste would whip up radical experiments. "We created night programs. We put fake grass on the streets during the day. We had pop-up parks, and pop-up parties. People suddenly had a taste of everything city life could be."

Melbourne's officials could see the incredible cost-benefit advantage. The green designs saved energy and water. Thousands of new jobs were created. The new commercial establishments and new residents paid more taxes. Policing costs went down. And all of this was done with planning efforts that cost a tiny fraction of what mainstream economic-development projects would have.

With its reputation growing, Village Well was hired to redo the Melbourne Central Shopping Center. This participatory process led to the decisions to blast open walls so that shoppers could see the flow of foot traffic, turn off the air conditioning, and cover the alleyways with roofs for all-weather use including a gorgeous piazza.

Rochecouste is now at work in other cities in Australia and his vision is spreading worldwide. In England he has been hired by London and the seaside town of Bournemouth. He's preparing master classes for fellow planners in New York City, Salt Lake City, San Francisco, and Toronto. And to extend his reach, he anticipates producing iPhone apps, online training, and "lots of three-minute videos."

"Economic development," says Rochecouste, "needs a paradigm shift. It needs to embrace deeper democracy, deeper engagement. It's not just about the economics of money but cultural economics and human economics. It should be a transformative process, connecting head, heart, and hand. We need a more integrated approach, where we bring in more strategic interventions—more events, more residential units over commercial spaces, more buy local campaigns, more food security. And we can't forget the joy and the celebration."

Rochecouste compliments the economic-development community in Melbourne for being very open to change. He also believes public policy played a positive role. The city allows districts to place their own levy on businesses, and the resulting funds were used to pay for Main Street projects. Melbourne currently has about 140 such districts.

As a pollinator business, Village Well has been extraordinarily successful, but Rochecouste has deliberately kept the firm small. For more than twenty-five years, it has had a staff of ten to twenty people at any given time. The typical annual revenues are between $600,000 and $800,000.

Does Rochecouste see the Village Well as an economic developer? "In a way, yes. We serve as both an activator and a developer. We're the glue in the economic-development equation that brings everything together. We deliver not just a plan but a process."

Most economic developers, he believes, have their priorities backwards. "They start with hardware, not software. They deliver designs, buildings, and roads, and wind up cleaning up the mess later. You've got to start with place and the people living there, and they have to participate in your process. They have to drive the finance and the infrastructure."

Planning in a Chaotic World

Planning came into vogue a century ago when progressive politicians were convinced that science, technology, and intelligence could be put to use to perfect an imperfect economy. In the years since, planning has had at least as many failures as successes. For every national highway system we treasure, there are also massive road subsidies that have saddled us with an unwise dependence on cars, nonlocal commerce, and imported oil. Our ambitious national war on poverty has saved many retirees from destitution because of Social Security, but condemned millions of inner-city families to live in failed housing projects. And none of our economic planning, from the Federal Reserve to the federal jobs program, prevented the near collapse of the global economy in 2008.

"Man makes plans," says Ernesto Sirolli, whom we will meet in chapter 4, "and God laughs. There are too many variables to predict. If you are too narrow in your plans, war, famine, or some other crisis can destroy everything."

Local economy planners think small. The great libertarian writer, Friedrich Hayek, argued that knowledge is too specific to a situation or a place to be generalized.[48] And the more one tries to figure out what's right, not for just a firm, but for a state, a country, or the world, the more likely one is to lose critical insights and information along the way. A pollinator approach to economic development means assuming a new modesty about planning. A pollinator doesn't ever conceive of a big outside company saving a community. Instead a pollinator plans business by business, block by block, community by community. Getting a few things right is far better than continuing to get everything wrong.

CHAPTER 3

Purchasing

Pumping Up the Sales Volume

F or the roughly two hundred communities that have formed local business alliances affiliated with either BALLE or AMIBA, the starting place is often a buy-local campaign. The focus on consumer action makes sense, since a consumer makes purchasing choices daily, sometimes many times per day, which affords multiple entry points into changing behavior. The other *P*s occur much more irregularly. Investment decisions, for example, are harder to organize action around since most people make decisions, say, about where they invest their pension funds, only rarely. Shifting purchasing decisions also carries the potential of a huge payback. If a modest fraction of a community's consumers shift a modest fraction of their expenditures toward local business, the economic boost can be extraordinary. One recent study in British Columbia, for example, found that a shift of just 10 percent of purchases in the province could create 31,000 new jobs paying $940 million in new wages.[49]

Thousands of other US communities without formal business alliances also are promoting local purchasing through farmers markets, energy cooperatives, credit unions, and Transition Town initiatives. Walk through any downtown area in the United States, even in a small rural community, and you see some signage or advertising that encourages residents to buy local. Stickers on stores indicate which are locally owned. Handbooks and websites direct consumers to local restaurants serving local food. Community consciousness is now being shaped by public service ads, debates, speakers, films, handbooks, events, buttons, bumper stickers, you name it.

As impressive and effective as these campaigns have been, however, they all share one basic flaw: There's no income stream. And so BALLE network heads, AMIBA organizers, farmers market directors, and Transition Town volunteers are constantly scrambling to raise cash. Grassroots efforts turn to bake sales and door-to-door collections. More sophisticated nonprofits submit proposals to local foundations or seek sponsorships. The result, as noted in the Introduction, is an uneven stream of money and an unpredictable flow of activities, always vulnerable to the next donor who says "no."

As the most commonly deployed P, purchasing initiatives have attracted the most pollinator innovations. The smartest BALLE and AMIBA networks quickly understood the need for earned income and turned to buy-local coupon books.

Coupon Culture

One of the oldest and most respected local business alliances in the BALLE network is Sustainable Connections, based in Bellingham, Washington, a town of eighty-three thousand about a two-hour drive north of Seattle. In the earliest days of BALLE, the founders and leaders of Sustainable Connections, Michelle and Derek Long, also worked part time as the initial executive directors of BALLE itself. Today, Michelle is full-time director of BALLE, while Derek runs Sustainable Connections, which has grown to more than five hundred member businesses. The accomplishments of Sustainable Connections are impressive:

- Its Local First campaign tactics—now widely copied around the United States and Canada—include store signs, posters, advertisements, and almost every other conceivable form of marketing to motivate residents to buy local. An independent survey by Applied Research Northwest found that a whopping 69 percent of Bellingham consumers are now paying attention to the local character of businesses, 58 percent have begun localizing their purchasing habits, and business proprietors regard Local First as one of the most compelling reasons they are thriving. Another study in 2011 by Civic Economics ranked Bellingham as the number two town in the country for retail vibrancy.[50]

- Sustainable Connections' energy program has mobilized one in ten residents to buy local "green power"—the second highest percentage in the United States. Following that accomplishment, a community energy challenge was launched that has helped retrofit 425 commercial buildings and 1,800 homes, reduced carbon emissions by 6,500 metric tons per year (the equivalent of getting 1,350 cars off the road), and created 80 new jobs. The number of farmers in surrounding Whatcom County marketing directly to consumers increased 44 percent between 2002 and 2007, twice the statewide rate. The value of direct sales—a key strategy for boosting farmers' income—increased 125 percent over the same period, quintuple the state rate.

- So impressive have these accomplishments been that in 2009 the Natural Resources Defense Council named Bellingham as the #1 "smarter" small city in the United States. In 2014 the website Livability .com ranked Bellingham as having the eighth best downtown in the nation, noting that the "area highlights how a local living economy can work."[51]

Today, Sustainable Connections employs fifteen people full time, more than Bellingham's Chamber of Commerce or the Northwest Economic Council (a nonprofit that leads economic-development initiatives).[52] That works out to be one staff person for every 5,500 residents. (At that level of performance, how many staff might your local business alliance have?) From the outset Sustainable Connections has sought to develop earned income streams, and today it derives 51 percent of its revenue from public and private contracts, 20 percent from program income, and 12 percent from membership fees. Only 17 percent comes from foundation or individual donations.

Sustainable Connections's first revenue-generating product was a coupon booklet called *Where the Locals Go*. The business model was simple: Convince Sustainable Connections members to submit coupons to drive consumer traffic to member businesses—say, 10 percent off your next meal at Pepper Sisters. Insert lots of graphics to make the booklet visually attractive and draw consumers' attention. Sprinkle in quotes and interesting statistics to educate users about the local economy. And then sell the product through the participating businesses, including local bookstores.

The woman primarily responsible for this project since the fourth edition has been Michelle Grandy. Hired in 2005, Grandy became the fourth employee for Sustainable Connections (Michelle and Derek Long were the first two). After obtaining a degree in communications, Grandy took a job as a graphic designer in a print shop. She then went to work for Brown and Cole, a regional grocery chain with twenty stores in Washington State. She saw first-hand the carnage that occurred when Wal-Mart rolled into rural Washington and forced her employer to start laying off people: "I felt sad, frustrated, and hopeless." Both experiences wound up being perfect preparation for her new job at Sustainable Connections. She knew she had landed at the right place when Craig Cole, president of Brown and Cole, became one of the first corporate sponsors of Sustainable Connections' "Think Local First" campaign.

Grandy's responsibilities were to serve as Sustainable Connections' membership coordinator and office manager. She was surprised, however, that she really did not need to go knocking on the doors of potential members. Derek and Michelle Long were attracting lots of press—not just locally but nationally—and Bellingham businesses were flocking to join. As membership climbed quickly from two hundred to six hundred businesses, Grandy was fielding most of the phone calls and e-mails, and happily signing the businesses up.

The second edition of the coupon book was already in progress when Grandy arrived. The Longs had launched the project to challenge the myth that local businesses were not competitive. As residents used the coupons, they would identify great deals, become more familiar with the full range of local business offerings, and shift their loyalty toward these businesses.

Grandy ultimately persuaded one hundred local businesses to place coupons in the second edition, and in subsequent editions nudged that number up to 250. About thirty of these businesses agreed to serve as sales points for the coupon book, and each was given a visually attractive sales display. They consigned the booklets to be sold at an agreed price of $10. For every fifteen booklets a local business did sell, it got one additional copy for free that it could sell for cash or give away as a reward. All the marketing was very grassroots, with posters and signs around town encouraging residents to buy the coupon book.

In most of the years that followed, Grandy was able to sell 2,500 copies of the booklet, and that pretty much covered her costs. Consumers were happy with the discounts, and businesses saw a clear boost in customer traffic. As staff grew and Grandy had more time to do extra marketing, she convinced realtors to give the booklet to new home buyers to introduce them to the Bellingham business community. Tourists also bought copies at the city's visitors' center.

Grandy knew another potential revenue stream was advertising, but decided not to pursue it. Instead, participation in the coupon book was wrapped into the overall package of membership benefits each business got for its annual Sustainable Connections dues. Each coupon contained basic information about the sponsoring business, so in a sense advertising was already happening. Grandy would only charge nonmember businesses that wanted to advertise, like Puget Sound Energy, a local utility. A member business also could pay a premium if it wanted to insert more coupons than its allotment.

Asked if any businesses complained about losing money from the discounts, Grandy was hard-pressed to think of an example. A local pet store, she recalled, complained about a customer who bought multiple copies of the coupon book and then used them repeatedly. But that was about it.

After many years of steadily selling 2,500 copies, give or take, the 2013 edition saw a big drop off to 1,600. Grandy speculates that the novelty had worn off. Plus, the rise of other big "deal" companies like Groupon and LivingSocial, which provide deeper discounts for very short periods of time, say 40 percent for a day, had reshaped the coupon market. Consumers got used to the steady supply of huge discounts for free, and businesses began to wonder why they should bother with clunky year-round coupons when consumers seemed increasingly numb to relatively small discounts?

As a result, Sustainable Connections has decided to discontinue *Where the Locals Go*. Grandy says that she and her colleagues are thinking about creating a mobile app that might reward local purchasing. If they go this direction, they might get serious about selling advertising. An app might also help with what professionals call "the analytics"—the details on who exactly is buying the coupons, and how exactly consumers are using them. Information like this can help fine tune the product, the advertising, and the sales strategy.

It's worth noting that other BALLE networks that have published coupon books, such as Ft. Collins, Colorado, have encountered similar challenges. The effort barely breaks even, and even that result depends on hundreds of hours of volunteer labor. (In Bellingham, the expense accounting didn't tally the costs of all the staff who dedicated many hours to the project.)

That said, there still may be an underlying model for a successful pollinator business here. Perhaps the combination of more advertising and more consumers engaging through an app might do the trick. Perhaps greater scale could help—2,500 businesses instead of 250. Perhaps a coupon book specialist working in several cities that spread the fixed costs of staff, printing, marketing, app design, and so forth over enough copies could make the economics work.

Grandy has urged her colleagues to study closely a product called the Chinook Book. Founded in Portland, Oregon, in 1999 by Celilo Group Media, the Chinook Book offers coupons for socially responsible businesses in the San Francisco Bay Area, Denver, Portland, Seattle, and the Twin Cities. While it doesn't focus on local businesses per se—some chains, like Whole Foods, participate—it does demand that any business meet exacting standards on sustainability and other measures of good corporate citizenship. In 2012, the various Chinook Books collectively listed 4,700 businesses, and their users redeemed nearly a million deals worth $19.7 million.

The importance of scale is also underscored by the success of Groupon. That company started when founder Andrew Mason had trouble cancelling a phone contract in 2006, and decided that his complaint might have a shot at changing corporate policy if enough users with similar problems organized themselves into a single, powerful virtual community. By 2008, the idea of creating a "tipping point" of consumers morphed into deep discounts that consumers would buy in advance, with the proceeds split between Groupon and the participating business. The company then grew so spectacularly that in 2010 Google offered to buy it for $6 billion. Groupon turned Google down, instead taking itself public. In 2014 its annual revenue is expected to be $3 billion and earnings about $200 million.

Not a few local economy advocates detest Groupon. They complain that it's creating a "coupon culture," where consumers have no loyalty to any businesses and just keep chasing the deal of the week. They also point to some early examples of small businesses that were so overwhelmed by the stampede of Groupon customers desperately seeking deals that they lost their shirts.

This criticism, however, misses three important points about Groupon.[53] First, the vast majority of the companies using Groupon's services actually are local businesses, and Groupon sees itself as primarily a service provider to local economies. Second, Groupon admits that it made serious mistakes in the beginning that have since led to some important changes. The company now gives more specific guidance to clients on how to manage discounts effectively and avoid dangerous stampedes. Today nearly 90 percent of Groupon clients are satisfied with their experience, and many use its services repeatedly. Third, Groupon ultimately does what many Local First organizations have wanted to do, which is to mobilize more customers for client businesses, only with a professionalism that comes with its scale. It provides consumers with an easy-to-use app and it provides businesses with extensive analytics, enhancing everyone's experience.

If Groupon were owned by the local economy movement, we would regard it as the secret weapon for local marketing. It's not, of course. It's a publicly traded company that, like other nonlocal businesses, takes money from the community and respends much of it elsewhere. But I believe that, in the short run, BALLE and AMIBA networks might be wise to partner with Groupon, where their members can take advantage of the Groupon tools and get a cut of the action for their efforts (Groupon's top management has indicated interest in forging these relationships). In the long run, locally owned purchasing pollinators might begin to offer Groupon-like services themselves.

Advertising Pure and Simple

Another way to market local businesses is to give away a publication singing their praises for free and pay for it with lots of advertising. That's the framework used in major metro areas by weekly papers like the *San Francisco Bay Guardian* and *The Village Voice*, which are geared to young hipsters and provide helpful information on local music, art, cinema, restaurants, and events. In rural and suburban America, freebie papers still get tossed in colorful wrappers on people's lawns with features about local civic life, all supported by local advertising. The growth of low-cost Internet advertising through sites like craigslist and through social markets via Facebook has challenged these models, just as it has challenged the entire newspaper industry, but the written word still is valued in small and rural communities. Moreover, because these papers are more "use-papers" than "newspapers," because their readership is narrowly defined and often prefers print to virtual formats, and because they have a small staff and overhead, these weeklies have survived the Internet onslaught better than the dailies.

While most weeklies have some stories about local business, I have yet to see a successful weekly with a sharp pollinator mission of mobilizing the public to buy local. Perhaps the pollinator that comes closest is the Edible magazine network which is all about promoting local food and farms. With a template from the central office in New Canaan, Connecticut, some eighty five licensees now prepare an exceptionally pretty and well-written magazine filled with features on local chefs, restaurants, farmers, and consumers committed to local food. Each regional edition, like *Edible Iowa River Valley*, then appears in racks strategically placed in restaurants, coffee houses, farmers markets, organic markets, wherever foodies hang out. Most regions allow anyone to take a copy for free.[54]

The founders and former managers of Edible Communities, Inc., were Tracey Ryder, a publisher and marketer, and Carole Topalian, a photographer. Their website says that the company is "currently adding new magazines at a rate of 10 per year." The mission statement evinces "a commitment to sustaining the unique local flavors and economic viability of the communities we serve. As individuals and professionals, we live, breathe, and literally eat these values."

Edible Portland, for example, launched in April 2006, through a social enterprise called Ecotrust, under the leadership of an entrepreneurial Oregonian named Deborah Kane. After building up Portland's Food Alliance, which connected local farmers and food producers with locavore consumers, Kane joined Ecotrust and became its vice president of food and farms. *Edible Portland* was one of her first projects.

Each *Edible* license usually requires a significant payment up front, and the licensee gets an exclusive right to distribute its local edition of the magazine to a carefully defined region. Some interviewees report a buy-in fee of $60,000, though this can be paid over several years. But the national office of Edible Communities at the time was so eager to have a presence in the Portland market that the fee was waived for Ecotrust. National advertising revenue gets split with the locals. If they want, licensees also can purchase a suite of services from the central office that includes design, printing, and distribution.

Asked to evaluate the viability of the *Edible Portland* business over her seven years of running it, Kane noted it "only broke even." One reason, she jokes, is that Ecotrust pays its staff a living wage with good benefits. Many other *Edibles* around the country, in contrast, rely on volunteer distributors, freelance writers, and advertising reps working on commission. Not a few of the license holders consider *Edible* a labor of love rather than a serious day job. Some don't pay themselves anything, and instead rely on a spouse's salary or inherited wealth. Others adopt it as a business that they casually run in their golden retirement years. But a few of the licensees run the magazine as a serious enterprise and are profitable.

Kane recently moved on to a job with the US Department of Agriculture, handing off *Edible Portland* to a new team. With a few years now under her belt, the current editor, Laura Ford, argues that getting too hung up on exact profit rates doesn't make sense, because many different aspects of the magazine are handled by different staff within Ecotrust, each of whom has multiple responsibilities. That said, Ecotrust does keep track, best it can, of expenses and revenues. In 2013, according to Ford, the magazine went in the red and it may not be profitable until 2015.

One reason *Edible Portland* has struggled is that the print industry is getting squeezed by the Internet. Advertisers are expecting more for their money. So *Edible Portland* has begun offering to local companies opportunities for digital advertising on its website and in its e-newsletter. Ad packages encourage companies to sponsor Ecotrust events, like its annual Local Hero Awards.

The typical issue of *Edible Portland*, says Ford, is between fifty-six and sixty-four pages, with about 40 percent of those being advertisements; the Ecotrust team produces nearly all the copy locally. There are recipes and short items about, say, what's now in season. A recent issue describes chili peppers grown in Oregon. (Who knew?) Then there are three or four more in-depth stories and profiles, usually on the benefits of local food. A popular series just covered local farm-to-school programs, including a Bend school district that raises pigs in the local program of Future Farmers of America and butchers them in a culinary classroom at the senior high.

Ecotrust publishes twenty thousand copies every quarter. The main distribution points are Whole Foods, New Seasons (Portland's local alternative grocery to Whole Foods), four food co-ops, farmers markets, garden centers, and restaurants.

To sharpen the editorial content and distribution, Ecotrust administers an annual survey. Readers have indicated, for example, that they are increasingly interested in local fisheries and in how local food can reach underserved populations.

Mindful that many of its licensees have been struggling, the national office has recently overhauled its strategy and support activities. In May 2013, Edible Communities was acquired by Lifestyle Media Partners, which is run by a "long-time media-junkie-type guy" (in his own words) named Eric Thorkilsen. The professional experience Thorkilsen brings includes thirty years working for Time-Warner and the launch of *Martha Stewart Living*, a brand that included a magazine, a television show, and imprinted books. Tracy Ryder still participates in the company and serves as the public face of the *Edible* network at industry events, but Thorkilsen is now the strategist focused on taking the business to the next level.

Thorkilsen's view is that a brand does best when its messages are conveyed over multiple media channels. "If you are just in a single-media business, perhaps just selling print advertising, you have a limited number of options to do business. If you are in a multiplatform business, you have a greater opportunity to have a relationship with a given advertiser."

Thorkilsen has built up the web presence of the *Edible* network, seamlessly connecting local sites with the national site, EdibleFeast.com. This helps networks, among other things, share articles for their magazines. He also has rebranded a public television show once called *Victory Gardens* (which covered only kitchen gardening) into *Victory Gardens Edible Feast* (which incorporates great *Edible* stories about local-food enterprises). The show, currently in its second season, reaches 85% of the United States and parts of Canada. All these media make *Edible* magazines more attractive to advertisers, which in turn increases the viability of every *Edible* licensee.

"The most critical basic skill that's an indicator of success for an *Edible* licensee," observes Thorkilsen, "is the ability to sell advertising." The scale of larger markets like New York and Boston also has helped them succeed, because there are more local food businesses to solicit for advertising, more interested readers, and more distribution points. But licensees in some smaller regions like Baja, Arizona, have done well, too, because there's less competition for advertising dollars.

With the magazine now distributing copies to 1.4 million readers, Thorkilsen is in no rush to expand. He sees up to 100 more markets in the United States and Canada, but his highest priority is finding the right people to lead local operations. He wants to find local publishers who will become not only great businesspeople but also great collaborators with other licensees in the network.

Back in Portland, Laura Ford thinks there's much more she herself can do to improve the success of *Edible Portland*. She wants to broaden the readership, shake up the design, and create more digital versions for easy downloading and reading on your smart phone. Ford and other *Edible* publishers also appreciate that printed material is giving way to online alternatives, and that more and more content will need to be virtual. Yet as this happens, many wonder whether the Internet will ever really be a reliable friend of local business.

Retaking the Web

To many local economy advocates, the Internet is the enemy. They have seen how Amazon has destroyed brick-and-mortar bookstores and how e-commerce generally threatens to eviscerate other retailers. They worry about Google and Facebook replacing geographically defined communities with virtual ones that diminish the importance of place. They view E-Trade and TD Ameritrade as tools that have increased the ease and speed with which locals pull their money out of their communities and put it instead into the slot machines of Wall Street. There's little doubt that the big winners of Web 1.0 and 2.0 were global behemoths and not local businesses. But Web 3.0 is another story entirely.

The Internet is ultimately a tool for sharing information. And if local businesses are as competitive as the data in chapter 1 suggest, then better information might be their savior. This is especially the case for myriad local companies that offer great value to their customers but lack marketing prowess and have difficulty reaching beyond a small loyal customer base.

It's telling that buy-local campaigns always boost consumer spending at local businesses. The point may seem obvious—sure, advertising works—but consider another possibility: If local goods and services were really inferior and too expensive, then a surge in consumers that tried local businesses and were disappointed might wind up backfiring into stronger loyalty to nonlocal alternatives. Why does this almost never happen?

One pollinator who sees the value of helping local businesses share more information is Colin Pape, the creator of the fast-growing ShopCity.com. Pape grew up in Midland, a small town of about sixteen thousand in Ontario, Canada, on the shores of Georgian Bay, an offshoot of the Great Lakes. His parents owned a retail paint store for twenty-eight years, and chatter at his family dinner table gave him a comprehensive education on the trials and tribulations of running a small business.

The year 2000 was a turning point for Midland. That was when Wal-Mart and Home Depot rolled into town. Pape, then 20 years old, had already proven his small-business chops by building websites for his parents' paint store and for their retailer friends. But when the chains invaded, he decided to marshal his programming talents for a pollinator mission to save the community's local businesses.

Pape built an online directory of local businesses called ShopMidland .com. For $450, Pape would write for a business a compelling narrative with professional photos. He effectively provided the first websites for many of the town's businesses. At the top of the ShopMidland.com site, Pape placed a then new search engine called Google that allowed users to search his site or search the web.

The site was launched through a "guerrilla marketing" campaign he and his college roommate undertook, plastering signs around town saying "ShopMidland.com: Support Your Community." Interest exploded. The Chamber of Commerce backed the effort. Soon Pape had one hundred businesses in the community signed up, each sporting signs promoting the website (today there are 1,500 participants). Even though by contemporary standards the site was "rudimentary," in Pape's own estimation, it was financially viable from the very beginning.

Seeing the same need in other communities, Pape looked to expand the model but immediately stepped into a pothole. From his small office above his parent's paint store, Pape hired sales representatives to recruit businesses in other nearby Ontario communities like Collingwood and Wasaga Beach. The response was tepid. Pape soon realized he had committed the same offense that the chains in Midland had. He and his reps were outsiders corrupting the meaning of "local." The lesson was that communities had to control and manage their own sites, and that's when he began a franchise model for expanding his business.

Pape went on a spree securing domains—ShopVictoria.ca, ShopLondon.ca, ShopHalifax.ca, and so on—for cities across Canada, but someone else had beat him to it in the United States. He assumed his competitor was a huge global conglomerate, but when he met Jim Terry, the two realized that they were both scrappy entrepreneurs and that by working together they had a better shot at bringing their vision to life. They decided to become partners. Terry is a native of San Jose, California, which explains why most of the ShopCity clients in the United States are California communities like Corona, Palo Alto, Menlo Park, and Mountain View.

A huge growth spurt occurred in 2012, when CanPages—the Canadian equivalent of Yellow Pages—was shutting down. Pape was able to recruit a small army of former CanPages employees who had intimate familiarity with each Canadian city's small business community. These reps started off as company employees, but then became ShopCity managers under the franchise model.

Today ShopCity can be found in twenty-five communities in Canada, seven locally owned and operated franchises and eighteen under ShopCity management. Another fifteen in the United States operate on an older model for self-service signups. Pape oversees a staff of fifteen people in the home office, who in turn work with what he calls "city managers" in each of the participating communities. Annual revenues have grown more than 2000% between 2011 and 2014, and now exceed $2 million.

The current expansion strategy is to recruit a city manager who then pays a licensing fee to own and operate the site and who takes responsibility for sales and marketing. ShopCity provides the platform, customizes it to suit the community's needs, trains the city manager, oversees all the billing, and provides technical support to the participating businesses. The city manager creates free profiles for as many businesses as possible, followed by a grassroots sign and sticker campaign to connect the online and offline worlds. After the initial launch, the focus shifts to getting partners onboard, including the Chamber of Commerce, business improvement associations, other local business groups, and nonprofits. These partners are provided with an opportunity to share in the revenue, as well as online tools such as a business directory and an events calendar that they can plug into their websites.

As was true with the original model, basic information about all the local businesses in the city is listed for free. Businesses that pay a subscription fee of $25 to $150 per month can expand and manage their own listings. Those paying a higher fee of $200 to $400 per month can hire ShopCity's staff to manage the listings for them. These fees are then split between ShopCity and the city manager, with the latter receiving about two-thirds of the revenue.

Pape admits that the first version of ShopMidland.com would be a flop today. There's much greater fragmentation of Internet users' attention, as they bounce between Facebook, Twitter, Google, Instagram, and thousands of other sites. It's a lot harder for any site to retain an audience.

ShopCity's sites consequently have had to become more sophisticated, and offer a more comprehensive database of local businesses and their products. Listed local businesses can now modify their content online and issue gift certificates and coupons, and showcase weekly deals. They can easily synchronize this information with their existing websites. Pape also would like to allow clients to use local currency for transactions (he recently integrated the use of the global, government-free, and controversial digital currency called bitcoin).

While participating communities are still learning how to master the ShopCity technology, some are already seeing significant profits. One of the network's most successful sites, ShopLondon.ca, grossed more than $300,000 in 2014, again with two-thirds going to the city manager. The site, run by Rick Kloss, has already paid off the initial investment. The former owner of a bowling alley, Kloss sympathizes with entrepreneurs who are overwhelmed running their business and don't have time to effectively tell their story.

In Midland, there is also a downtown storefront location designed to make the Internet more tangible to local businesses, and ShopCity believes this strategy is something they will encourage other communities to adopt at some point.

When asked to explain the metrics that participating cities and businesses use to prove to themselves that the platform is working, Pape laments that he lacks the comprehensive data of, say, Groupon, which can easily track what percentage of issued coupons are used, when, and where. But Pape can provide some data. "When downtown storefronts that were once vacant are filling up your site, and you're seeing 45,000 unique site visitors per month in a community of 30,000, you know you're doing something right."

Expansion since 2008 has required about $3 million in outside capital. Pape has been fortunate to find local investors in Midland. He is also putting together a direct public offering in California with the assistance of Cutting Edge Capital (discussed in chapter 6).

Asked if he would sell his business to a multinational company for $100 million, Pape says, "Absolutely not. We're thinking long term, and plan to be the folks running the company." After a pause, he adds, "Though it would be great validation."

Local Rewards Cards

The next horizon for local purchasing pollinators is the cards in your wallet. Most of your debit and credit cards have various benefit programs baked into them. Use your cards enough and you'll get gifts, discounts, frequent flier miles, and cash back. The moment I truly appreciated the power of these programs was when I observed how my aging mother, who had a high-interest savings account at a bank that required that she use her bank-issued debit card a certain number of times per month, would spend hours driving to a dozen filling stations, fill up a gallon or two, and charge the transaction just to make her quota.

From the perspective of local economy advocates, most of these cards are awful. Credit cards, even if nominally issued by a local bank, are run through national networks like VISA that skim every local transaction for global financial conglomerates. The loyalty programs of these cards are mostly redeemable at big box chains, even if the rewards are earned through local small business. To add injury to insult, local proprietors have to pay a huge processing fee for every transaction. And credit cards often leave their users with large balances that suck more wealth out of communities in the form of interest payments, fees, and penalties. Debit cards do not increase people's debt, but if they are issued by a nonlocal bank, the various transaction fees represent another leak out of the community.

A former executive at Union Bank, the third largest bank in California, has concluded, however, that there is a way to make debit cards promising pollinators. Arno Hesse came to the United States from Germany as a young adult for "a change of air, romance, and business school" at UC Berkeley. He bristles at being called a banker, because his real interests are organizational culture and how business can best effect social change.

Union Bank was not a bad place to work when the financial crisis hit in 2008, because the bank had not been investing in subprime mortgages. But as Hesse traveled up and down California, he saw the growing fallout from a highly profitable Wall Street on local economies. In his own neighborhood of Bernal Heights, which is south of the Mission District in San Francisco and sits on a large hill, capital sources for neighborhood businesses had slowed to a trickle. He was frustrated that the operating logic of traditional banking meant that even well-meaning community bankers were putting most of their capital into big business and overlooking smaller ones. How, he wondered, could community finance work more effectively from the bottom up?

Hesse has a rare combination of skills. He's a good economist who can think abstractly about complex systems, but he also has a pragmatic sense of how to assemble a business, one step at a time. He wanted to create a tool that could equip local businesses with more credit. The first designs of this tool materialized when he met Guillaume Lebleu, a Frenchman in the United States, who is a talented banking technologist and an expert on financial transaction systems.

As a reminder and incentive to keep the money circulating locally, Hesse and Lebleu created stickers for $5 bills that Bernal Heights residents could purchase at a neighborhood center. Then they convinced local businesses in the neighborhood to give small perks for customers who presented marked bills. The coffee shop might upgrade your cup size, or the grocer might give you an extra apple. Proceeds from the sales of the stickers went to a local nonprofit. Hesse viewed this simple program as "creating a good cycle," and Bernal Bucks, as they were called, generated lots of media buzz.

Hesse knew, though, that the project could do a lot more. He understood that Bernal Heights residents were spending most of their money, not through cash, but through the cards in their wallet. So he approached his neighborhood banking institution, Community Trust Federal Credit Union, which had "community development" in the charter. By pointing out how his proposed program would bring more members through the door, he convinced the credit union to issue a debit card branded with the Bernal Bucks logo and a drawing of the neighborhood's famous hill.

Today every expenditure made with the card at a participating local business earns a cardholder 5 percent back to respend at any of the participating businesses. The stores and restaurants can afford the giveaways, because they are in the form of products and services (similar to what airlines give with frequent-flier programs). Technically, it's the rewards that are called Bernal Bucks, since they cannot be spent in chain stores. The credit union also agreed to share its interchange fees (running about 1.2 percent per transaction) with the Bernal Bucks project, so that Hesse and Lebleu could promote the card in the neighborhood and encourage members to use it at local businesses.

Since Bernal Bucks resembles hundreds of other local currency experiments across the United States, it's worth a moment to contrast the concepts. The whole idea of local currency is that residents of a given community will spend a homemade dollar (or a virtual dollar in a local electronic trading system) at a local business, which in turn must spend that dollar at another local business. Outsiders really have no use for these local tokens, and that puts pressure on users to spend them with insiders who will find them valuable. Local currency therefore encourages the community to localize more and more of its spending, which pumps up the local multiplier, and increases local income, wealth, and jobs.

Hesse and Lebleu had studied the best local currency systems in the United States, such as BerkShares and Ithaca HOURS, and concluded that Bernal Bucks could improve on these models in three important ways. The first problem afflicting most local currencies is marketing: How do you convince the broad public, not just a few aging hippies, to carry unfamiliar dollars or undertake unfamiliar rituals for processing local currencies? The average consumer craves convenience, familiarity, and simplicity. The vast majority of local currency communities see only a tiny fraction of their populations using the currency for a tiny fraction of their transactions. The absence of critical mass usually relegates the currency to a nice idea that exerts only a small influence on the local economy. Bernal Bucks, in contrast, by piggybacking on a familiar debit card, has had no problem being widely adopted in the neighborhood.

The second problem that besets local currency systems is that almost none are pollinators with a coherent mechanism for self-financing. They rely instead on volunteers and small donations to cover the costs of administering and marketing the system. This compounds the first problem of marginalization. Bernal Bucks captures a percentage of the normal interchange fee that businesses are paying to banks anyway, so businesses don't perceive it as an additional cost. And local merchants are much happier to have that fee support a program like Bernal Bucks. Not a few are annoyed that merchant-funded reward programs effectively tax local businesses to pay for rewards at 7-Eleven and Wal-Mart. With Bernal Bucks, at least the merchants are supporting other local businesses.

The third problem with local currencies, according to Hesse, is that they "typically wind up at the local grocery store, which then has no idea where to spend it." Bernal Bucks could be vulnerable to this, too, if, for example, all the users suddenly tried to redeem all their Bernal Bucks rewards at just one local coffee shop. That could force the shop to pay out more than its fair share of rewards—potentially even more than it took in as earnings from the card program. So Bernal Bucks established a basic rule that every business only has to redeem up to the number of Bernal Bucks awards that it issued. Card users can see online which businesses have current rewards offers. Thus far, "liquidity" in the system hasn't been a problem, and at any given time perks are available at 70–80 percent of the businesses. The fact is that residents tend to sit on their rewards for a while, just like holders of frequent flier miles do.

The partnership with the credit union adds another advantage to Bernal Bucks—data. Every day, the Bernal Bucks team receives reports from Community Trust about where the cards were used and how much was spent. This in turn enables them to update participants' points online. (The credit union otherwise has no involvement in the administration of the rewards.)

When Bernal Bucks was formally launched on June 21, 2011, Hesse and his colleagues made a big splash at a neighborhood party, signing up businesses to carry the card and residents to set up accounts at the credit union. It didn't hurt that the day before, the Board of Supervisors for the city and county of San Francisco passed a "Certificate of Honor" for Bernal Bucks "for launching an innovative and cutting-edge economic-development project that supports local businesses and community-based organizations."

The Bernal Bucks debit card, of course, can be used at any business, even a chain like Home Depot. But Hesse and Leblue were happily surprised to discover that 81 percent of all the dollars that flowed through the card were spent at the thirty local businesses officially participating. More impressively, card holders increased their spending at these participating businesses by 41 percent.

So how's Bernal Bucks doing as a business? Hesse says, "The program is essentially running itself." It involves hundreds of households, with even more family members. Its transactions have grown every quarter since its inception. "The tables have turned. Now businesses come to us." Hesse is reluctant to share the exact revenue being generated, but it's enough, he says, "to finance a part-time administrator."

If several hundred households can finance a part-time employee, then surely several thousand households can finance a full-timer. Local business alliances have taken notice. Hesse periodically provides telephone advice to interested networks, but most have gotten stymied in their conversations with their credit union. Smaller credit unions don't have the resources to launch new programs, and larger credit unions with multiple branches are less willing to start a program just for one community. But Hesse remains optimistic that the Bernal Bucks will soon have siblings. Indeed, his team expects that similar programs around the country will use their software and hire them for technical assistance.

Hesse and Lebleu are now developing other online tools for local economies like Credibles, which allows consumers to invest in local food businesses by prepaying their tabs. We'll visit Credibles in chapter 6.

Local Gift Cards

A recurrent theme in these stories about purchasing pollinators is that local businesses have a love–hate relationship with discounting. They understand that sometimes you need a special deal to attract first-time customers or to solidify loyalty with existing customers. But it riles them when they see loyal customers bring in coupons by the wheelbarrow. Their own margins are pretty thin already, and they cannot afford to start losing money on Groupon-style deep discounts. This explains why metrics are so important. Local businesses need to be convinced that the discounts are bringing in new customers, and that these customers over time are spending more money. This also explains the appeal of gift cards.

Unlike debit or credit cards, a gift card can be designed without fees being imposed on local businesses. The reason is a funny term called *shrinkage*. It's widely known that once someone receives a gift card, perhaps in a Christmas stocking or inside a birthday card, they stick it in a drawer and forget about it. Some cards get lost. Others get partially used and then disappear. The unspent surplus, often running 15–25 percent of the total value issued, is the shrinkage. Until recently many of these cards had expiration dates as well, but that practice is now illegal. Shrinkage offers yet another way to finance purchasing pollinators.

One entrepreneur who saw the value in helping locals get into the gift card business was Jessie Radies, based in Edmonton, the second largest city in the western Canadian province of Alberta. It's hard to believe that a woman with many years of experience in the fast-food industry, who worked for companies like PepsiCo (including its KFC and Taco Bell franchises), Dairy Queen, and Orange Julius, could find herself an advocate for local businesses. But Radies and her husband decided to buy an existing restaurant in the year 2000. Radies oversaw the marketing and front-of-the-house operations, while her husband was in charge of the kitchen. They changed everything—the concept, the branding, the layout, the food, even the name. The Blue Pear became one of the top restaurants in Edmonton, offering not only great local food but also live music and local art. They built the rest of their lives around the restaurant. They had two daughters and loved the flexibility that the restaurant afforded them as parents.

But Radies was not blind to the challenges: "We had no scale." She and her husband were consummate foodies, dined out around town, and realized that other great restaurants in Edmonton had exactly the same problem. They couldn't bulk purchase foodstuffs, their hiring couldn't compete against the high-paying "oil patch" jobs in the surrounding area, and they couldn't market effectively on their own. A lightbulb went off in her head that the only way The Blue Pear could thrive would be to team up with other local restaurants. So over the next two years she approached her peers to work collaboratively, and "either they thought I was brilliant, or I was insane."

By 2004 Radies had convinced a dozen local restaurants, all committed to a great dining experience, to launch a joint advertising and promotion program. Under the branding of "Original Fare," the group included a coffee shop called Leva, the Blue Plate Diner, the high-end Jack's Grill, a family place called The Dish Bistro, and a neighborhood jewel called the Red Ox Inn. Each restaurant contributed $350 per month, the group met every other month, and Radies kept refining and expanding their collective marketing plan. She started with print advertising in foodie publications. She then created postcards featuring all the restaurants, and made sure that customers at one Original Fare restaurant would get goosed to try the others.

Radies introduced a gift card in 2006. She had met the head of a company called Powercard at a restaurant association gathering in Tucson, who convinced her that paper gift certificates were history. Most of Powercard's customers set up group loyalty programs, in which each purchase garnered credit for awards and discounts. But Radies wanted a gift card, so she created a branded Original Fare Card that could be purchased in various denominations between $25 and $200.

Using Powercard's software, Radies sold the cards online and then mailed them out to the purchasers. She didn't want each restaurant to sell the cards, because she worried that her program might compete with each restaurant's gift certificate program. Participating restaurants had a special reader to run the card through, and the transaction data were fed back to Radies. Once a month, Radies would reconcile the transactions, send reports to the restaurants, and cut them checks. Radies did not assess restaurants any special fee for the program, nor did she provide $1-to-$1 redemption. Instead, she redeemed 50 cents on every gift dollar used (later revising this to 75 cents) to ensure that her costs were covered.

While it's impossible to separate out the impact of the gift card program from other marketing done through Original Fare, the results were stunning. Within "a few years," according to Radies, The Blue Pear went from $110,000 of business to $500,000. The other restaurants reported similar boosts in sales, with many of the new customers coming as referrals from the other Original Fare restaurants.

During this period, the rules governing gift cards were overhauled throughout North America, including in Alberta. Gift cards can no longer expire. That said, a portion still tends to go unused. So once a year Radies' accountant estimates what percentage of the unused cards can be shifted from a liability to an asset, and the new money then helps defray administrative costs. Overall, Radies says, the program has always managed to pay for itself.

Other Edmonton businesses outside the restaurant sector were interested in this kind of joint advertising program, and asked if Radies would help them organize their sectors. Originally she said no—they should do this for themselves. But then she started to appreciate the economic impact of all local businesses. In her own neighborhood, where local businesses were really struggling, she could see the growth of poverty, homelessness, drugs, and prostitution. "When I started to understand the difference between local and nonlocal business, I could see, oh, that's how it happens." She decided to broaden her work to include all local businesses and to launch a BALLE network.

Today, the gift card program continues under the brand name Live Local Alberta. It's also tied in with a loyalty program—the more you eat at a participating restaurant, the more gift cards you earn. But the number of restaurants in the program has shrunk to a half dozen. Radies herself sold The Blue Pear, and others lost interest as the results got weaker. Radies attributes this to the spread of Groupon-like deep discounts and changing consumer behavior. "Getting points and getting a gift card just isn't enough anymore."

Radies is now debating whether to shut the program down or, perhaps, upgrade it to make it more profitable. How might she do the latter? Add more restaurants. Involve more consumers. Use a state-of-the-art technology platform that e-mails to people or sends to their phones the virtual equivalent of cards. And use a technology provider who is passionate about local business.

The one place where all these innovations are coming together is Portland, Oregon.

Local Loyalty Cards

Katrina and Michael Scotto di Carlo want the local economy movement to have a killer app that will enable any community to create an efficient loyalty program that can underwrite its local business network. From a converted warehouse space in Portland (which they just moved out of), they and their small team have been quietly building a sophisticated marketing and technology platform called Supportland.

It's useful to step back and think about the big challenges of loyalty cards. How do you get the vast majority of a community to carry these cards? If businesses have to pay for processing the card, whether through a fee or just the time it takes to handle the transactions, how can you prove to them that the benefits exceed the costs? How can you spread the system from community to community cost effectively?

Working through the details of these questions, as we've seen already, requires two very different kinds of expertise: marketing and technology. Without creative marketing, even the most impressive technology platform sits unused in cyberspace. And without technology, a creative marketer is stuck with a primitive system like punch cards. What sets Katrina and Michael apart is that as a couple they have the perfect combination of skills.

Katrina is a 30-something marketing whiz who adores small business and has a knack for clever messaging. From the moment in the third grade when she had learned that slavery once thrived in the United States, Katrina also has been on a personal quest to conquer social injustice. In college she concluded that the best approach to justice is a healthy economy rooted in strong local businesses.

Michael is a decade older than Katrina, and when they met—randomly on a bus, fate would have it—he held a tenure-track position teaching computer science at Bellingham Technical College in Washington State. Michael moved to Berkeley, as Katrina got her undergraduate degree from UC Berkeley, and then they both moved to the Portland area where Michael took a new teaching job at Clark College. As they began to have kids, Michael was coming home every evening unsatisfied, worried about becoming a grumpy father because teaching did not provide much of an outlet for his entrepreneurial energy. Katrina challenged him to "come up with one big business idea that we could work on together for twenty years that would make the world a better place."

In 2005 Katrina and Michael became residents of St. Johns, an economically challenged community on an island about a fifteen-minute drive from downtown Portland. They could see that the neighborhood businesses were struggling because of the presence of nearby big box stores. That's what crystalized the idea of Supportland—a state-of-the-art rewards system to support local shoppers and independent businesses. Over the next three years they began a process of intensive market research. They studied the loyalty programs of Wal-Mart, Target, and Nordstrom. They came up with more than two dozen different ways of designing the program, and interviewed small businesses in Portland to decide which would be the most effective.

It was another four years before Michael left his day job, and when he did, friends and relatives thought they both were crazy giving up the family's one steady source of income. But Michael and Katrina were convinced they had a winning idea and tapped Michael's retirement savings.

Their first plan was to deploy their loyalty program in collaboration with the Sustainable Business Network of Portland, a BALLE affiliate. When the nondisclosure agreements were signed, however, SBN revealed that the organization was disbanding. That's when Katrina and Michael realized that they would need to recruit the businesses themselves. The mountain ahead suddenly got much bigger, though in retrospect it was a blessing, because they could now enjoy a more direct relationship with their independent business customers.

While Michael was busily leading two other developers in the computer programming equivalent of the Manhattan Project, Katrina was recruiting local businesses with another secret weapon—cartoons. The home page for Supportland and many of its cards still feature Portland iconography, with a cartoonish figure of Paul Bunyan standing on a stump, surrounded by deer, squirrels, and rabbits, with a "Buy Local" slogan to the right, and with an Oregon mountain peak in the background. Katrina put together a cartoon video, explaining how Supportland would work, and showed it around town to every innovative local business she could think of. Once she snagged a business, she went to its competitors. She was blown away by how deeply local businesses wanted to work together. Katrina also convinced one of the city's weekly newspapers, *The Portland Mercury*, to run a front-page story on Supportland a month before the grand opening. She promised first-time users one hundred free points—or what are now called "merits"—just for signing up. Cards were available for free at all the participating businesses.

Supportland officially launched in August 2010, with twenty-seven businesses and zero users. Within a month, about six thousand people had signed up. Today that number has grown to 150 businesses and 80,000 active users. With each business paying $49 per month, annual revenues will soon clear $100,000. A recent evaluation found that Supportland thus far has moved about $8 million of spending into local businesses, and has engaged its card holders to a much greater degree than similar loyalty programs.

The Supportland system is basically two products: a paperless punch-card system, allowing each "punch" to be used for rewards at the issuing business; and a loyalty program where users accumulate points that can be cashed in for rewards at businesses across the network. Whenever a customer presents a participating business with a Supportland card or a mobile app, the business just needs an Internet connection to fulfill the transaction. No special equipment is required. The first purchase by a consumer earns twenty merits, and each subsequent purchase five merits. Consumers can then redeem the points for discounts or giveaways at any of the participating businesses. Businesses also get credit for the merits they give out in the form of discounts on their monthly fee.

One challenge with loyalty systems, as we saw with Bernal Bucks, is how to protect the most popular businesses from being stampeded. Supportland handles this by asking each business to limit the number of rewards it offers, and when one business's monthly rewards inventory is depleted, users have to go to the other businesses. But there is a natural incentive for businesses to keep offering up rewards. Experience shows that the more rewards offered, the more customers pay attention to the business and rush through the door. Katrina points out that a big point earner is ultimately "an amazing customer. You only get points for engaging with the local economy. It's like all the businesses have come together to vet the best customers and send them to your shop to redeem their rewards. It's pretty cool."

Participating businesses also are permitted to play around (within limits) with the points they distribute. Some give more merits for customers who pay in cash. Some will award merits to anyone who just shows up for an event. Every Valentine's Day, Supportland doubles the value of points and the rewards are temporarily tapped out. "The messaging," says Katrina, "is that local businesses love you."

"What we discovered is that when users get a reward, they are a crazy evangelist for the program. 'Oh, you like my bag? I got it with Supportland points.' I got a massage once as a birthday present, and the whole massage was an experience of gratitude toward my friend! That's why we actually want people to get rewards."

You would think that Katrina and Michael and their half-dozen staff would be pounding the doors of more Portland businesses, pushing for more publicity, recruiting more card holders, and nudging them to use the cards more frequently. They are doing a bit of this, but Portland is no longer their priority. Remember their vision is to create a state-of-the-art platform that can easily spread to metropolitan areas around the world. From their twenty-year perspective, they are still in the R&D phase.

Over the past year the Supportland technical team, led by Michael, has begun working on an entirely new version of the platform that will increase the functionality for consumers and businesses alike. Any user will be able to give another user a virtual gift card to any business in the network. With their Supportland mobile app, users will be able to gather more information about nearby businesses (based on their GPS coordinates) and share it more easily with other consumers. And businesses will soon have much more data about their Supportland-affiliated customers.

For example, new analytical tools will tell a given business which other businesses in the network its customers have an affinity with. The results, Katrina explains, can be surprising. A coffee shop and a toy store that were several miles apart, had no prior relationship, and had never even set foot in one another's store, discovered that they had similar customers. Once Supportland let them know this, the businesses entered into what Katrina calls "a hookup": All toy store customers presenting a Supportland card got a free cookie at the coffee shop. Not a single one of these toy-store customers went to get their cookie within the expiration period, but a third still made it to the coffee shop at some point over the next year.

"And this," explains Katrina, "is because every time the toy store rang up a Supportland customer, the checkout employee would say, 'I just put an awesome chocolate chip cookie on your Supportland account.' The toy store gave that customer a deep sense of community. Those toy-store customers who did go to the coffee shop were 60 percent more frequent in their visits to the coffee shop than other customers. At the toy store, people who had gotten a cookie had a 38 percent higher retention rate at the toy store and were 40 percent more frequent with their visits. Isn't this wild? We calculated that the coffee shop made over $500 in profit from this campaign.

"When two businesses collaborate together to provide something for a customer, an unexpected gift is the holy grail. The experience of the customer gets a layer deeper each time another business is involved. If just one business provides you with a gift, it feels good, but it feels like that one business gave you something. If two businesses get together and give you something, then suddenly you have the community embracing you. That's the space the Supportland likes to play with."

Katrina views the most important service that Supportland provides as helping local businesses identify crossover partners and bringing them together to conceive joint rewards for their customers. It's basically Match.com for commerce, and a natural fit with a local business alliance.

Supportland is still bare bones, just past the seed funding phase, and not yet profitable. Katrina and Michael have raised several hundred thousand dollars already for the venture, primarily from friends, family, and angel investors in Portland. They are now trying to raise more capital, but in a way that protects the social enterprise mission of the company. Their advisory board includes: a business anthropologist who works with Fortune 500 companies; the head of a San Francisco-based product development company; a former tech executive at Yahoo!; and a Wall Street attorney with social consciousness. And me.

Supportland aspires to become a tech tool used by business alliances or similar groups all over the world. One of their first takers is the Seattle Good Business Network, which is now preparing to launch their loyalty program. Another taker is Victoria—the same community in British Columbia running a ShopCity site. Even in Portland, Katrina says she would like to find a group that would take on the "front end" of the relationship building with consumers and businesses. Ideally, Supportland would like to find clients of different scale—a small community, a neighborhood within a large metro, a downtown area—where they could test their assumptions. "Frankly, we really have our pick of communities, because there are so many people interested."

Will Supportland operators be a licensee or a franchise? Neither, according to Katrina. "We see ourselves as a platform providing a service. We provide the business network with all the technology, the billing infrastructure, the help-desk support, and the basic functionality. What we need is a local business alliance that plays with the system and brings its members on board. Each alliance will retain its own branding, except our tools will say 'Powered by Supportland.' So, if a local business alliance runs a holiday campaign, we'd encourage an interactive marketing piece that involves Supportland. The benefit to them is that now they have the data to prove whether that campaign was a success. We want their members to pay dues, not as a gift, but rather because the alliance is really improving their bottom lines."

Evolving Consumer Consciousness

A thread running through all these stories is the changing relationship between consumers and businesses. The simplistic models in Economics 101 assume that consumers are only interested in price. Lower the price of a widget and consumers will buy more of it. While price matters, smart consumers increasingly pay attention to many other considerations as well: What's the quality of the widget? How long will it last? What's the reputation of the company selling it? How easily can it be returned if it's defective? Or repaired if it breaks down? These factors alone often motivate a consumer today to spend a little more on an item from a trustworthy local business.

But the next generation of consumers might be not only smart but also principled. A growing number already care about how a product was made. Did it involve child labor? Does the company dump toxics into the ocean? Are its lobbyists supporting unsavory politicians? And, of course, is the company supporting the community? Does it hire local? Contribute to local charities? Pay local taxes?

The success of deep discounters over the past generation, from Wal-Mart to Amazon to Groupon, was all about price. And price, too, was the focal point of the early pollinator models like coupon books and loyalty programs. But purchasing pollinators increasingly appreciate that loyalty built on price is superficial and fleeting. Loyalty needs to be built on smart shopping and on an inspiring vision. Purchasing pollinators are all about building a meaningful sense of community: a community of local businesses that partner together; a community of consumers that support community-nurturing local businesses; and a community of these kinds of communities across the world.

CHAPTER 4

People

Training the Talent

"**R**ight Livelihood," explains E. F. Schumacher in *Small Is Beautiful*, "is one of the requirements of the Buddha's Noble Eightfold Path. It is clear, therefore, that there must be such a thing as Buddhist economics."[55] Schumacher goes on to describe Buddhist economics as "people-centered," a field that gives "a man a chance to utilise and develop his faculties; to enable him to overcome his ego-centredness by joining with other people in a common task; and to bring forth the goods and services needed for a becoming existence."[56] Schumacher's vision of local economic development was rooted in entrepreneurship.

People is perhaps the one *P* category to which mainstream economic development has been most attentive. The profession has spawned many kinds of programs providing resources to would-be entrepreneurs, including courses, mentors, incubators, industrial-development parks, and workforce-development programs, all aimed at transforming human capacity into prosperous local production.

These mainstream programs go off the rails, however, when they convince graduates that success means taking their companies "public" and deserting the home community. An otherwise excellent publication put out by the National Business Incubation Association (NBIA), called *Best Practices in Rural Business Incubation*, contains the following odd paragraph:

[Jennifer Simon, director of the Ohio University Innovation Center,] wants to solve a problem that bedevils numerous incubation programs. . . . "People here are working constantly to create companies and products, but they may never become fully integrated in the community. That means that when they graduate, they haven't established loyalty to the region and might relocate."[57]

And why is it that the companies graduating from incubators might not be integrating into the community? Might it be that the programs forgot to limit themselves to local entrepreneurs? Hundreds of programs around the United States foolishly attract businesses to set up shop in their incubators, invest tens of thousands of dollars per company in services and rent subsidies, and then are surprised and disappointed when, two years later, they graduate and fly off elsewhere. Wake up and smell the local coffee!

People pollinators focus exclusively on local businesses already woven into the fabric of their community. In this chapter, we begin by describing the work of one of the world's most influential people pollinators, Ernesto Sirolli. We then look at a new kind of business school in British Columbia, and a high school teaching food entrepreneurship in Paraguay that's now spreading worldwide. Finally we see interesting new ways of thinking about business incubation—at a deli in Michigan, at a spin-off Maker Works, and at a social enterprise "accelerator" in Seattle.

"Shut Up and Listen"

Ernesto Sirolli is perhaps the closest anyone comes to being a pollinator rock star. His TED Talk (TED stands for technology, entertainment, and design) on his philosophy for promoting entrepreneurship through a form of business counseling that he calls "enterprise facilitation" has been downloaded nearly two million times. A list of the top thirty global advocates against poverty and hunger, circulated by the website Top Masters in Health Care, ranks Sirolli at eleven. When I interviewed him, he had just finished a grueling trip with stops in Singapore, Italy, and Australia, before he returned to his current home in Sacramento, California. Ernesto Sirolli is part academic (he has a degree in political science from Rome University and a PhD from Murdoch University in Australia), part advocate (he has written two compelling books on how to promote entrepreneurship), and part entertainer (his storytelling is filled with humor, passion, and grace).

I first met him in Australia, at an annual meeting of SEGRA (Sustainable Economic Growth for Regional Australia). Even though Australia is geographically vast, more than 90 percent of the population is concentrated along its east coast; SEGRA is all about supporting the thousands of towns everywhere else in the country. One of those remote outposts is Esperance—a ten-thousand-person fishing village on the west coast of Australia and, as Sirolli explained with Italian charm and sweeping arm gestures, ground zero for his first experiences as a people pollinator.

In 1985, Sirolli helped Maurie Green, an unemployed fish processor living in Esperance, get a loan to move his fish-smoking equipment to a commercial venue. When that business took off, the fishermen supplying tuna to Green asked for Sirolli's help to find export markets for their fish in Japan. He ultimately secured a price for their catch some six times greater than what the local processor was offering. He then helped sheep farmers figure out how to make money from old ewes. And he wrapped up his work by training Brian Willoughby to continue this work as an enterprise facilitator and appointing an overseeing Local Enterprise Initiatives Committee.

Sirolli's orientation of Willoughby went something like this: "Brian . . . there are only two things that I don't want you to do in this job. Anything else you can do, but don't ever initiate anything and don't ever motivate anybody."[58] A community should know that "an enterprise facilitator" is available to help, argues Sirolli, but the initiative always must come from the entrepreneur. And that entrepreneur must have complete passion and love for his or her business.

Recent trends in the global economy, Sirolli believes, make enterprise facilitation more urgent. More women have entered the workforce and are interested in starting their own businesses. Older people who have been laid off and discarded by the mainstream economy are looking to launch new businesses to supplement their income. Younger people are looking for more control over their working lives through their own firms.

The demand side of the economy is changing too. "Customers," Sirolli wrote in his first book, *Ripples in the Zambezi*, "demand variety, quality, service and ethics in business. . . . These new trends have spurred new ways of winning market share through niche marketing: personalized, customized, labor-intensive, intelligence-intensive, client-centered, highly localized, cooperative endeavors."[59]

The title of that book refers to another formative experience Sirolli had while working for the Italian Agency of Technology Cooperation (ASIP). The government agency had resolved to create a "training farm" in a village near the Zambezi River in Zambia. The plan was to train thirty locals to use communally owned technology—tractors, trucks, seeds, and so forth—and ultimately give them ownership of the farm. The first day went well. The trainees were supposed to return the next morning but didn't. In fact, they vanished for a week. The reason, it turned out, was they had more than enough food to feed their families and didn't feel that they needed to work more than one day per week. This, from ASIP's perspective, was a problem. So the Italian trainers started selling to the Zambian locals various western items, such as sunglasses, radios, and booze, which guaranteed that they needed more money. To the satisfaction of the ASIP staff, the locals now came to the project every day.

"I could not believe we were doing this," writes Sirolli. "Here we were, talking about aid, technical cooperating, and caring for these people, and what did we do? We got them hooked on beer so they would want more money and would come to work every day to get it."[60]

The crop that these farmers wound up growing was the Italians' favorite vegetable—tomatoes. The harvest was splendid. But just as it was ready to be picked, it disappeared. "Approaching the field the Italians . . . didn't take long to figure out what had happened. They could see the ripples in the Zambezi. The best-fed hippos of the entire river system were enjoying their after-dinner siesta literally a stone's throw away from what had been the pride and joy of the Italian continent."[61]

Sirolli was appalled with what his high-minded Italian colleagues were doing, and found solace in E. F. Schumacher's recently published *Small Is Beautiful*. "Fundamentally, [Schumacher] said two things to me: (1) If people don't ask for help, leave them alone. (2) There is no good or bad technology to carry out a task—only an appropriate or inappropriate one."[62]

Sirolli began to think about how to make economic development more effective. He incorporated the ideas of two influential humanistic psychologists: Abraham Maslow, who conceptualized a "hierarchy of needs" that defined human development as moving from material to emotional and ultimately spiritual well-being; and Carl Rogers, who theorized that the best therapists should help clients not to overcome this or that childhood trauma but rather to achieve their full human potential.

At the time, Sirolli was living in the small city of Fremantle in Western Australia. With a grant of $900, he introduced several local sandal-makers, mostly younger hippies, to an elder leather craftsman who was—of course!—Italian. The informal workshop was a spectacular success and evolved into the Fremantle Shoemakers' Cooperative. When he showed the city the results of this low-cost "long-term job creation scheme," city officials were "speechless with delight," reported Sirolli. "So was I, and I would have been more so if I had known then that the $900 project would last ten years, train two dozen people in varying degrees of skill, and propel some of them into further careers in orthopedic shoemaking, special footwear, and even an academic degree in podiatry."[63]

That small project laid the foundation for Sirolli's work in Esperance in 1985, and then elsewhere. The results have been extraordinary:

- In the first three years in Esperance, he and Brian Willoughby created 45 businesses, 77 new jobs, and $4.3 million in new annual sales. In the years following, three dozen other communities in Western Australia were sufficiently impressed to adopt Sirolli's methodology.
- Sirolli was invited to create an enterprise facilitator in Waimate Plains, a 3,000 person town in New Zealand's northern island. Three years later they had 207 new businesses and 400 new jobs. By 1998 some 70 New Zealand communities had deployed enterprise facilitators.
- In the mid-1990s Sirolli took his work to some of the poorest communities in Minnesota and South Dakota. Vince Robinson, the appointed enterprise facilitator of Lincoln County, Minnesota, reported that in six years they had helped start 55 businesses, expand 61 others, and create 180 jobs, all at a cost of $1,833 per job.

Since then Sirolli's work has gone truly global. Over just the past year, he has had initiatives in Ecuador, the Congo, Nepal, Ghana, and Wales. "We are purely responsive, and we go wherever we are invited. We try to stay as diversified geographically as possible." Sirolli estimates that since Esperance, he has personally trained 150 enterprise facilitators, who themselves have collectively trained another 150.

As I read through *Ripples in the Zambezi* and listened to Sirolli's various talks, I realized that his strategy was similar to Lou Stein's in West Virginia, even though the two have never met or even heard of one another. Roll up your sleeves and help passionate start-up entrepreneurs realize their dreams. Get modest loans or other capital into their hands. Listen to the problems they identify, and offer to help solve them in ways large and small. Help existing businesses find larger chunks of capital. None of this, as they say, is rocket science.

Sirolli has elaborated his long list of entrepreneurship do's and don'ts into courses, lectures, and his latest book, *How to Start a Business and Ignite Your Life*. For example, he points out that "business is a team sport." Every successful business needs to have a great product, great marketing, and great bookkeeping—and rarely does one entrepreneur excel at all three things. An essential exercise for an entrepreneur, therefore, is to figure out his or her weakness, and then recruit a team—as partners, staff, or board members—who fill the gap. He also argues that an enterprise facilitator, following Carl Rogers' ideas on therapy, should say little or nothing until asked.

The Sirolli Institute has never raised a dime from funders. Its model is to charge fees for services, and then to help the clients raise funds locally from events, donors, or foundations. In South Dakota, the enterprise facilitator's salary is paid by forty-two different entities. Once results start materializing, the local government is often willing to start underwriting the work. In Wales, the economic-development department is now considering putting an enterprise facilitator on its staff.

Even though Sirolli does not ask businesses being "facilitated" to pay for services, he reports that the vast majority do give back. "Those businesses collaborate, share resources, and trade among themselves. Some become members of our enterprise facilitation resource board."

At one point the Sirolli Institute had as many as ten full-time and five part-time staff. "But we decided to let go of the ambition to become an in-house training organization." Now the institute enters partnerships with other groups to take on the training. It has working relationships with six business schools around the world, including the prestigious Haas School at UC Berkeley. While Sirolli is a critic of international aid, progressive aid organizations like Oxfam have used his techniques to train personnel in international development, and forty universities use his books for their courses.

Reflecting on his growing fame, Sirolli credits the millennial generation. "They have an extraordinary level of need to learn about concrete approaches to transform their own passion into a business. I had not realized how desperate the situation is out there, but they are our hope for the future." Student groups at universities around the world are now asking him to help them push their economics and business departments to teach enterprise facilitation.

"I thought I was a middle-aged fool who would disappear in obscurity," Sirolli says about his life's work. "Instead, I'm a spokesperson for a movement with no name."

Reinventing Business School

Ernesto Sirolli is one of thousands of entrepreneurship teachers worldwide. Around the United States, for example, the Small Business Administration finances a network of sixty-three Small Business Development Centers (with nine hundred affiliated sites), where entrepreneurs can find volunteers, professionals, and mentors willing to help them write business plans and improve their business skills. A nonprofit called SCORE organizes retirees into mentors for early-stage businesspeople. Many community-development corporations, which were created during the 1960s War on Poverty, provide critical support to low-income entrepreneurs. All these institutions are almost entirely funded through government grants and other donations.

It's worth pointing out that there is one institution that has long had a successful business model teaching people how to run businesses, and that's the modern business school. But as Sirolli argues, MBA courses are focused on training managers, not entrepreneurs. Getting a traditional

MBA, he says, is "the worst thing you can do." There are, though, some options for entrepreneurs looking for an MBA that's supportive of local business. Both the Presidio School of Management in San Francisco and the Bainbridge Graduate Institute in Seattle—two newer business schools—do an excellent job focusing on training social entrepreneurs who wish to start community enterprises.

Even so, business schools are at best imperfect pollinators. Most depend on alumni gifts and foundation grants, though they do at least cover some costs through tuition. And there's another important obstacle: How many entrepreneurs can afford to quit their day jobs and go back to business school? Finding more modest programs that offer more specialized assistance is a more relevant option. The one school I've come to know that comes the closest to embodying a pollinator model is the Community Economic Development (CED) program at Simon Fraser University (SFU) in Vancouver, British Columbia. The adult-education course is almost entirely self-financing, and its curriculum focuses exclusively on localization. Running it now is a 42-year old dynamo named Nicole Chaland.

When she was an undergraduate student in economics, Chaland puzzled over the contradictions between the rosy assessment of First World development initiatives presented by her professors and the depressing news accounts about globalization's awful "race to the bottom." She traveled to the Philippines to form her own opinion, and concluded that "it wasn't a black-and-white story." The factory she was studying there forbade its workers from forming a union, but not a cooperative. She could see how the coop was providing financial services and loans to its members, and this began her lifelong interest in do-it-yourself models of economic empowerment. Her practical research at the factory was part of a class she was taking from SFU's CED program. Because she was studying in a pre-Internet era, Chaland was undertaking distance education the old fashioned way—through the mail.

When Chaland returned to Canada, she landed a job with the British Columbia Institute for Co-operative Studies at the University of Victoria, one of several initiatives by the recently created British Columbia Ministry of Community Development, Co-operatives, and Volunteers. Her assignment was to write case studies of exemplary co-ops, and she wound up interviewing fifty co-op founders. "It was a great thing for a young person looking for how to make her way in the co-op economy."

That experience was short lived. When the provincial government was voted out, the co-op ministry was shut down and its projects defunded. "I should have learned not to depend on government grants," she says, but then she immediately took a job with another nonprofit, the Canadian Community Economic Development Network (CCEDNet), which itself was grant-dependent on the national government and foundations. "For the next five years I was living on the edge. We had six-month contracts, and you never knew at the end of month five if you would have to move into your car."

In other respects, however, the CCEDNet job was terrific. Her mission was to build a movement for community economic development in Canada, and to find, mobilize, and organize groups for this emerging network. She interviewed three hundred organizations, built a huge database, and published her findings.

"I was both impressed and confused by the sector. I was impressed with the level of entrepreneurship of most of these groups, because only about half their money came from the government. The rest came from sales, donations, investment income, and membership fees. But I was confused by their mission. Some of the organizations were place-based, some were attached to disadvantaged groups. Way too many people were doing only what they were funded to do."

Then came a golden opportunity in 2008. The SFU program from which Chaland had taken her distance-learning course in the Philippines was in trouble. The university was increasingly frustrated that it was unable to create a financial model that worked. The overseers wanted to incorporate more practitioners to teach the classes. The solution was to partner with CCEDNet, and appoint Chaland director of the CED program.

Chaland immediately realized that what was killing the program was the huge university overhead. Revenues from the program had been supporting three part-time, unionized staff, some of whom were only tangentially involved. With the program's financial administration now technically outside the university, Chaland was able to slash these expenses and take the program through what she called "a lean start-up." She talked with her customers (that is, students) and learned that they wanted more up-to-date models of community and economic development. She overhauled the course designs, reshaped the program's marketing and branding, and incorporated basic business principles into day-to-day operations. "We used to be everything to everybody. Now we focus on people who are building a local living economy."

The more entrepreneurial Chaland herself became, however, the less well the program fit within CCEDNet, the nonprofit mother ship. She herself didn't want to rely on grants forever. She wanted partners and investors who truly valued the program and were prepared to take some risk. So she spun out the program in 2013, and it has thrived ever since.

The program is still technically SFU's—the certificates it hands out formally come from the university—but Chaland negotiated a new financial deal that just pays the university a modest per-student enrollment fee. Chaland occasionally relies on an SFU professor to teach, but mostly contracts with outsiders. She currently has a stable of eight instructors, and I am one of them. Several times per year, I fly to western Canada to teach an intensive two or three days to a twenty to twenty-five person cohort, most of whom are entrepreneurs, run social enterprises, or practice local economic development. The typical cohort spends 135 hours together. It meets for three full weeks of courses spread over seven months, and then does distance learning between these weeks via the Internet.

Chaland argues that the program's emphasis on combining theory and practice provides her students with an especially rich learning experience. Her teachers tend to have more stories to share, and a more coherent worldview. And from my perspective at least, the students are also well prepared to take the material and run with it.

Unlike 99 percent of university programs throughout the world, Chaland's is 100 percent financed by fees. "Hey, our philosophy is that we need to make the economy more self-reliant, and we need to walk the talk." Every student pays $4,800 per certificate. She has secured a few grants primarily to support scholarships for low-income students. She also recently raised $25,000 for an investment fund of sorts. The students run an annual social innovation challenge, in which any one student, or group, may present projects for funding—basically a *Shark Tank* for projects that localize the economy.

Among Chaland's priorities now are to create an active alumni association for mentoring current students and also to help launch the Centre for Social Impact in Victoria, the provincial capital where she lives, a several hour boat-ride away from Vancouver. The Centre is a work hub where entrepreneurs can rent space as small as a desk, use co-owned office equipment, and collaborate with like-minded thinkers. "It's a pretty straight-forward theory of change. Bring together people, and you get a deeper level of impact." The Centre pays for itself through memberships, rentals, and fees. And this is just the beginning, as far as Chaland is concerned. Next up is a social venture accelerator, a concept we will explore shortly.

Foodie High Schools

Sirolli, Chaland, and most entrepreneurship programs work with adults, but young people are hungry for these skills as well. Filling this gap in the United States have been myriad "youth entrepreneurship" programs. The Network for Teaching Entrepreneurship (NFTE), for example, provides basic business skills to hundreds of thousands of young people, particularly in low-income communities. To finance these admirable programs, NFTE's founder, Steve Mariotti, has probably raised hundreds of millions of dollars from government agencies and foundations. But is it possible to convert these programs into self-financing pollinators? An intriguing answer comes from Paraguay.

"We change peasants into rural entrepreneurs," says Martin Burt, executive director of Fundación Paraguaya, a nonprofit foundation that since 1985 has been providing microlending and sustainable training to Paraguay's farmers and other agricultural workers, with some of their funding focused specifically on women and young people. Fundación Paraguaya's Escuela Agrícola Orgánica Financieramente Autosufficiente (Financially Self-Sufficient Organic Farm School) offers a solid high school education focusing on strong agricultural practices, business skills, and entrepreneurship. The school is located in Cerrito, an area outside the rural town of Benjamín Aceval, about 46 kilometers from Asunción, Paraguay's capital and largest city.

"What sets our model apart from other approaches," says Burt, "is that we have found a way to combine quality, relevance, and affordability. Our model offers high quality agricultural education at the secondary level, yet does not require poor students to pay any more than a token tuition fee."

The roots of the school go back to the early 1950s, when the San Francisco Missionary Brothers, a small Franciscan congregation, founded La Escuela Agrícola San Francisco de Asis, a parochial boarding school for the area's poor boys. By 1980, the school had seventy students, 62 hectares of partially forested yet cultivatable land, and 7,000 square meters of facility and conference space. It had also run into the ground financially. The congregation of the LaSalle Brothers, another local congregation, took over the school, but again became mired in money problems and prepared to shut it down in 2002.

Around this time, the leaders of Fundación Paraguaya met at their annual staff retreat. When they learned that the Farm School was on the verge of closing, they saw an opportunity. Why not reinvent the school as a model for teaching sustainable agriculture?

"There's a natural assumption that the food chain starts with the farmer who knows how to farm," observes Nik Kafka, director of Fundación Paraguaya's sister organization based in the United Kingdom, Teach a Man to Fish. "But the reality in most developing countries . . . is that that just isn't the case. The educational system is set up to deliver people a piece of paper that shows their academic prowess, but students aren't really learning how to be farmers, and this is the missing link in the food chain."

So the foundation set out to design the Farm School to be that missing link. As a condition for buying the school, the foundation made a commitment to educate rural, low-income kids in a boarding school model; to develop new sustainable business programs for teaching purposes; and to rebuild the school's finances, facilities, and training programs. Within the first year, 2002, it rewrote the curriculum and got it approved by the Ministries of Education and Agriculture and Livestock, transitioned to organic farming practices, and made the teachers more accountable to the financial health of the institution. Four years later, the school went co-ed, and soon after it created a cluster of campus-based, revenue-generating enterprises so that the school could operate financially self-sufficiently. In

2008 the Ministry of Education granted the school permission to issue its graduates certificates in hostelry and tourism, in addition to the certificates in agriculture and training technicians.

Today, the Farm School operates as an independent entity under the foundation's nonprofit umbrella. It employs twenty full- and part-time staff, including administrators, teachers, cooks, and other support personnel. Sometimes interns from around the world support the staff, offering additional training and services in exchange for room and board.

When Fundación Paraguaya first took over, it also committed to weaning the Farm School back to financial health in five years or less, and it resolved to walk the talk of entrepreneurship—to make the school market-driven and financially self-sufficient. It immediately stopped taking state subsidies. It did raise some grant money from foundations and other entities, but viewed these as investments in its social enterprise.

To achieve self-sufficiency, the school developed sixteen sub-enterprises on campus, including a hotel, a dairy, a restaurant, and a farmers market. Each of these enterprises is designed to provide experiential education for the students and to generate additional revenue for the school. For example, Hotel Cerrito and its surrounding chalets can accommodate up to 140 guests at once, and can be used as a conference center and a destination for tourists and travelers. The facilities generate up to 30 percent of the school's annual revenue, but also train students interested in hotel management and hospitality. The school's dairy processes the milk produced on campus into *dulce de leche*, yogurt, and cheese. Students make the products, bring them to market, and sell them, which gives them experience with food processing, packaging, and retail.

Community experience is regarded as essential. For example, students must take turns running the school's farmers market stands. By being involved in local markets, students learn customer service, merchandising, financial management, and production, all while meeting people in the community. "Our greatest teacher—the market—gives us big, important classes all the time," explains Jose Luis Salomón, a former director of the Farm School.

In other programs, students learn how to meet Grow Biointensive organic standards, employing soil conservation practices to produce more food on less land. They also learn AgroWin, a basic software program that helps farmers easily organize and analyze accounting, budgeting, inventory, and production data. And they are introduced to solar energy, composting, and vermiculture (farming with worms).

According to Luis Fernando Sanabria, the chief operating officer of Fundación Paraguaya, by 2007, the Farm School reported an annual growth rate of 10–15 percent and annual revenue reached US $300,000—an operational break-even point. The school now operates debt-free and has also generated a cash reserve to be used for teachers' retirements.

The program takes local economics very seriously. For instance, with the exception of durable goods like vehicles, computers, and hardware, the school purchases all of its supplies locally—within an hour's drive— and teaches its students how to best use local resources. It tries to hire its instructors locally and provides them with good salaries. And it has played a role in improving the local food system, generating nearly 70 percent of its income by selling locally grown organic food to local markets. It is also very conscious of its energy impact on the surrounding community, and strives to minimize its carbon footprint with its new solar energy panels and composting program.

For Paraguayan communities generally, the school has become an invaluable resource. According to Fulbright scholar Sarita Role Schaffer, who lived at the Farm School and studied its operations for two years, "Each year the school graduates roughly fifty young people who return to their communities not just to grow food, but to transform their local food systems by launching rural enterprises that introduce innovations at all points on the food supply chain. The Farm School graduates inject their communities with the vital intellectual inputs required to generate lasting social, environmental, and economic wealth from locally available resources." Students also become extension agents and teachers.

The school has earned numerous awards from such entities as the Inter-American Development Bank, the BBC World Challenge, the Skoll Foundation, and the United Nations Educational, Scientific, and Cultural Organization (UNESCO). Through conferences the foundation organizes, it has become a model for other agricultural schools in Paraguay, Latin

America, and around the world. For example, Fundación Paraguaya has since founded three other schools in Paraguay, one of which is an all-girls school based in a forest reserve designated by UNESCO as a "biosphere for humanity."[64] Its teaching businesses include growing tree seedlings, developing reforestation plans, and selling yerba mate, which grows in the understory of the forest. In Tunisia, the foundation is partnering with the MasterCard Foundation to replicate the model in five schools there. Some are even thinking about ways of deploying the model in poor neighborhoods in developed countries.

"The Financially Self-Sufficient Organic Farm School is not a pilot, it's a paradigm," says Nik Kafka proudly. "It's self-sufficient, which means it is endlessly replicable . . . It's literally a revolution in the making and with potentially the same impact as the microfinance revolution. For the people who got in early on microfinance, they're the ones with the biggest smiles on their faces today. And the people who get in early on education that pays for itself will be the people smiling very happily in twenty or thirty years, too."

The Little Deli That Could

Entrepreneurship training does not happen just in schools. It happens within businesses every day. Any smart company that moves past its start-up phase begins grooming managers. But a people pollinator goes further, deliberately trying to use its internal training practices to spawn new local businesses in the community. An exemplar of this is Zingerman's Community of Businesses in Ann Arbor, Michigan.

Zingerman's started in 1982, when Paul Saginaw and Ari Weinzweig launched a deli that served great local sandwiches and purveyed fine, arti-san-made food products from around the world. They became a nationally recognized food sensation, winning corned-beef tasting competitions in New York City and becoming one of the top sellers of traditional cheeses in the United States.

After a decade of success, Saginaw dragged his partner outside and said, "Hey, we've been at this for ten years, we achieved our original vision, but how could we impact our community still more? Where do we want to be ten years from now? If nothing else, we owe it to the people working for us to provide great growth opportunities."

They could see neighboring businesses trying to copy their success. "We got complacent," admits Saginaw. "We thought we owned the market, but people aren't stupid and understand what parts of your business are successful. Competitors come along and offer 50 percent of your quality at 75 percent of the price, embarrass you, and make you look like you're ripping off the public."

Saginaw and Weinzweig decided to grow the company in new ways, to take on new challenges, to give their best employees entrepreneurship growth opportunities within the company. The solution, however, was not to become a deli chain. "We knew," says Saginaw, "we wanted to have just one store and that we were not going to grow by replicating ourselves. For us, by definition, if there was more than one store, it wasn't unique anymore. This wasn't a political belief or ideology; it was a lifestyle we wanted to live." That lifestyle meant getting to know the employees and customers, and continually fine-tuning their goods and services to meet the needs of the Ann Arbor community.

Some think that staying local means repudiating growth. To the contrary, Zingerman's has grown spectacularly in one place. Saginaw clarifies: "We grow deep."

So, in the early 1990s Saginaw and Weinzweig prepared a strategic plan to grow the company around what came into and out of the deli. The first company they created, to localize the bread served in the deli, was Zingerman's Bakehouse, established in 1992. Zingerman's Creamery, which produces cheese and ice cream, was created in 2001. Zingerman's Coffee Company, which roasts beans, was established in 2004. Zingerman's Candy Manufactory was opened in 2009.

At the same time Zingerman's looked at value-adding opportunities for its foodstuffs businesses. It created Zingerman's Mail Order Company in 1994 to market its coffee cakes and other delicacies nationally. That same year it opened a consulting business, focused initially on teaching Zingerman's approach to good customer service, called ZingTrain. It built a sit-down restaurant in 2003 called Zingerman's Roadhouse. The most recent addition is Zingerman's Cornman Farms, which provides local ingredients—everything from heirloom tomatoes to goats' milk—to the Roadhouse. A rebuilt barn also serves as a reception hall for Zingerman's-catered weddings, bar mitzvahs, and other events.

In all the Zingerman's Community of Business (ZCoB) comprises ten enterprises that collectively sell about $50 million of goods and services each year, and employ almost seven hundred people in the Ann Arbor area. And more enterprises are on the way. A food cart called San Street, which is aspiring to become a traditional sit-down Korean restaurant, will probably be Zingerman's next business.

Each of these enterprises is independently owned and run as a separate business, yet operates as part of the ZCoB. As a ZCoB business, it must follow certain rules to carry the Zingerman's brand: it must meet standards of quality, it must prioritize sourcing from and selling to fellow ZCoB businesses, it must embrace certain social responsibility principles, and its partners must participate in biweekly meetings. But in the end each business is truly independent—and that's what qualifies Zingerman's as a pollinator.

"We have a two-year associates degree," jokes Saginaw, who quickly points out that "the path to partnership is usually longer." Any potential partner must show exceptional skill within his or her enterprises. He or she must go through an internal leadership-development program. And he or she must get involved in activities outside his or her day-to-day responsibilities, such as teaching a ZCoB-wide class. "This isn't just a six-month boot camp."

Every Zingerman's employee discovers that creating and co-owning another ZCoB entity is possible. "We let them know," says Saginaw, "that money will never be a roadblock. We'll figure it out." Saginaw and Weinzweig have seeded some of the ZCoB businesses through funds from their own holding company called Dancing Sandwich Enterprises. Sometimes they've arranged a loan from a third party. Sometimes they have personally loaned the money and asked the employee to pay it back as a salary deduction. In any event, Saginaw emphasizes, "he or she has to have skin in the game."

When Saginaw and Weinzweig formally announced their vision for a community of businesses, they thought they would be opening the floodgates and that lots of new employees would want to run new businesses. But only a few employees really demonstrated that level of commitment. Would-be entrepreneurs have to present a written vision of their idea, and to go through the Zingerman's leadership program. The process naturally weeds out people. "At every stage," Saginaw clarifies, "the decision is never 'no.' It's either 'yes' or 'not yet.'"

Besides serving as a pollinator for its own branded businesses within Ann Arbor, Zingerman's has sought to strengthen other local businesses through ZingTrain. The roots of ZingTrain go back to when Saginaw first met Weinzweig and both were working at a restaurant called Maude's, along with a young woman named Maggie Bayless. Years later, after Bayless got her MBA at the University of Michigan and had successful stints working for General Motors, SoHo Beverages, and a local training and consulting firm, she approached her old buddies to discuss joining them. She had read their vision for "A Community of Businesses" and saw a need to create a training infrastructure for it internally, as well as an opportunity to share information externally with other companies.

At the time, Zingerman's had been receiving many inquiries from outsiders about how to start similar businesses. So, the partners set Bayless to work documenting the key systems operating within Zingerman's and then preparing courses to teach them—and ZingTrain was born. "Because we were practitioners, not just trainers, we believed we had a real competitive advantage in the marketplace," says Saginaw. "We're not just motivational speakers."

The "systems" that Bayless documented and began teaching included: models for training the trainers; open-book accounting (which allows all stakeholders to review the books online in real time); management techniques; marketing and merchandizing; human resources; and visioning future businesses. Bayless herself also had new ideas about training. She was critical of most courses that just dumped material on students. It was far better to recognize that they had many different learning styles, and to focus not on skills per se but on results—better products, better customer satisfaction, and better bottom lines.

When Bayless, in partnership with Saginaw and Weinzweig, launched ZingTrain in 1994, the initial clients were other ZCoB businesses at the time: the Deli and the Bakehouse. Today, twenty years later, 99 percent of ZingTrain's clients are from outside the ZCoB. For many years, customer service was the most popular training topic, but now there's equal demand for visioning and open-book management.

Seminars open to the general public are held at Zingerman's training facility, and provide a mix of lectures, small groups, individual reflection, and engagement with ZCoB partners and staff. Most sessions are capped at thirty to thirty-five participants, each paying $1,250–$1,500 for a two-day seminar. Attendees are encouraged to sit with strangers and learn from one another as well as from ZingTrain trainers. Usually one or two people per company participate, and most are small- to mid-sized privately held companies or nonprofits. If a company wishes to send more students, or wants to bring ZingTrain to its location, it is encouraged to contract for a private, tailored session.

ZingTrain has been profitable for most of its history, but in the early stages Bayless had to invest sweat equity. She took no salary for the first year, and then a very low salary of $1,000 per month. She was lucky that her husband had a full-time job with benefits, because the start-up occurred when she had a two-year-old child and was pregnant with another. But one of the reasons she wanted to work with ZCoB instead of a Fortune 500 company was to have flexibility for her family life.

The crash of the US economy in 2008 was a wrenching period for ZingTrain. Before then, the company had been growing and hiring steadily. Then, suddenly, sales fell off, and Bayless had to commence the emotionally painful process of downsizing, cutting, and reorganizing. "But because we were an open-book company, there were no surprises. Everyone knew that our cash was running out and that we had to make cuts." There was also a silver lining. When sales came back, the leaner company quickly became very profitable. For the fiscal year that ended in July 2014, ZingTrain had $1.8 million in sales, with a 16 percent net operating profit, and paid out $63,000 to eleven staff in profit shares.

Now things are chugging along again. ZingTrain recently moved into its current space with two dedicated training rooms (previously trainings were held in the upstairs of the Deli). This allows the company to invite private clients to come to Ann Arbor for trainings and gives ZingTrain the flexibility to offer trainings even during the Deli's busiest days. Another recent innovation is to design courses in partnership with other organizations. For example, it is working with NEW, an Ann Arbor group, to pilot a nonprofit leadership academy.

The two-day commitment required for ZingTrain seminars makes them especially popular with entrepreneurs who don't have time to go to business school or even attend a multi-week course. Bayless estimates that ZingTrain now delivers about twenty-five public seminars per year, with an average of twenty to twenty-five people per seminar, plus an equal number of private seminars. "We now are reaching over a thousand people per year. And all of this has happened without much advertising," she adds. "I don't have a real desire to change anything right now, but I know it will need to change for the future. That's a job for the next generation to figure out."

Bayless sees her final challenge as finding her own replacement, preferably one or two younger people who are web savvy. It's time, she believes, to start reinforcing some of the company's in-person offerings with online learning experiences, and she is looking for that expertise as she hires the next ZingTrain trainers.

Reflecting both on ZingTrain and the ZCoB, Paul Saginaw says, "What we are is a better business incubator. It's a corruption if you start up and sell out. ZingTrain won't turn away customers, but local businesses are our priorities, especially those that embrace the principles of local living economies."

Let's Make It, Baby

Another Zingerman's success story involves Tom Root, currently a partner at the ZCoB Mail Order Company. Unlike Bayless, Root took his pollinator idea outside Zingerman's. His Maker Works is an 11,000-square-foot facility with an electronics lab, 3-D printers, and a full assortment of tools for textile fabrication, woodworking, and metalworking. It works like a health club: buy a membership, take a few lessons, and get access to all the toys. Only the members are geeks, students, inventors, and wannabe manufacturers.

Root sees his company as part of the national maker movement. He recounts a presidential debate between Barack Obama and John McCain in 2008, when the topic turned to energy independence. "Tom Brokaw asked if the federal government should fund a Manhattan-style project for energy independence or one hundred thousand interesting experiments in garages," recalls Root. "To me the answer was obvious."

The maker movement, he says, "is a social movement that is teaching people how to make and repair physical things. Why are there such limited woodworking or metalworking classes in the Ann Arbor school system? How can we have manufacturing jobs if we don't teach people how to make things? And how can we achieve sustainability if we don't move from throwaway consumption to repairing things?"

Root points out that spaces like his have existed for years, though they were primarily organized as nonprofit clubs. Maker Works is the first in the nation explicitly to operate as a for-profit business. Many of its features were inspired by a network of facilities called the TechShop. The first TechShop was started in Palo Alto—the heart of Silicon Valley—by Jim Newton, who was then science advisor to *Mythbusters* on the Discovery Network. In fact, Root spoke at length with Newton and discussed opening a TechShop in Detroit. But it soon became clear that the TechShop was still figuring out its business model, so Root decided to proceed on his own with a local partner, Dale Grover.

Root has long been thinking like a pollinator. "Here in southeast Michigan, we've demonstrated the problem of depending on one monolithic employer like the automobile industry. The same thing happened in Youngstown, where I grew up, and where the community imploded after the exit of the steel industry. As a country, we've got to put an emphasis back on trade knowledge, on doing not thinking, on reality instead of virtual reality. Every community needs to bring back manufacturing."

Operations was Root's specialty at Zingerman's Mail Order Company—specifically, lean manufacturing. The goal of lean manufacturing is to bring batch size down to as small as economically possible—even one unit—so that production never exceeds the book of orders. This prevents wasteful overproduction, unnecessary storage, and excess inventory.

One element of lean manufacturing that Root sees coming is community-based production. If you need parts for your washing machine, why order parts that will take several days to reach you. Instead, your local

3-D printer can print the parts, at least if plastic composites can work. Alternatively, it can print a mold for the parts, and the corner manufacturer then can pour the appropriate metal, glass, or whatever into the mold for your pickup in a few hours.

Prior to working for Zingerman's, Root was a web designer. His interest in software led to learning about robotics. And then Zingerman's imbued him with a deep belief that business ought to serve community. Maker Works, in a sense, brings all these interests together.

While Root considered plugging Maker Works as another ZCoB enterprise, he concluded that it was just too far afield from the food businesses that characterized Zingerman's brand. That said, Paul Saginaw is now one of the company's biggest fans.

Maker Works has been open for three years and has issued 680 membership cards. In any given month, Root reckons, about a fifth of the membership is active. The default membership is thirty days, providing unlimited access but a limited number of hours each day per tool. Another option gives all-hours access. The newest option provides a punch card for ten sessions usable over the course of a year. Besides collecting member fees, the business also sublets space and gets fees for classes and sponsoring special events (like birthday or bachelor parties). The business has reached the break-even point, but is not quite able to pay Root a salary yet.

Most of Root's clients are not hobbyists and tinkerers, but business people who already have viable products. Three years into its operations, Maker Works has proved invaluable for three local companies that were then adopted by major venture capitalists. One company makes computerized vision machines that Chrysler is using to ensure that its products have the right electronic tags as they proceed along the assembly line. Another company developed a heat pump, based on Stirling engine principles, that radically reduces energy consumption for industrial operations requiring hot or cold streams of air. Several University of Michigan engineers have used Maker Works to develop a fuel-injected, two-cycle engine, which can be found in motorized "tuk tuks" throughout the developing world.

Root also sees high school and college students as one of his target audiences. Currently, Maker Works is providing spaces and classes to five FIRST robotics teams that are participating in the annual robotics competition started by Dean Kamen, best known for inventing the Segway. FIRST has high school students, supported by adult mentors and local sponsors, create 300-pound robots to participate in a grand futuristic spectacle.

Kids are on Root's mind in another way too. One reason he wanted to become an entrepreneur was to have more control over his time. Right now he has two kids, ages 4 and 9, who share his passion for making toys. Their latest creation, working together at daddy's business, is a compressed air rocket launcher.

To feed his family, Root maintains his day job at Zingerman's Mail Order Company, and uses the rest of his time to help manage Maker Works. If things continue to go well, he may have to step away from Zingerman's. If he does, his next priority will be to replicate the model elsewhere. He estimates that he and his partner have invested $500,000–$600,000 thus far, but that a second site would not require as much capital. "There was a lot of programmatic trial and error at the outset, a lot of resources spent developing programs and classes, and we wouldn't need to do this again. The equipment and space expenses, however, would be the same."

Root appreciates that as the maker movement grows, so will his competition. TechShop has eight sites around the country, including one nearby in Allen Park, Michigan. The website HackSpaces.com shows about 1,800 maker-friendly sites around the world and 350 more planned—mostly nonprofits with no business structure.

Does Root regard Maker Works as a business incubator? "We set out not to be an incubator—a common space where you could get lots of advice and counsel from experts in the field. Our belief was that there were lots of people in our community already doing that, and we didn't have anything to contribute. What we did think we could add was this: I may be able to get legal counsel, marketing counsel, etc., but if there's any physical aspect to my business, where can I go to make a prototype? That ends up being one of the more difficult and expensive aspects to starting a business."

"We do tours here all the time," Root adds, "and we talk about our mission and our triple-bottom-line approach: people, planet, profit. At the end of the tour, I always say, 'Do you remember the movie *The Matrix*?,' and of course they do. Well, unbeknownst to you, I gave you the red pill.

Now you understand that there's the idea of a triple-bottom-line company, the idea of an open-book finance company, the idea of a shared economy, and you cannot uninstall that software. You have now become a foot soldier in perpetuating that meme. You will now go into the world and think, perhaps subconsciously, that clearly there ought to be a makers' space."

Fledglings

An idea that has come up again and again in this chapter is the importance of shared space. Shared classroom spaces, like those provided by Simon Fraser University or by ZingTrain, allow like-minded entrepreneurs to give peer support to one another. Shared working spaces, like the Centre for Social Impact in Victoria and sixty-three Impact Hubs worldwide, provide low-cost ways for early-stage entrepreneurs to cover some of their fixed costs. Shared equipment at Maker Works provides an afford-able entry point for would-be manufacturers. All of these benefits are also possible with a business incubator.

The first business incubator was created in Batavia, New York, in 1959, with the term originating not only from the mission but also from the fact that one of the first residents was a chicken business. The concept spread dramatically in the 1980s, and today, according to the National Business Incubation Association (NBIA), a trade association for the profession, there are more than 1,100 incubators operating in North America. During this period North American incubators are estimated to have created 19,000 companies and more than 245,000 jobs.

One reason a community will create an incubator is to improve the survival rate of startups. NBIA claims that 87 percent of incubated compa-nies are still operating, substantially better than new companies without incubation. That statistic is probably an exaggeration—incubators select stronger businesses in the first place—but there's no doubt that their cheap (or free) space and suite of services are useful to early-stage companies. These services can include assistance with planning, marketing, technol-ogy, finance, equipment, human resources, procurement—almost any business need imaginable. Most incubators expect companies to gradu-ate—that is, leave—within two or three years. About half of all incubators also make some of their services available to early-stage local companies that do not reside in the incubator.

While incubators could be self-financing, few choose to be. Most depend on annual allocations from federal agencies, local governments, or foundations. This reality was driven home to me as I was helping two groups in Southern Illinois, the Mount Carmel Area Economic Alliance and the Greater Wabash Regional Planning Commission, think through whether an incubator made sense for their economic development agenda. Given the lightly populated nature of the region—Wabash County itself has only twelve thousand residents, and even adding six adjacent counties yields a regional population of only one hundred thousand—I reviewed carefully NBIA's extensive literature on incubators in rural regions. Its 2013 report on best practices looked at one hundred such programs in the United States, and then presented detailed case studies on what the authors regarded as the top nine performers. Half were nowhere close to self-sufficient, and three got about three-quarters of the way there by charging rents slightly below market rates. Of the two that were almost self-financing, one, in Quincy, Illinois, was the beneficiary of the city buying a large, abandoned building for the project.

The one rural incubator that really did seem to be self-reliant was in Northwest Wisconsin, where ten counties and five Native American tribes teamed up in 1959 to form the Northwest Regional Planning Commission. The area covers almost 11,000 square miles, contains 230 units of local government, and still only has a population of 179,000. Its design innovation was to create a network of ten small facilities with a total of 170,000 square feet spread across the region. "Circuit riders" move from site to site and provide various forms of technical assistance. Among the resources the network makes available to incubating businesses are six loan funds, an equity fund, an international trade council, and a public–private support group that facilitates mentoring relationships. Altogether in 2013 the network reports graduating twenty-two new businesses with ninety-three jobs.

A new approach to incubation called "acceleration" appeared in 2005, when Paul Graham established the Y Combinator in Silicon Valley. According to NBIA, "Seed accelerators invest in founding teams that are put through a fast-paced process to validate products and markets and solidify follow-on funding rounds." The time scale for an accelerated company is typically weeks or months, not years. Many accelerators put some funds into the businesses they accept into their program, and unlike venture capital funds, they don't seek to take control of the businesses. Instead, they only ask for a tiny piece of the company's equity.

Y Combinator pitches itself to entrepreneurs who have "spent a lot of time figuring out how to make things people want." It specializes in developing web and mobile applications, though it funds a range of start-ups, and then helps founders identify and pitch their start-ups to investors and acquirers. It also helps start-ups navigate the nitty gritty of getting a company off the ground: paperwork, legalities, hiring, patent questions. They'll even help mediate disputes between founders.

At the end of the day, however, Y Combinator and most other accelerators are uninterested in local business. An exception is Fledge, based in Seattle and run by Michael "Luni" Libes. Unlike his competitors, Luni wants to nurture triple-bottom-line businesses with important social missions. Fledge promotes itself as "the conscious company accelerator," focusing on "entrepreneurs who aim to make an impact in the world, improving lives, the environment, health, and communities, and making a more sustainable world."

Fledge welcomes applicants from all over the planet. Its first ten-week session in 2014 had three teams from Tanzania, and the second session that year had teams from Ethiopia, Kenya, China, and the Republic of Georgia, along with a few from the United States. "We take the best from wherever they apply," says Luni.

Twice a year, Fledge brings seven teams to Impact Hub Seattle. It gives them each $20,000, provides them with ten weeks of intensive support, has them present publicly at graduation ("Demo Day"), and then continues to assist them after they return to their hometowns.

Luni is himself a serial entrepreneur who helped start five software companies over twenty years before launching Fledge. In mentoring students at the Bainbridge Graduate Institute, he repeatedly heard stories about venture capitalists (VCs) and angel investors pronouncing their proposed companies not "venture scale." He was convinced that there was a need for an accelerator focused on local, socially-conscious businesses. He understood that one reason these VCs were not very interested in social companies was the difficulty of exiting. "If you're successful in the tech world, big companies like Google, Cisco, or Apple will buy you out. In the impact space, there's a lot of talk of companies 'selling out' as opposed to being acquired."

"So," explains Luni, "Fledge uniquely uses a model where we invest in companies, get some equity, and the company is required to repurchase that equity from us using a very small percentage of future revenues."

This approach, he says, is good for both Fledge and the company. "For us, the most important benefit is that we no longer have to invest in companies that have hockey-stick growth. We can instead bet on companies that will make a few hundred thousand dollars or a million dollars a year. This could be a perfectly good lifestyle company or something that's local to a city. We can still make a good rate of return on these companies. We're not betting on unicorns. We just need a bunch of local products and local services that do reasonably well."

Since Fledge is only two years old, the model remains unproven. "It takes time. It's not an instant return on investment. But frankly that's true of traditional equity in the tech world, where it takes six to seven years to get a return. We're just starting to get some returns. We get quarterly reports from all our incubated companies on revenue, growth, and prospects, and all the indicators thus far look good. In three years I'm hoping to be able to say this model works great."

When Luni is asked to identify his favorite graduates, he bristles, "Hey, I have four children—and no favorites. So I have thirty-two fledglings and, again, no favorites." But he does have plenty of success stories. Two graduates from the first class are illustrative:

- Burn Manufacturing set up a factory in Kenya to build modern cooking stoves that use half the fuel of their competitors. Consumers who purchase the stoves start saving money within three months. Since graduation, the company has raised $5 million from both public and private investors, including General Electric and the US Agency for International Development.

- Community Sourced Capital was started by students at the Bainbridge Graduate Institute, where faculty members also serve as advisers and mentors for Fledge. It pools small loans (called "squares") from customers or fans of a local business (called "squareholders") into one larger loan, and thus far their pitches have moved hundreds of thousands of VC dollars into local business. Squareholders then become natural cheerleaders for their businesses, because the better the borrower does, the faster they get paid back.

Since it will take several years before expected royalty payments cover the bills, Fledge has had to raise a significant amount of start-up capital. Luni mobilized his contacts in the Seattle area to bring in several angel investors. But, he notes, "whether you are all grant-funded or for-profit, you're constrained by the amount of money you have. There are only so many teams we can work with, a small number. Our programs are highly exclusive—we get over a hundred applicants per cohort, and we take seven at a time. I'm turning away over 95 percent of customers, and so are all of my peers."

To assist some of the companies he turns away, Luni has launched a new program within Fledge called Kick. The idea is to make the Fledge curricula available in other locations, especially to entrepreneurs who don't have a business plan or haven't yet proven the viability of their plan. Some of these entrepreneurs may have other jobs or family obligations that make it impossible for them to come to Seattle. A key requirement is that the entrepreneur must raise his or her tuition through crowdfunding.

"Everyone who applies to Kick is accepted," explains the Fledge website. "We do not choose who can participate. But, we do want to ensure that you are serious about your idea. To do that, as proof of sincerity, and as proof of viability, we ask you to convince at least ten supporters to donate toward your entrepreneurial efforts. A true 'wisdom of the crowd.'"

"Kick is a six-week program," says Luni, "and provides the same world-class guidance as Fledge. We launched the program in January 2014 and it's in seven different countries now. Future plans are to get this in fifty, sixty, one hundred different cities."

Luni criticizes conventional business incubators for moving too slowly: "I've done a lot of research on incubator programs, and there's no company coming out of those local programs that is the next Dropbox or Airbnb, both of which came out of the Y Combinator. I think most incubators are missing the urgency of getting companies off the ground. They put too much 'patient' in patient capital. They also put too many eggs in one basket, inviting a few companies in for six, twelve, eighteen months instead of trying to teach every entrepreneur. One thing I've clearly seen in twenty plus years as an entrepreneur is that no investor ever knows in advance what's really going to work."

An important virtue of Fledge and Kick is that, compared to incubators, they spread more money over many more businesses. Moreover, the royalty model is not looking for a few home runs, as VCs are, but modest success from most of the graduates. "In the VC world," says Luni, "three out of ten have to be successful for them to make money. The same is true with federal government loans—and the two biggest loans the United States did in clean tech this past year went bust. It seems we should spread the wealth around and help as many entrepreneurs as possible. Our aim is to help 120 companies in ten years with Fledge, and hundreds of thousands with Kick."

The Royalty Treatment

Luni's instincts seem right. Given how poor our powers of prediction are, people pollinators would be wise not to pick a few big winners but instead to support as many wannabe entrepreneurs as possible. And his concept of applying a royalty stream to the beneficiaries is ingenious. If you have a good year, you pay back more through royalties; if you have an awful year, you pay back less. Royalties also provide another viable means of financing a nonprofit social enterprise.

But why should the royalty repayments be limited to the entrepreneurship services provided by business accelerators? Why couldn't Ernesto Sirolli use royalties to pay for enterprise facilitation? And why couldn't Nicole Chaland move away from charging tuition up front and toward collecting royalties later? ZingTrain could do the same. Even Maker Works could add a revenue stream from royalties from its members.

I asked Sirolli if he ever considered using royalty payments as a way of underwriting his enterprise facilitation. He said "no." In his experience start-up businesses take an average of five years to make a profit, and he does not want to do anything to impede their reaching that point. Fair enough. But we did agree that the five-year window would not apply to established businesses, and that royalty-based compensation could work for their expansions.

But Luni's model also could work for start-ups as well. Remember, Luni takes a small ownership piece of the company, and allows the entrepreneur to buy back shares. A company eager to reach profitability sooner would just need to be willing to share its ownership with the people pollinator a little longer.

What I like most about the royalty framework is this: Every beneficiary of every economic-development program should have to give something to support successor generations of entrepreneurs. Nothing onerous, and no entrepreneur should have to lose control of his or her business, as venture capitalists require. But a few percentage points of revenue or profit for the pollinator's assistance constitute a small price to pay for a brilliant future for other local businesses in the community.

CHAPTER 5

_____

Partnerships

Teaming Up to Win

T he alternative to picking a few winners and dissing the rest of the business community, as mainstream economic development does, is to create mutually rewarding partnerships among every local business in town. Partner pollinators do this by helping to organize local business teams. They enable team members to become more competitive than they would be if they were to go it alone. And if you can improve the bottom line of your team members through joint marketing, joint financing, joint procurement, joint selling, joint whatever, they will be happy to share the costs. Therein lies a powerful business model for partner pollinators.

Partnership is of course the goal of the Chamber of Commerce and its chapters spread across North America, and Chambers do provide members with a variety of valuable services: discounts on health insurance, informative lunches, introductions to potential buyers, collective lobbying and litigation. The irresolvable problem with Chambers, however, is that the interests of their local and nonlocal business members are often at odds. Many Chambers, for example, oppose buy-local campaigns because they do not want to offend nonlocal members. Others uncritically support public incentives that benefit one or two big members without considering the ways in which these programs might weaken the competitiveness of the rest. In recent years the national office of the US Chamber of Commerce has lobbied fiercely against eliminating tax advantages for US corporations overseas (many receive tax credits for foreign taxes paid), even though the only beneficiaries are a relatively small number of globe-trotting members and the ultimate impact is to put a relatively greater tax burden on small businesses.

Out of these contradictions have emerged a new generation of local business alliances affiliated with BALLE and AMIBA. Generally speaking, these alliances provide services to their members in exchange for dues, but the business models for these alliances are still works in progress. So we begin this chapter by looking at two networks that have come close to paying their own way. One, in Arizona, emphasizes breadth of the membership. The other, in Calgary, Alberta, emphasizes depth. We then look at three other partnerships built around joint procurement in Tucson, joint delivery in northwestern Canada, and joint marketplaces in Seattle and Philadelphia.

Raising Arizona

Among the eighty-odd networks of BALLE, one of the largest is Local First Arizona, which operates primarily in Phoenix and Tucson. Many first-generation BALLE and AMIBA networks had difficulty growing their memberships beyond several hundred businesses, which meant they had difficulty covering even a single staff person's salary. Local First Arizona has 2,600 members and is still growing by forty to fifty members per month. It was able to achieve this stunning scale thanks to one of the most dynamic leaders in BALLE, Kimber Lanning, who participated in the first cohort of BALLE's Local Economy Fellowship Program and now serves on BALLE's Board of Directors.

No one ever needed to convince Lanning about the importance of local business. All of her immediate relatives—parents, grandparents, aunts, uncles, brothers—were self-employed small business people. Lanning herself started a series of small businesses when she was 19, including a popular local record store and art gallery in Phoenix. But in the early 2000s, she became alarmed at the onslaught of chain stores invading her city. "I did not know there was BALLE; I did not know there was anybody else in the country doing what I had in mind. What was going on in Phoenix at that time was that it was hemorrhaging bright young people who would leave, because they felt Arizona didn't have any soul."

By "soul," Lanning explains, "they meant a connection to place." And the same young people who were her record-store customers, whom she adored, were the first ones splitting town. "I started developing theories around what connects people to place, and I came to believe that it all came together with locally owned businesses. If we let people know where locally owned businesses are, we would have more luck making people feel like part of this place and building civic pride."

Finding the soul of Phoenix is not easy. The newer part of the city bears as much relationship with its surrounding environment as a space port would to the moon. Its long blocks are set out on a mind-numbing grid that keeps people in their cars as they drive from one artificial, air-conditioned environment to another. "So you see a chain," Lanning points out, "and then you drive 45 miles per hour to the next intersection, you whiz past all the locally owned businesses, and you stop at the corner and you see another chain."

But the city center, with older building stock and shorter blocks, was ripe for infill development with local businesses. Seeing this potential, Lanning was furious that the city was spending big bucks to attract nonlocal chain stores. One chain, BassPro, got $32 million. Cabela's sporting goods empire got $68 million. All these subsidies were wrecking "the very local businesses that are paying the taxes and giving the city soul."

"So I just started knocking on doors," Lanning recalls. "I went to two of the oldest locally owned businesses in the area where my record store was—a bookstore and a restaurant. We'd meet once a week and talk about pooling resources for marketing. We called ourselves Arizona Chain Reaction."

In 2003 Lanning and her colleagues put together a directory "to let people know where the locals are and [to] speak out as a united front against bad policy deals." Three years later she sold one of her stores to be able to devote herself full-time to organizing local businesses and renamed the organization Local First Arizona (LFA). Like other BALLE networks, it focused primarily on changing consumer behavior. Outreach paid off and soon Lanning was flooded with requests for interviews concerning buy-local campaigns.

Today, LFA has thirteen staff working out of offices in Phoenix, Tucson, and Cottonwood, a rural town in northern Arizona. Besides Lanning, there are three membership coordinators, a local food specialist, a development director, a volunteer coordinator, an events manager, northern and southern Arizona directors, a Spanish-speaking business director, a community outreach coordinator, and a communications person. Supporting them is an army of volunteers who must go through a training program where they become ambassadors of Local First Arizona—or ALFAs.

Financing this expanding operation has required diverse sources of revenue. About a third comes from member dues; a third from earned revenue including events, sales, and advertising; and a third from grants. Lanning is deeply principled about how she raises the funds to keep her staff working. She insists, for example, that her development staff not raise money from big banks like Bank of America or big chains like PetSmart.

How has LFA grown to be the biggest and fastest-growing BALLE network in the United States? There are at least five reasons for Lanning's extraordinary success.

First and foremost is Lanning's sheer tenacity as a consummate networker 24/7. She reckons she does public speaking over sixty times a year and meets with potential new members daily. "It's all about the relationships. I'm constantly meeting people, driving all over the city, talking about our initiatives. I speak at Rotary Clubs, Chambers, neighborhood groups, any business network—and lately at major state events like the Arizona Leadership Forum."

To build up her relationships around Phoenix, Lanning accepted a bunch of invitations to serve on local boards—at one point seven of them. "Many of them were somewhat prestigious in terms of who else was on the board, so that opened a lot of doors. Whether it was utilities companies or giant nonprofit organizations, suddenly I was there as a colleague at the table."

Second, Lanning has wooed unlikely partners by sharing the spotlight. "Local First can do all the work, but in the end I happily give away any award I receive. Building trust and partnership is what matters."

Third, Lanning has kept the price of admission low, with dues starting below $50 per year. In fact, until 2006, dues were free. At that point she had eight hundred members. When she introduced a small dues require-ment, membership dropped to 250 (most have since come back). "My strategy has been to make it super cheap to fill the directory, and then slowly ratchet up the dues, as we begin to have more and more benefits and services available. Now I can justify charging more. I've got seven members that have agreed to pay $5,000 a year, and that never would have happened a few years ago."

Fourth, Lanning has reached out to the nontraditional communities of business. For example, she created a special program, Fuerza Local, to involve the large number of Spanish-speaking businesses. "We've been having mixers *en Español*. My Spanish isn't great and I've hired a tutor to strengthen that, but we have two completely fluent staff. We created a steering committee of business owners from the Latino community to help us shape that program. We've translated nineteen pages on our website, we have bookmarks and brochures in Spanish, as well as morning and evening meetings with Spanish-speaking businesses."

Lanning appreciates that the barriers between her businesses are not just about language, so she is creating what she calls an "accelerator" to teach Latino business owners how to connect better with the mainstream Phoenix economy. "Most of the folks in Fuerza Local will pay with cash or borrow at really high interest rates, because they don't have a relationship with a bank and don't have a credit score. We're going to try to teach them how to get bank ready, so they can have more access to capital. They're stunted right now, because they go down to the check-cashing place and pay 36 percent interest. We're also trying to help them with things like social-media marketing and customer service."

Another target of Lanning's outreach is rural communities. Being a statewide organization, Arizona Local First sweeps in not just Phoenix and Tucson, but the hundreds of small desert outposts in between. "Our state cut the tourism budget, so rural areas have been hit really hard. There are all these great towns that were built between 1870 and 1930; they have great building stock. Sometimes you'll get someone from New York who's sick of the rat race, and opens up this five-star restaurant in a little town of fifteen thousand people. And then you've got three distinct wine areas, where vineyards are starting to win national awards. So we're trying to build some civic pride and get more people traveling within Arizona. Right now, Arizonans spends $6.5 billion per year vacationing in California. So we have a goal of redirecting 10 percent of that into our rural communities. On our website you can see WeekendZona, where we are hosting weekend getaways with a variety of adventures and great food, all available by just driving out of town an hour."

Fifth, Lanning has a penchant for clever, low-cost marketing. Reflecting on her Shift The Way You Shop initiative, Lanning says, "We had a huge ad campaign on the light rail system going through the city for four and a half months. Our metro paid for it, because they believe in the work we do. Originally it was only supposed to be for sixty days but they loved it so much they left it up for over four months. So our only expense was just to produce the advertising 'wrap;' they gave us the space for free. The local theater here, which is like a minichain, has given us slides before the movies, and that total package is worth $40,000. One of our sustaining members is an advertising agency, and they traded outdoor billboards for us, so we had billboards throughout the valley that said 'Shift The Way You Shop.' It was amazing!"

Even Lanning wonders sometimes if she has gone too far. "Our local grocery store has my voice on the overhead, saying 'I'm Kimber Lanning and I'd like to thank you for choosing our hometown grocers,' so people get it from all sides, they must think, oh man, I'm so sick of this woman!"

Ultimately, what holds the LFA network together—what convinces 2,600 members to pay their dues, to volunteer time, to participate in events—are the collaborative relationships that improve the competitiveness of the member businesses.

Relationships, Lanning contends, allow her to do things that her members could never do on their own. "We partner with the Phoenix Art Museum on a culinary festival that's at the museum. I work with a community-development corporation called Roosevelt Row and we do food-truck events and we partner on dessert competitions that build local food awareness. We partner with organizations and member businesses to do social-media workshops. We teach member businesses to start thinking like a team."

By getting businesses to work together, Lanning has been able to score some huge public policy victories. Perhaps the most important one started with a trip in 2006 to Austin, Texas, to meet Dan Houston, one of the principals of Civic Economics. A few years earlier, Houston and his colleagues had prepared a pioneering study on the relative economic advantages of local businesses over chains. Lanning contracted with them to study the potential economic benefits of local procurement in Arizona.

"We introduced legislation all the way back in 2007 that would change the way procurement is done, and I quickly realized that government officials didn't even understand the issue. So I started looking around at what kind of study we could do. Meanwhile this office supply company called Wist had been a big supporter of ours. And we decided this would be a great case study for us to demonstrate the difference in impact."

The study showed that for every $100 in procurement from Wist, about $33 gets directly respent in the state. Staples, which was winning most state contracts, respent about $5 in the state. OfficeMax, another chain that has a supply facility in Arizona, respent about $12. Roughly speaking then, a procurement contract with Wist instead of Staples would generate six times more direct economic benefits for the state, including tax collections. Could a procurement system that ignored these effects possibly be rational?

Lanning took the study to some of the area's leading economists and asked them to "blow holes in it." They couldn't. "And they said yeah, this is true, you've got a good point here." Lanning estimates that she has shared this study with more than twenty-thousand people. "That was the study that got the Arizona Public Service utility to switch their million-dollar contract over to the local office supplier," she adds. "SCF Arizona also switched a $300,000 per year contract over to Wist. And we changed the purchasing procedures for the city of Phoenix." When I interviewed her, Phoenix was anticipating spending an additional $20 million locally over the prior year.

The public policy establishment also has come to appreciate LFA. "When I started this I was focused on the central Phoenix corridor. At the height of the recession, about the end of 2009, the city at large was 18 percent down in sales tax revenue, with the exception of the area that we were working in, which was only 3 percent down. So we got a letter of appreciation from the mayor's office."

Lanning tells the story of a friend who's the vice president at the city's big utility company. "He called me up and said 'congratulations.' And I said, 'What for?' And he said, 'because you did it.' And I said, 'did what?'

And he said, 'You successfully changed the way people think. I'm sitting in board meetings, with top level CEOs, and they're talking about buying locally, and they're talking about how we're going to build civic pride and how we're going to be competitive moving forward. And they're having this conversation when you're nowhere around!'"

REAP What Calgarians Sow

If Local First Arizona stands for the virtue of a local business alliance recruiting many members paying modest dues, its counterpart in Calgary demonstrates the virtue of digging deeply with a small number of members who pay more dearly for an extensive suite of services. In recent years Calgary has become the Saudi Arabia of North America, with a booming oil sands industry nearby that has excited oilmen pushing for "energy independence" and terrified climate-change activists fearing the release of an enormous new pool of carbon into the atmosphere. Global energy giants have descended on this city of one million residents (the third largest city in Canada), and local businesses have felt shunted aside by municipal leaders. Taking up their cause has been a slender bespectacled woman with flowing blonde hair and a big smile named Stephanie Jackman.

Jackman was a marketing whiz working for a major Canadian communications firm with clients like Unilever. Her passion, though, was protecting the planet. She decided it was time for a job shift. In 2005 she founded a nonprofit called REAP, which stands for Respect for the Earth and All People, to promote businesses rooted in community that care about global sustainability.[65] Ever attentive to messaging, Jackman understood the other connotations of REAP: reaping rewards, reaping wheat, reaping what you sow.

Today REAP has only 120 members. In a letter that she sent to her members in 2013, Jackman reports that together they are responsible for 7,500 local jobs, $4 billion in annual revenue, and $8.5 million per year in charitable contributions. These businesses also participate in a "green power" purchasing program that has reduced Calgary's carbon-dioxide emissions by 1,800 metric tons. But part of Jackman's success is as a pollinator, for more than almost any other local business alliance in North

America, she has successfully provided a raft of services for which her businesses are willing to pay top dollar—and she has not needed to depend on any additional money from foundations or philanthropists.

Jackman created a website for REAP, and then she and her husband promptly packed up their possessions to travel around the world for a year. Throughout the trip she regularly blogged on the site—about the different forms of development and business she was seeing, about how millions of people were moving into crowded megacities, about how local businesses everywhere were being threatened by global corporations. She wrote about the great sustainability innovations she saw in Curitiba, Brazil, and the necessity of wearing a gas mask to avoid choking from the pollution in Beijing. She was starting conversations about sustainability with fellow Calgarians, and by the time she returned, a substantial audience was participating. From the outset, Jackman was determined to provide valuable marketing services to her members that they would pay for. She set up six tiers of membership, based on companies' annual revenues, with annual dues ranging from $1,200 to $12,000. In the autumn of 2007 she had signed up three founding members—a beauty salon, a green coaching service, and a health-care provider—and within a year she added twenty more.

Jackman quickly realized that for most of her members, she was their primary marketing and communications firm. Most small businesses cannot afford to hire a mainstream ad agency, so an initiative like REAP was a godsend. She gave her members an online presence through a REAP directory. She wrote articles about them. She distributed a coupon book called the REAP Passport (which she ultimately abandoned). She helped give her members visibility at trade shows. She went on Canadian Broadcasting Corporation radio shows to let the mass public know about her members. She distributed REAP logos to her members for their own advertising, so that the entire REAP brand would gain local visibility and acceptance.

Perhaps her most successful initiative was to get ads published in the main newspaper in town, the *Calgary Herald*. She prepared each ad around a theme. One ad, for example, spoke about the problems of automobiles and their emissions in Calgary, and concluded with pitches for local bicycle shops that were REAP members. Twice each year she also published an ad with a complete list of all her members.

Over time, however, Jackman could see that she was offering more value to her smaller businesses than the larger ones. The biggest businesses wanted to enjoy the "halo effect" of being associated with a community of sustainable businesses, but they had their own marketing programs. Jackman decided to simplify her fee structure to better reflect the reasons why businesses were joining the network and the prices they were willing to pay. Instead of six tiers of membership fees, REAP now had only three: $1,200 for businesses generating under $1 million in annual revenue; $3,000 for businesses making more than $1 million a year that wanted all the programming except the *Herald* advertising; and $5,000 for the works. Jackman had convinced the paper to offer REAP space at a deep discount. The *Herald* saw value in doing this to recruit small businesses for future advertising. The paper also had announced its commitment to make its operations more environmentally sustainable, and the deal with REAP— supporting a nonprofit trying to green the city's businesses—provided an easy win.

In REAP's early days, Jackman emphasized member businesses' commitment to environmental stewardship, but after conducting focus groups on her messaging she realized that there was more marketing traction in the concept of "local." From the beginning, local ownership was a condition for REAP membership, but Jackman hadn't highlighted it much. In 2011 she made the tagline for her messages "be local," and membership doubled within a year.

The shift in messaging reframed REAP's relationship with the *Herald*. Like other papers under siege from the web, the *Herald* could see that one of its few ways forward was to focus more aggressively on local news and local business. The paper agreed to prepare a "Be Local" supplement twice a year. Each insert contains articles about REAP businesses, which reporters write in close consultation with Jackman, and then Jackman in turn sells advertising for the insert to her members and gets a commission. Again, a win–win proposition.

Jackman is keenly aware, however, that the newspaper industry is dying, and that she needs to come up with another pollinator offshoot to provide value to her members. Reviving the coupon book is out, says Jackman, because REAP never did figure out how to make it work financially. She's more sold on increasing the digital presence of her members through REAP's online and social-media initiatives.

One new way Jackman is helping members tell their story is through an awards program. Nominees are presented on the REAP website through daily feature blogs, and visitors have three months to vote for their favorites. Some fourteen thousand votes were tallied in the first year, and more than thirty-two thousand in the second year, demonstrating that the program is an effective vehicle for community engagement. At a gala awards dinner each fall, eight members are given "Bee Local" statues, shaped like nature's favorite pollinators and made locally out of recycled computer parts. The winners also receive special coverage in the business section of the *Herald*.

Another popular new program is the REAP Savour Sustainability Dinners. Each event is at a REAP member restaurant, and participants get a lavish four-course dinner. During each course, a featured farmer or food producer explains a key item in the course. The chef describes his or her own local cooking philosophy and practices. And often, says Jackman, the topic turns to community economic development.

Calgary's economic-development office has been guilty of the usual attract-and-retain sins, but also has long been a member of REAP. Last year the city's mayor pressed the department to start being more responsive to local businesses, and it has since intensified its collaborations with REAP and with another organization, THRIVE, that promotes community development and poverty reduction in the city.

Like other pollinators, Jackman manages her expenses carefully. For much of REAP's history just she, several part-timers, and an occasional volunteer intern were the only staff. One of her members recently agreed to underwrite another staff person to run the awards program and blog daily. Is she tempted to increase her budget by resorting to grant writing? "No way," says Jackman. "We recently applied for three grants, and each went nowhere. It was a total waste of time."

Butts in the Seats

Greater affinity means greater action. While Chambers of Commerce are reduced to milquetoast gab associations for fear of alienating the nonlocal members, local business alliances can marshal sharper messages and programs because of the tighter affinity among their members. And even greater affinity is possible when local businesses work together in a specific sector, like food.

We saw in the previous chapter how Edmonton's Original Fare, a group of local food restaurants, was able to put together not only a joint marketing campaign but also a gift card program. Edmonton's Original Fare was inspired by the Council of Independent Restaurants of America, which at its peak had affiliates in nineteen US cities but went defunct in 2008 when the Internal Revenue Service yanked its tax-exempt status. Some of the affiliates still operate, however, and one of the best known is Tucson Originals, which since 1999 has been trying to fight chain restaurants by sharpening the public's appreciation of the city's local restaurants. Today, the organization has forty-two member restaurants, and a strong track record helping Tucson's independent eateries thrive.

Like Edmonton's Original Fare, Tucson Originals provides its members with a joint advertising program and a gift card, though the latter works somewhat differently than Edmonton's. Part of every member's restaurant "dues" is an agreement to honor up to $650 of Tucson Originals gift cards annually. The central office sells the cards online, and keeps the proceeds.

But as a partner pollinator, Tucson Originals has provided one other powerful service for its members—joint procurement. We have two focuses," says Sam Alboy, the organization's current president, "Get folks into restaurants, and find ways to make our member businesses more profitable. We say 'butts in the seats, and less money spent.'"

If you want to see the virtues of joint procurement, visit your local True Value or Ace Hardware stores. These stores are 100 percent independently owned, and no two stores look alike. Each member hardware store carries different merchandise and is arranged in different ways, with different prices, different service arrangements, and different advertising pitches. The stores are members of powerful producer cooperatives that scour the planet for great vendors, purchase in bulk, and then deliver the savings to their members.[66] This is how independent hardware stores have been able to compete effectively against chains like Lowe's and Home Depot. Similar producer cooperatives have helped improve the competitiveness of independent retailers of groceries, bicycles, pharmaceuticals, auto parts, carpet sellers, florists, and tire stores.

Tucson Originals is not structured as a producer cooperative per se—though it could be—but it does negotiate discounts and rebates from key suppliers on behalf of its members. For example, from a bulk supplier like Ecolab, it might be able to ensure that all its members receive the same "corporate rate" that Applebee's does for the purchase of dishwashing soap. Another supplier, such as the local RC Cola distributor, might be persuaded to rebate $2.50 for every crate sold, split between Tucson Originals and the purchasing member. Last year Tucson Originals received a total of $26,000 in rebates from its member purchases, and member restaurants significantly more than that.

The organization surveys its members annually to figure out the top twenty-five products that every restaurant uses, and then coordinates their collective pitches to vendors. Discounts and rebates have been negotiated with the suppliers of linens, pest-control programs, and payroll services.

There's no one fee to participate in the purchasing program—it's just one of many benefits of membership. Larger, older, more successful members mentor smaller, younger, struggling ones. Says Alboy, "We try to build relationships so that these restaurants will make it. In all our meetings we share best practices, and new members can bring issues forward. So, if someone says, 'hey, I want to apply for a liquor license, but I don't know how to do it,' another member might say 'here's a resource you can utilize to do that.'"

Ultimately the most compelling reason to join Tucson Originals, argues Alboy, is the caché that comes from being part of the rich culinary heritage of the region. "These businesses are your neighbors and friends who contribute endlessly to the betterment of our community. They are the first to give when there is a need."

Alboy runs a restaurant called Mama's Hawaiian Bar-B-Cue. When he opened the restaurant, a friend, Jonathan Landeen, the owner of another eatery called Jonathan's Cork, invited him to join Tucson Originals. Alboy immediately started to see the benefits to his bottom line: "It's about relationships. It's cool when you're working with an insurance guy, and then he gets catering from you for his office. It brings the circle to a full closure.

This money is staying in the town rather than going to the bottom of a corporation's ledger book."

Alboy recently stepped in to run the organization because he felt that his expertise, putting management systems in place, is what the organization needs now, in its fifteenth year. "When we started," says Alboy, "eating local was something that we had to broadcast. Now the message is widely accepted. In that sense, we've accomplished what we set out to do. But at the same time we're still trying to get people to shift more of their eating habits to local restaurants and support the local economy."

Tucson Originals recently has doubled the size of the businesses it represents. The collective purchases by its members exceed $80 million per year. It has extended its membership to many different participants in the local food movement: to magazines such as *Edible Tucson*; to the foodie blogs; to the nonprofits working in food deserts. "We've become more of a coalition," says Alboy. "We have sixteen businesses that are not restaurants per se but want to be restaurant-affiliated, like a bottling company or beer purveyor or a pest-control company or a taxicab company. They support us now in an auxiliary function." These "preferred purveyors" provide discounts and rebates.

Programming has shifted accordingly, says Alboy. "When we talk in meetings, it's still very restaurant specific, so we may do a presentation on health-care reform, human resources, or food costing. But now we're also teaching our preferred purveyors: How do you talk to a local restaurant? How do you meet its needs? How do you interface with restaurateurs in a positive way? We're functioning more like a restaurant association than just a purchasing and buying club."

The organization has only one paid staff member, and depends heavily on volunteer work done by its member restaurants. Its only other real expense is advertising. Last year it spent $100,000 promoting its members through joint ads. "None of our restaurants can come up with that kind of money," says Alboy, "But by piggybacking on Tucson Originals, they get a strong website, strong lead generation, and things like that—basically exposure equal to what a large chain gets. We've turned our profitability as an organization into better exposure for our member restaurants."

Another revenue stream comes from gift certificates donated by member restaurants, and then sold through the organization's website. Still another comes from events. "When we do events," explains Alboy, "we make sure there's some money going directly back to the restaurant— maybe 50 percent to the restaurant that's hosting, and then 50 percent to our organization, which ultimately goes into advertising supporting the restaurant anyway."

"We are also looking for revenue from sponsorships. Large, local companies are willing to become sponsors in return for advertising slots in our community map, for example. The printing of our brochure cost the organization $5,000 a year ago, but with sponsorships our cost is now $2,300. That's revenue that we've never gotten before."

Altogether, Tucson Originals is "totally self-sustaining," beams Alboy. "No grant funding! And everything is basically generated by our members—through purchasing, advertising, and events."

Special Delivery

Local businesses are trying to compete not only on price but also on convenience, because consumers value their time. Why should I drive around from local store to store when I can get everything I need with one stop at a Wal-Mart or at a megamall? Indeed, why go shopping at all when Amazon and a zillion other online companies will over-night me what I need for a few extra bucks? The best answer to these tough questions might be a local delivery company that can rush to you exactly what you're looking for in an hour. Amazon understands this emerging threat, which is why it's reportedly looking at deploying a squadron of delivery drones coast to coast (as is Google). But who needs an expensive, flying robot when a living wage local driver can do the job more effectively?

We're all used to having pizza and Chinese food delivered within an hour, but what about other products? The importance of door-to-door delivery was driven home to me some years ago when I was home alone with my two young children on a Saturday night. Somewhere around ten o'clock I realized that I was out of diapers—and I was unable to go shopping. I would have paid a home delivery company $100 for a single diaper that night. And it got me thinking: There are probably one hundred million Americans who are single parents, disabled, sick, elderly, or carless and periodically in similar predicaments. What a great business opportunity!

Of course, it was hardly an original idea. Over the next decade all of us have seen a proliferation of food delivery businesses. Chain grocers like Safeway now have teamed up with delivery services like Peapod. The options have expanded in metro areas for home delivery of not just fast food but gourmet meals. Even the friendly local milkman is making a comeback.

It's just a matter of time before local businesses organize their own local delivery companies. And, in fact, it almost happened in Edmonton, Canada. When Jessie Radies moved on from Edmonton's Original Fare and created a BALLE-affiliated business alliance, she was looking for creative ways to finance it. She decided to apply her food enterprise skills to creating a fresh-food delivery business.

"Eat Local First" in Edmonton started as a marketing campaign, with grocery stores displaying posters that conveyed the story of the farmer responsible for the apples or beef below. Radies quickly understood the big challenge facing local food advocates: Many farmers want to sell locally and many grocers and restaurants want to carry locally grown foodstuffs, yet connecting the two sides is exceedingly difficult. Why? Because over the last two generations we have systematically dismantled the distribution systems—the sorters, packagers, warehouse managers, wholesalers, and truckers—who used to weave food supply and demand together.

Radies incorporated a nonprofit to launch a home delivery service for local food producers. She put together a business plan and secured a $350,000 loan from a social enterprise fund. She bought a truck, rented a warehouse, hired a staff, and obtained a license to a computer software system to manage the online orders. Initially she promised to deliver food "door to door, piece by piece, but it turned out to be the most complicated and inefficient way to do it." She tried weekly deliveries, but customers wanted the products faster. She played around with selling set boxes of fresh food, like the kind subscribers get from their local community-supported agriculture (CSA) schemes, but the unforgivingly harsh winters in Edmonton made year-round business impossible. "We didn't know what we were doing, and we were way under-resourced."

In the end the venture lasted just two years, from 2009 to 2010. "We learned a lot and sold almost $1 million of product," recalls Radies, "but we didn't have a large enough consumer base and enough population density. We needed two to three times the volume to make this work and another year of experience. Perhaps another $500,000 in capital would have done the trick. And if we had a little more experience, perhaps we could have brought in farmers as partners—or perhaps other nonprofits."

Radies concedes that she misunderstood the market. She targeted locavores and community activists, the people who were her closest allies in her local economy work. "But we needed to go after busy moms with two incomes. People will identify one way, but act another. The biggest enthusiasts buy the least. The biggest buyers just want convenience."

During this period Radies learned about another entrepreneur, David Van Seters, who was making the local food delivery model work one Canadian province to the west. In Vancouver, British Columbia, Van Seters had developed a company called Small Potatoes Urban Delivery (SPUD), which delivered farm-fresh fruits, vegetables, dairy products, breads, meats, prepared meals, you name it, to homes and offices. "Everything he shared with me convinced me to get out of the business. We needed larger scale, more capital, deeper commitment, more seriousness of purpose."

Radies now focuses on scale in a different way. Her current day job is to be a consultant to major regional institutions on how they can increase their local food purchasing. For example, she is reorganizing the procurement policies and programs of a local convention center around local farmers. She's also working with the Food Development Center, run by the province of Alberta, to improve the market penetration of new local food products.

What Radies didn't have in resources, Van Seters did—in spades. Indeed, today SPUD is North America's largest delivery service of local and organic food, thriving not only in Vancouver but also in Edmonton (Radies's turf), Victoria, Calgary, Los Angeles, Seattle, and the San Francisco Bay Area. (SPUD tried but failed to catch fire in Portland, Oregon.)

A short cartoon video on SPUD.com quickly demonstrates its value proposition. A harried housewife is shown trying to pack her kids into the car, anxiously working her way through traffic, watching her kids grab unhealthy cereals from the shelves, and then waiting in an interminable checkout line. Enter SPUD. Now she can order quickly online, get free delivery of fresher food, enjoy more time at home with her kids, and still make her yoga class!

Van Seters has been thinking like a pollinator for more than two decades. After earning an undergraduate degree in environmental biology, he spent six years working as an environmental consultant to assess and clean up industrial pollution. He decided to skill up with an MBA, but about two-thirds of the way through the program he had an epiphany that his whole approach to environmental protection was wrong. A far smarter approach than cleaning up industrial messes would be to prevent pollution in the first place using the tools of business he was learning about.

When he graduated, he decided that instead of going back to environmental consulting, he would become an environmental business consultant. He shopped his idea with the country's biggest business-consulting firms. They all turned him down flat, saying that they did not offer environmental services. However, one of the firms, KPMG, agreed to hire him to set up an Asia Pacific practice, based on a brief time he spent working in the Canadian High Commission in Hong Kong. He agreed, but only on the condition that he be allowed to spend some time testing out the market for environmental business services. The latter succeeded beyond his wildest expectations, and KPMG let him work his green beat full time.

Van Seters found markets for recyclable materials, assessed the economics of sustainable transportation, wrote environmental business guides, and prepared full-cost accounting studies. But after five years, he got tired of advising others; he wanted to get directly involved in sustainable business himself. He left KPMG and created his own consulting firm called Sustainability Ventures, with the goal of launching innovative companies in the four sectors he regarded as the most environmentally important: transportation, food, buildings, and finance. One client hired him to do a community food study, and he became aware of the growing inefficiency and inequity of long-distance food distribution. Local distribution, he realized, could potentially reduce prices for consumers and raise incomes for farmers, while providing consumers with a fresher, tastier, healthier diet. That was the origin of SPUD, in 1997.

He recruited a friend, Deb Joy, who had successfully run two Body Shop stores, to help launch the company. He prepared a business plan, and poured in his life savings. "We grossly underestimated the cost of almost everything," Van Seters reflects. "We underestimated the costs of delivery vehicles, the cost to pack groceries, even the staff costs."

Van Seters had to raise additional capital. He convinced an angel investor to provide a big loan (and then later to transform it into an equity stake). He secured traditional bank finance. He hit up friends and family, and bootstrapped every inch of the way. "There was zero interest from the 'ag' industry. Some small local farmers were engaged, but not ag funders or government agencies supporting agriculture."

In the early days, SPUD's competitors were CSAs and the like, which focused on produce. "Our goal from day one was to provide a full range of groceries so our customers could avoid shopping trips." A typical small grocery store, Van Seters points out, has at least 6,000 items. SPUD sought to have at least the 1,500 most popular items in stock.

To reach a minimum economy of scale, Van Seters argues, the first SPUD network in Vancouver needed to make five hundred deliveries per week. This allowed SPUD to fully use one warehouse. Then as the business grew, the warehouse could be expanded a little at a time.

"We were also able to make it work," explains Van Seters, "because we sold a product that people would buy every week or two. And we delivered to each neighborhood only once a week on a set route. We did this to reduce our carbon footprint, but the result was that each of our trucks could deliver up to one hundred orders in a day. Typical food delivery companies average only thirty orders per truck per day, because their trucks are crisscrossing all over town to meet customer-imposed delivery times."

After four years of successful operations in Vancouver, Van Seters was approached by another local delivery company in Victoria to see if he was interested in buying the company. He was, and this began the steady expansion of SPUD across the west coast of North America, with each region buying as locally as possible.

Van Seters left SPUD in 2010, after twelve years, though he remains a shareholder. For the company to grow to the next level, it needed a different kind of CEO and Van Seters was keen to pursue new green business opportunities. With SPUD, he had helped crack the code for cost-effective local food delivery. Now competitors were copying and improving on his model: Relay Foods in Charlottesville, Virginia; Greenling in Austin, Texas; and Urban Harvest in Kelowna, British Columbia. "It was time to crack the sustainability code in other sectors."

Van Seters dusted off his old firm, Sustainability Ventures, and is now helping to create other kinds of sustainable business. He has an ownership stake in an energy-finance company that allows developers and building owners to install energy-saving equipment with no upfront cost by capitalizing and selling off future cash-flow savings. He's helping to develop an electric bike company that "allows me to get to my clients faster than I can by bus or car, get some exercise, and not arrive sweaty." He's also prototyping new businesses that facilitate the sharing of idle, wasted assets—home sharing, car sharing, tool sharing, office sharing—and has been working to implement a reusable items drop-off program at all of Metro Vancouver's waste disposal facilities (which cuts waste and provides a new source of low-cost goods for low-income residents, at zero cost to taxpayers).

Asked whether he sees local delivery moving beyond food, say to diapers, he points out that a generation ago parents commonly would hand over their bags of used cloth diapers to cleaning services and would exchange them for a bag of folded, clean, fresh-smelling diapers. Consumers might have more resistance to this now, but one characteristic of diaper delivery that makes it work is that users have a steady need for the service week after week.

What about other goods? "Maybe for books—Amazon has already proven that works." But Van Seters observes that these deliveries are more intermittent than food or diapers. Much larger warehouses would be required, with more carefully orchestrated delivery algorithms and a state-of-the art ordering system. He cites a local green office supply company that wasn't able to make it, because it couldn't compete against Staples's deep discounts and free delivery service. Maybe this is an area where Amazon, Staples, and other global players will continue to enjoy a competitive advantage.

Where the local food delivery industry is expanding, Van Seters notes, is bringing food to low-income consumers. Indeed, many local food advocates are coming around to the position that expanded direct delivery services might be a better solution for food deserts than building new grocery stores. In less than three years, well over sixty mobile food markets, most of them run by nonprofits, have rolled into low-income communities. They usually need to get some kind of subsidy to provide food that's cheaper than what's available at grocery stores. But these are all tiny operations (Van Seters estimates that only a few have more than one vehicle), and will probably never become self-financing pollinators.

The business gears in Van Seters's head are turning. Perhaps these mobile markets could become viable businesses if they served both main-stream and low-income neighborhoods, with the former cross-subsidizing the latter. Perhaps customers could be issued a membership card, with the system automatically applying deeper discounts to low-income food bank members. Perhaps the company could launch targeted fundraising campaigns to support discounts.

"But a bigger problem must be overcome," insists Van Seters. "Direct delivery is seen as a luxury that comes with a price premium, not a discount. A cognitive shift needs to happen. We had a survey on the SPUD site for people to estimate how much they believe they would save each week by avoiding a trip to the grocery store. Factoring in the time for driving and parking, or taking a bus, they typically estimated saving about $30 per week. It's a challenge for people to remember this when they rush to take advantage of a small discount at a chain store."

Van Seters expects attitudes to shift as the direct delivery business grows and matures. "We will become more cost competitive than bricks-and-mortar stores in the long run. The more food items a company like SPUD sells, the more cost effective it becomes. When Whole Foods expands in a metropolitan area, it may need eight to ten stores to achieve full penetration, with each new store costing millions of dollars. SPUD only needs one warehouse per metro area. And when SPUD doubles its volume, it only needs to expand its warehouse by about 10 percent. That's how we will get to scale."

Local Business Destinations

Just as direct delivery companies can help local businesses compete against online marketers, public markets can help them go head to head against conventional shopping malls. Why can't a great destination with one hundred local businesses offer the same convenience, variety, and fun as a shopping mall with one hundred nonlocal businesses? Indeed, the mind-numbing similarity of shopping malls across the United States, whether one is in Bangor, Houston, or San Jose, with the same cookie-cutter Gap, Brookstone, Starbucks, LensCrafters, Dunkin' Donuts, and the like, underscores why local malls, with the regional character that can only come from one-of-a-kind restaurants and retailers, are almost always more satisfying experiences.

We know what successful local business malls once looked like. They were called downtowns, and in cities large and small, downtowns were the place to meet, to shop, to have coffee, to see a movie, to find romance. Then shopping malls rolled across suburbia, many anchored by department stores like Target and Wal-Mart, all sucking the life out of downtowns like Dracula. Communities struck back with downtown revitalization programs, some working under the umbrella of the Main Street Center of the National Trust for Historic Preservation, but too many of these programs wound up creating quaint destinations for tourists while daily commerce proceeded briskly at the suburban mall.

A better approach to winning back shoppers may be to transform empty or underused spaces into informal malls where local vendors can sell their wares. These destinations, depending on their focus, go by names like flea markets, night markets, farmers markets, swap markets, and antique markets. In just the United States, it's worth noting, the number of farmers markets has increased from 1,755 to 8,268 in two decades. These markets serve multiple functions. They provide many entrepreneurs with their first public sales space, which can be a stepping stone to renting a storefront. Far more so than rigidly policed shopping malls, these markets are in tune with local culture, and likely to attract jugglers, clowns, and street artists. They are more welcoming for spenders and nonspenders alike.

About thirty US cities have gone a step farther to create permanent, indoor local business malls under the moniker of "public market." Among the best known are the Ferry Plaza Farmers Market in San Francisco, Pike Place Market in Seattle, Reading Terminal Market in Philadelphia, Eastern Market in Detroit, Haymarket Square in Boston, and West Side Market in Cleveland. The "public" part of the name reflects not so much the owner-ship (most public markets are at least partially owned by a nonprofit or a private consortium) as the spirit of the endeavor. Public markets are like the agora in Roman times, or the farmers markets springing back to life worldwide. As we saw with the story about the revitalization of public markets in Melbourne in chapter 2, these are the places with something exciting for everyone—young and old, rich and poor, black and white, shoppers and dawdlers.

No serious tourist to Seattle will miss visiting the Pike Place Market, one of the first continuously operated farmers markets in the country. Opened in 1907, Pike Place originally was designed to break the monopoly of produce wholesalers and provide farmers with a place to sell fruits and vegetables directly to consumers. It has since expanded into eight adjacent buildings near the city's central waterfront, and its roster of local busi-nesses includes fishmongers (famous for tossing around the largest catch of the day), butchers, restaurants, bakeries, small grocers, crafts sellers, and even a comic book shop. It attracts ten million visitors annually.

Pike Place was originally owned by two enterprising realtors, Frank and John Goodwin. In the early 1960s the owners and other developers proposed replacing the market with Pike Plaza, incorporating a hotel, office buildings, apartments, a hockey arena, and a parking garage. The proposal met massive public resistance, and in 1971 the city council proclaimed the market a historic preservation zone and put the whole operation under a quasi-governmental body called the Pike Place Market Preservation and Development Authority. A nonprofit, the Pike Place Market Foundation, was created by the Authority to raise funds, and it prototyped an early version of a crowdfunding campaign. Between 1985 and 1987 about forty-five thousand donors contributed at least $35 to have their names inscribed on a tile in the top arcade, raising $1.6 million for renovations and other social services administered by the market such as a free clinic and childcare center.

The Reading Terminal Market in Philadelphia is another must-see destination by visitors. At lunchtime it's mobbed by thousands of business people and blue-collar workers, who mingle with tourists. A business professor studying the market in the early 2000s estimated that annual sales by vendors exceeded $30 million. In 2013 reported sales exceeded $50 million. The market's local businesses represent a mix of a dozen purveyors of fresh produce, fish, and meats (including several groups of Amish farmers), two dozen sellers of other grocery items (including dairy products, coffee, spices, and baked goods), eight vendors of nonfood items (such as crafts, gifts, flowers, and books), and three dozen food court vendors serving primarily breakfasts and lunches. One of the tenants is a nonprofit called Fair Food, which promotes local food and runs a farm stand that carries products from about ninety different local farmers and local food producers.

Like Pike Place, the Reading Terminal Market started as a farmers market in the center of the city and remains committed to preserving that core function. Unlike Pike Place, however, the Reading Terminal Market is 100 percent self-financing. It is a nonprofit and has a thirty-year lease on the building from the Pennsylvania Convention Center Authority, a state agency. According to Paul Steinke, the market's general manager until late 2014, "We don't get any subsidy from the government or foundations. We get approximately 90 percent or more of our revenue from tenant rents." Much of the rest comes from an annual fundraiser that nets around $100,000.

Steinke says that all the businesses in the Reading Terminal Market are local, though "we don't have a formal definition of 'local.' You can't be a chain or franchise, first and foremost. Also, Fair Food's definition is that the food should come from within a 100-mile radius of the city, and that's our rule of thumb. We do have one tenant, however, who is a lamb producer and whose farm is in Virginia."

Like any business, the Reading Terminal Market has stakeholders with radically different needs. The market wants to collect more rent, while the tenants want to pay less. To preserve the original produce focus, farmers and fresh-food purveyors are given lower rates than others. Vendors in more heavily trafficked locations pay more dearly than those in remote corners. Meal-serving vendors pay the highest rents and sales-percentage fees, though many complain about the intrusive nature of reporting their daily business and about the fee structure. As general manager, Steinke must continually juggle these conflicting needs, and it's not always easy. In 2003 the market's fresh-food purveyors petitioned management to lower rents, warning that the existing rent and fee structure threatened their economic viability, and it took three years to negotiate an acceptable resolution.

Reading Terminal Market has sought to harmonize the needs of its stakeholders through inclusive governance. The mayor of Philadelphia gets to name one person to the board of the nonprofit, the city council another. The merchant's association, which represents the tenants, also names a member. The merchant's association has monthly meetings and invites the general manager to attend. Says Steinke, "I present what's going on at the market every month, and these meetings do have an influence on what we do and how we do it. It's definitely a two-way street."

Plans are now afoot for the market to create other pollinator businesses. It's reopening the "City Kitchen," a demonstration space where regular culinary classes and events can be held. It's also partnering with Instacart, a home delivery service for groceries, that will allow most of the market's merchants to sell their products online and then deliver them directly throughout the Philadelphia area.

What advice would Steinke give to other communities that wish to create a public market? "Everyone wants one, but they're not easy to start and sustain. Finding a location that is affordable but also gives access to large numbers of customers is vital. Those two things work against each other—the most lucrative locations carry the most expensive real estate costs. We have the advantage of having been here since 1892, on a site that a start-up probably could not get today."

That said, there are intriguing examples of new public markets being developed. In Colorado Springs, I helped a local group put together a business plan for a new public market where vendors will operate along-side a "food hub" and possibly a small-scale meat-processing facility. A local realtor believes that the envisioned relationships and transactions between local farmers and eaters will be so transformational that he is offering the public market a long-term lease in the center of a major commercial and residential development project with significant up-front financing. The developer and the public market board are now working together to make the project a key element in revitalizing the city center.

The Economics of Collaboration

Harvard biologist E. O. Wilson argues that evolution favors groups that work together altruistically.[67] We've seen in this chapter examples of that logic playing out with local businesses. The stories of partner pollinators here show how groups of local businesses can improve their competitiveness through joint branding (Local First Arizona), joint marketing (REAP in Calgary), joint procurement (Tucson Originals), joint delivery (SPUD), and joint locations (Reading Terminal Market). These examples hardly exhaust the list of ways in which collaboration can reduce costs and increase profits.

Partnerships also provide another way to think about economies of scale. Mainstream economic developers and business advisers tend to judge businesses by their size. Bigger is better, and bigger businesses achieve better economies of scale. But partnerships offer local businesses the possibility to achieve almost any economy of scale, not through endless growth, but through carefully constructed collaborations. What limits local businesses from creating these partnerships is the absence, not of good models, but of needed capital. And that's why purse pollinators are so important.

CHAPTER 6

Purse

Ending Investment Apartheid

*I*n my last book, *Local Dollars, Local Sense*, I argued that the most urgent need for growing local business is more capital.[68] We know that the home-based, small, and medium-scale businesses that make up the universe of locally owned businesses constitute about half the US economy (by output and jobs). We know that these businesses are at least as profitable as their Fortune 500 counterparts, and that trends in the global economy are likely to increase their competitiveness. We should therefore expect that if our capital markets were functioning efficiently, at least half of our short-term savings in banks would be reinvested in local businesses, as would at least half of our long-term savings in securities (stocks, bonds, pension funds, mutual funds, and insurance funds). If only. Far less than half of banking capital goes into local business, and almost no securities capital. This represents a huge capital market failure, and fixing this failure must be a top goal for local economic development.

The reasons for this capital market failure are complicated, but I would finger two principal culprits. The first is the dramatic consolidation of banking institutions, which has strangled community investment. If you deposit your money in a single-branch bank, it almost automatically will be reinvested locally. If that bank has multiple locations, your money will move to those projects where investments have greater payoffs. If it has many branches spread over a vast geographic terrain, chances are good that your money will move from rural areas to urban areas, from poor neighborhoods to rich neighborhoods, and—most disturbingly—from nonwhite to white communities. The government's response to this problem could have been to limit the size of banks to guarantee that capital stayed local, and if it had done so a generation ago, much of the financial crisis of 2008 could have been avoided. But instead, in 1977, federal lawmakers decided to impose on nonlocal banks a weak, poorly enforced mandate to keep some money local called the Community Reinvestment Act (CRA).

The Devil's bargain of the CRA was this: If you, nonlocal banks, do a reasonably good job of ensuring that your branches invest locally, we will permit you to grow through interstate branching, consolidation, and mergers. Following the teachings of community organizer Saul Alinsky, activists were delighted to use the CRA as a lever to push big banks into putting more money into low-income housing and community-development corporations. Trillions of dollars of capital poured into worthy community projects this way. Conservative critics called this extortion, and believe that the mandate motivated many banks to invest in subprime housing and to issue mortgages to people who could not afford them, laying the tinder for the massive defaults of 2008. While there is truth to the advocates' and skeptics' positions, I believe that the debate misses a more fundamental point: The CRA created a permission slip for massive consolidation and the emergence of megabanks like Bank of America that never should have been allowed in the first place.

As the financial crisis unfolded early in Barack Obama's first term as president, the newly elected Democratic majority on Capitol Hill felt compelled to pass reform legislation in the form of "Dodd-Frank" (named for the cosponsors, Senator Chris Dodd of Connecticut and Representative Barney Frank of Massachusetts). Again, Congress could have broken up the big banks and restored community finance, but instead it imposed stiff new regulations on all banks, with no awareness that these were irritating but doable for large banks but utterly unaffordable for small banks. As a result, a heartbreaking new wave of bank consolidation is under way.

The second reason for our capital market failure can be traced back to the 1930s and 1940s, when three laws were passed concerning securities, exchanges, and investment companies. I call this legal regime "investment apartheid," because it created two classes of Americans with very different rights. If you are in the top 1 percent of income earners or wealth holders, you are considered an "accredited investor" and are allowed to invest in any business, any time, no questions asked. The other 99 percent are "unaccredited investors" and may not even invest a penny in a business until it has performed legal disclosures that easily can cost $25,000–$100,000.[69] Smaller businesses that cannot afford these fees must forgo raising capital from the general public, which has left the general public stuck investing in Fortune 500 companies.

While our banking and securities laws are quite different, both sprang from a similar mindset of New Deal paternalism. Both legislative frameworks came from politicians who were trying to protect the little guy, but ultimately offered legal protections that were both too little and too much. They were too little because they failed to prevent the growth of banking and securities behemoths and unable to stave off the dangers of monopoly. And they were too much because their regulatory burdens effectively destroyed local investment by making it mind-bogglingly expensive.

That's the bad news. The good news is that despite outdated public policies favoring nonlocal business, a local investment revolution is under way worldwide. At the heart of *Local Dollars, Local Sense* are dozens of stories of average Americans who have developed powerful strategies to work around these laws and in the process have begun to end investment apartheid. Here, for example, are some of the kinds of local investment tools Americans are deploying today:

Move Your Money. You can move your day-to-day financial activities, including your checking, loans, credit cards, and mortgage, to a local bank or credit union. These are the institutions that recycle short-term savings locally—so much so that even though local and regional banks account for only 20 percent of the assets of all US banks, they provide more than half of all the loans to small businesses.

Start a Credit Union. If your community doesn't have a local bank or credit union, you can start one. Credit unions are easier and cheaper to launch than banks, and many communities have small credit unions managed by part-timers or volunteers. (That said, creating any financial institution is a demanding undertaking, with many legal, accounting, and capital-raising requirements.)

Create Targeted CDs. By law, local banks and credit unions must be very conservative with their money, so they are often wary of loaning money to any local businesses without full collateral. A few banks, such as Ithaca's Alternatives Credit Union, have agreed to set up special certificates of deposits (CDs) that fully collateralize loans to high-priority local businesses. Eastern Bank in Boston has a CD that allows depositors to collateralize a line of credit to Equal Exchange, a local fair-trade company. You can work with your local bank or credit union to set up similar lending mechanisms for your favorite local businesses.

Stretch Your Co-op. One of the fundamental principles governing a cooperative is to assist other co-ops. When one cooperative invests in the legal paperwork required, say, to borrow money from its members, it's happy to share those documents with other co-ops—which brings down the legal cost of involving unaccredited investors. Some co-ops, like Weaver Street Market in North Carolina, pay their members handsomely to borrow money for building new stores. Others, like Co-op Power in western Massachusetts, invest member capital in supplier businesses. The La Montañita Co-op in New Mexico has created a revolving loan fund so that members' capital can support local farmers and food processors.

Donate Locally. Your charitable giving can do "double duty" if you target local nonprofits that support local business. For example, the Twin Pines Cooperative Foundation, based in northern California, has helped set up foundations across the country that support the creation and expansion of local co-ops.

Sponsor Local Businesses. Last year, Kickstarter alone raised $480 million for small businesses and projects. Even though all you get for your money is a T-shirt or token of appreciation, you know that you are one of thousands of small contributors helping to get a big idea off the ground. Note that it's important to scan these sites for businesses in your own community (most peer-to-peer Internet crowdfunding is nonlocal). A new generation of websites, like Lucky Ant and Community Funded, specifically facilitate local sponsorships.

Tap Internet Lending Sites. Kiva and Kiva Zip facilitate peer-to-peer lending to microentrepreneurs, mostly in the global South but increasingly in US inner cities. Both dot-orgs, they only pay back principal. Prosper and the Lending Club, both dot-coms, also pay interest (now averaging close to 10 percent per year). You could encourage your local businesses to use these sites for loans and your investors to scour them for local business investment opportunities. Alternatively, you could take advantage of several cutting-edge, peer-to-peer lending sites that focus on community finance, such as Solar Mosaic and Community Sourced Capital.

Weave Investor Networks. The Local Investment Opportunities Network (LION) of Port Townsend, Washington, brings together local investors and businesses each month to establish "preexisting relationships" that facilitate the circulation of business plans. New LIONs are spreading around the country. Unlike traditional angel-investor networks, to which entrepreneurs present their business plans at periodic dinners, LIONs often involve unaccredited (nonwealthy) investors, though the exact rules for doing so vary from state to state.

Harness Federal Programs. Various national programs provide generous tax deductions for local investors who support antipoverty initiatives through New Markets Tax Credits, and provide other benefits to designated community-development corporations and community-development financial institutions. Make sure accredited investors and foundations in your region are fully aware of these opportunities, and encourage them to participate.

Promote Program-Related Investments. By law, foundations must give away at least 5 percent of their assets each year. The other 95 percent is typically invested in distant stocks and bonds. Work with your local foundations to help them move that 95 percent (or even just 1 percent) into local business. If these businesses are "program related" and the investment does not succeed, the foundation also can apply losses to its annual grant-giving obligations.

Issue Slow Munis. Your local government issues bonds all the time, often to support dumb economic-development projects like corporate attractions or industrial-development parks. How about issuing bonds to finance local businesses? Several communities have debated proposals to create "food bonds," the proceeds of which might go into a local fund that collateralizes loans from local banks and credit unions to high-priority local food businesses. Properly structured, the interest income from these bonds could be tax exempt, and the bonds could be purchased by any resident of your community.

Take Your Local Businesses Public. The original US securities laws created pathways for small businesses to sell stock to the public through "direct public offerings." Even though these "exemptions" to a full securities registration can be costly, new technologies, methods, and laws are bringing down these costs—as we will elaborate later in this chapter.

Move Your Public Money. Where is your city doing its banking? If it's not local, lobby for a change. The state-owned Bank of North Dakota does this on a statewide basis, placing local tax collections and federal government transfer payments on deposit in local banks before the funds are needed. More than a half dozen states are looking seriously at creating their own public banks.

Create a Local Investment Fund. Pools of capital are preferable to one-off investments because they diversify risk. There are a thousand local-investment pools around the country, most of them linked with local economic-development programs, though nearly all of them are only open to accredited investors. A few, however, have structured themselves to allow unaccredited investors to participate.

Create a Local Mutual Fund. There are 7,500 mutual funds in the United States (in which unaccredited investors can readily invest), but not a single one invests in local small business. There is no legal reason why a locally focused mutual fund could not be formed, though the start-up costs would be significant. The toughest requirement for mutual funds is that 85 percent of the fund must be liquid, which might be accomplished through "slow munis." The other 15 percent could be local stock.

Lobby Your Pension Fund. In the absence of local pension funds, you can lobby your workplace pension funds to put some money in local stocks and bonds. Most managers of these funds will claim—incorrectly—that local investment is illegal under the US Employee Retirement Income

Security Act (ERISA). Point out to them that many of the local investments outlined here outperform the US stock market, and therefore are
completely legitimate investments for fiduciaries managing these funds.

Form a Local Investment Club. You and your friends can form your own
investment fund on the cheap as a "club." The legal requirement is that
all your decisions must be made together, as a group. A great example
is No Small Potatoes, a project of Slow Money Maine, which makes
loans to farms, fishermen, and food businesses.

Prepare a Community List. Knowledge is power. Imagine a local craigslist of
all the local investment opportunities in your community—that is, all
the local businesses that have jumped through the right legal hoops to
sell securities to unaccredited investors. A list like this is easy to create
and invaluable for potential local investors. What can and cannot be
listed varies by state, but general information about companies looking
for capital is usually permissible (and if it isn't, the state can and should
amend its securities laws accordingly).

Spread Self-Directed IRAs. Tax-deferred investing through an IRA or 401k
typically must be done through mutual funds, which means your money
is stuck on Wall Street. By rolling over your funds into a self-directed
IRA, however, you can direct a custodian (for about $200–$300 per year,
if you shop carefully) to invest instead in any and all of the items above.
The only restriction is that you cannot invest in your family's business
or home. But you can invest in your neighbor's business or home, and
your neighbor can invest in yours!

Get Residents to Rethink Their Finances. There's a widespread mythology,
spread by the investment industry, that patiently leaving one's money
on Wall Street will generate the best returns for retirement, college,
or other long-term needs. In fact, far better returns can be achieved
through investing in one's own home, in energy efficiency measures
in your residence, and in one's own education. And the single best way
to localize your money and improve your rate of return is to wean
yourself off nonlocal credit cards.

Start a Slow Money Chapter. Across the United States and in other countries as well, groups inspired by Woody Tasch's book, *Slow Money*,
are exploring all these strategies with the goal of placing 1 percent

of investment in local farms and food businesses. The twenty active US chapters, which involve both professional investors and newbies, have created thirteen investment clubs and have already mobilized $38 million into more than 350 small food enterprises.

From a pollinator perspective, some of these tools are social inventions with no obvious business model. Local investment clubs, for example, are usually labors of love among the participants, and by law they can't hire anyone to make decisions for the club.[70] But most of these tools—banks, credit unions, cooperatives, mutual funds—amount to local variations of proven models of financial businesses that charge fees for various services.

What follows are four stories that suggest the coming tsunami of purse pollinators. We begin by looking at one of the most impressive credit unions in North America, Vancity. We then look at the status of securities reform in the United States through the eyes of two young companies, Cutting Edge Capital and Mission Markets. We return to Canada to see an extraordinary network of local investment funds in Nova Scotia that could provide a powerful model for the United States. Finally, we look at Credibles, which dances on the edges of securities law by allowing users to prepurchase local food and food services.

The World's Local Bank

To most Americans, says comedian Kathleen Madigan, visiting Canada is like climbing into your attic—you suddenly remember how much good stuff is up there. Its financial innovations are relevant to Americans because many of its securities and banking laws are similar to those in the United States, and have become more so since the countries signed (with Mexico) the North American Free Trade Agreement and various other trade agreements "harmonizing" financial rules. Both countries, for example, are dominated by big banks. There is, however, one important difference: In Canada small local banks are almost unheard of, but some of its credit unions are significantly larger and more powerful than their American counterparts. And an example that would blow most Americans away is Vancity, located in Vancouver, British Columbia.

Credit unions are consumer cooperatives that provide financial services. That means they are controlled democratically by their members. Every member of a credit union receives one vote irrespective of how much capital he or she has invested. One in three Canadians belongs to a credit union—and in British Columbia 41 percent of the residents do. (In the United States, about one in four are members.) A thousand Canadian communities have access to at least one credit union, and in 362 of them the local credit union provides the only source of financial services. The largest credit union in the English-speaking parts of the country by far, with assets of $18 billion, is Vancity. (The Desjardins Group in French-speaking Quebec is larger still, with assets of $190 billion.)

The Canadian credit union movement spread rapidly before World War II, but Vancity didn't get organized until 1946, receiving the 169th charter from the federal government to operate. It became the first financial institution in Vancouver to provide mortgages to residents living in the city's working-class east side. The founding members also wanted to create a pool large enough to qualify for health insurance (this was before Canada nationalized its health-care system). Over the years, Vancity has grown dramatically, in part by merging with fifty-three other credit unions in the Vancouver metropolitan area and surrounding regions.

Canadian credit unions are all local, in the sense that the federal government restricts their operations to the home province. This limitation was recently relaxed, but Vancity shocked the country's financial commentariat by announcing that, despite its size, it would be sticking to British Columbia. Unlike one of its biggest competitors, HSBC, which misleadingly advertises itself as the "World's Local Bank," Vancity is genuinely committed to being the world's best local bank—which means being the best financial institution possible for British Columbia.

Today, Vancity provides every mainstream banking service to about five hundred thousand members, 80 percent of whom live in metropolitan Vancouver. You can finance your house, your education, your automobile, you name it. You can get debit cards, credit cards, and prepaid cards. You have access to a state-of-the-art banking system and to ATMs across the province. You can get assistance with tax preparation and retirement plans. Unlike the vast majority of US credit unions, Vancity also provides an extensive suite of services to its business members. A recent survey of more than thirteen thousand small and medium-scale businesses in Canada grabbed headlines by showing that they rated the business services of credit unions superior to those of banks. Credits unions have lower fees, pay higher returns, suffer fewer defaults, and provide more personal service. The Global Alliance for Banking on Values also has named Vancity as one of the twenty-five best banks in the world.

But it would be a mistake to think of Vancity as just a well-run bank. It's on a pollinator mission to transform the local economy. In 1961 Vancity was the first major financial institution in Canada to extend loans to women without requiring a man to be a cosigner. In 1967 it introduced savings accounts that calculated and added interest daily, a fairer way of growing members' money. The firsts in Canada then started snowballing: Canada's first socially responsible mutual fund (1986); the first Registered Education Savings Plan (1988); the first Community Investment Deposit Program (1993), which reduced interest rates by 1 percent and passes on that amount to promising community projects; the first youth credit union in an elementary school (1996); the first bank to award funding for environmentally sound transportation projects (2001); the first loan program for people with disabilities (2001); the first marketing program targeting gays and lesbians (2002); the first home-lending program for energy efficiency installations (2004); the first bike-sharing initiative (2007); and the first mainstream financial alternative to payday lending (2014).

Vancity's green business manager today is Maureen Cureton. She became a member about twenty-five years ago. "I had my epiphany about the importance of banking when I had to start paying back my student loan," she recalls. "I heard about the great things Vancity was doing. That percolated for a bit and then I said, you know what, I need to pay my money to some financial institution, and I want to direct it to one that cares about community and our environment. So I became a member."

Cureton completed a major in environmental management (with a de facto minor on the national rowing team), and went on to work for a green technology company that recycled fish waste. She did a stint at the Rocky Mountain Institute, Amory Lovins's resource-efficiency think tank, where she coauthored two books: *Homemade Money: How to Save Energy and Dollars in Your Home*, and *Green Development: Integrating Ecology and Real Estate*. She returned to Canada for an MBA, continued consulting, writing, and teaching, and planned on entering a PhD program on sustainability strategy in business, when Vancity offered her a one-year project contract in 2006. That one year has since stretched into happily ever after.

Cureton's first position was as a project manager charged with extending Vancity's sustainability work beyond its internal operations to help "green up" its business members. If they improved their triple-bottom-line performance, the credit union reckoned, all of Vancouver would benefit, as would the credit union's membership. Over time, Vancity dissolved the sustainability department and spread its sustainability practices across every department. Cureton's role then evolved to her current position. She is now essentially a full-time, bank-financed pollinator dedicated to strengthening local businesses across the city. "It's not just about helping our members' environmental performance any more. It's also about designing financial services in a way that better assists businesses that share our values."

With thirty-eight thousand business member accounts, Cureton knows she cannot possibly help more than a tiny fraction directly. So she partners with organizations that themselves connect with many businesses. For example, through a partnership with a grassroots group called ClimateSmart, she has been able to help many of her local business members reduce their greenhouse-gas emissions. Vancity provided seed capital for ClimateSmart and later helped finance some of its projects by, for example, underwriting scholarships for local entrepreneurs to take its training courses. Her priority is to reach local businesses with a "juicy carbon footprint"—small manufacturers rather than a home-based business. Consequently she recently helped finance a ClimateSmart study on how food processors could reduce their greenhouse gases.

But what's really in this for Vancity? "We just did a survey," explains Cureton, "and most of our members said they were proud of what Vancity does in environmental and social leadership." Cureton believes that her members want her to lead. She sits on numerous municipal and provincial committees advising on environmental policies. "They want us at the table, because they want that financial institution perspective, and they know Vancity is committed to environmental leadership."

But there are limits too. "Over time what we've come to learn is while our members want us to do the right thing, they want us to lead with our values-based banking, but they don't want it coming out of their pockets. So we are getting the message out now that we are a competitive banker, providing the same products and services as other financial institutions, but we do it with a triple-bottom-line orientation. That's why our branding is 'We Make Good Money for You.' We're still seeing great growth in our revenues, we're always profitable, and we continue to have competitive rates. Our market research also tells us that this branding resonates with our community, and I know we are attracting more and more businesses that share our environmental and social values."

Vancity positions itself as a "trusted advisor" to its business clients. Sometimes a business comes to Cureton through her community engagement; other times the business is referred to her after having a conversation with a loan officer or an account manager. When those businesses with special environmental needs or opportunities arrive at her desk, she looks for programs or partnerships that can link them with "our tribe of businesses with similar values."

"For example," she explains, "one of my amazing businesses is Tacofino, which is committed to local food and wanted to green its operations. It has one restaurant and several food trucks." When Tacofino asked Vancity to finance another restaurant, she offered to connect it with a biodiesel co-op; it could dispose of its cooking oil there, save disposal costs, and in exchange get a discount on biofuel to run its trucks. "The company now has that relationship," she says. "I also gave its managers a ClimateSmart scholarship, and connected them with a local energy consultant to help them find more strategic and operational solutions for improving their environmental performance. I could have done a walk-through myself, but I decided it would be better to pay another wonderful business member, SES Consulting, engineers with expertise in energy efficiency, to do it. Then I was at another event, and witnessed Tacofino give SES's contact information to two other businesses, telling them you've got to talk with these guys—they're amazing. So much of what I do these days is serve as a connector—it's not just about the freebies and grants."

In case you forgot, we're talking about a staff person at a bank. And the bank deploys other staff to work in fields like low-income housing, antipoverty social enterprises, aboriginal businesses, and so forth.

"When I first came to Vancity," says Cureton, "they had me as the one and only consultant giving businesses one-on-one advice on their eco-footprints, and then they had a bunch of grants that were really only for not-for-profits. Now it's about leveraging our resources in a variety of ways to help build a community of businesses and nonprofits that share our values and support each other.

"I continue to get excited about our partnerships. One of the ones I'm working on this year is the Zero Waste Challenge with Metro Vancouver. The aim is to help businesses and the community overall move toward zero waste. With a new municipal ban on food scraps from landfills, restaurants and food processors are looking for solutions. Much of the 'waste' is quality food that is still edible, and we have many people living in poverty in Vancouver. So we're exploring the logistics for redirecting this food to organizations that feed people in need.

"We want to help create more opportunities for building a circular economy, where one business's waste can be used by another. I have a business member who disassembles products and sends out metals to be recycled. But if it had a machine to shred the metal, it would get three times the price. That machine is expensive, so rather than finance one business to make that purchase, I'm suggesting that the business colocate with a similar company to share the equipment and space. We designed a mortgage years ago to encourage homeowners to colocate, so why not businesses? We gave a little grant money to explore the establishment of a zero waste hub. Now two local recycling businesses have colocated and several more businesses are considering moving into neighboring buildings."

Cureton argues that many more of British Columbia's businesses should be sharing space, equipment, resources, and staff to achieve economic and resource efficiency. "I'm working with Passive House, a developer in Victoria building a sixplex, which is unusual. The company uses an amazing energy efficient building technology. You tend to see it in 4,000- or 7,000-square-foot houses for the privileged. Passive House is building an apartment complex with 900-square-foot condos that's groundbreaking in Canada. So financing for this was new for all of us. Sometimes when businesses do something that's different, it scares the bankers. So I help my colleagues understand the benefits and risks, and push internally to get my lending colleagues more comfortable with these ventures."

Vancity set up an internal loan fund for projects like these. "It's not something we advertise. But when our bankers think a project is too risky, we might backstop part of the project with this fund. We'll cover the loss if the project goes sideways. The goal is to build up a track record of successful financing in newer areas, so that in the future bankers are comfortable financing without a backstop."

Cureton and her colleagues involved in community investment also are shifting Vancity's own purchasing practices. They developed a list of values-based business members to promote purchasing from them. They introduced their purchasing department to local businesses like Fairware (an ethical SWAG supplier), green printing companies, and numerous local and organic caterers. Besides boosting these clients, this policy is helping Vancity employees feel connected to the values-based business community they serve.

Vancity is also committed to addressing poverty in the region, and in 2011 it became one of Canada's largest "living wage" employers. (A living wage ensures that a full-time breadwinner for a family of four earns above the national poverty line.) Besides ensuring that its employees are paid a living wage, Vancity is shifting its supply chain to those companies paying living wages. By December 2014, forty-three of the bank's suppliers had pledged to pay their own employees living wages.

In the years ahead, Cureton would like to see Vancity offer members the option of directing their deposits toward certain local priorities like renewable energy, recycling, affordable housing, First Nations' ventures, and so on. "We finance all these things anyway, but it would be great to give members opportunities to choose where their deposited dollars get invested."

Another project piloted this year was a local rewards program. Vancity basically implemented some of the innovations of the purchasing pollinators discussed earlier: a website, an app, and a loyalty program leading consumers to member businesses. The first test was in Victoria with 135 Vancity business members.

Vancity offers a powerful pollinator template that other banks and credit unions could embrace worldwide. It applies conservative banking practices to local business lending, but then supplements it with a suite of services that increase the probability of borrowing businesses succeeding.

It also must be said that one reason for Vancity's success is its scale. Small credit unions in the United States would readily attest that the absence of scale greatly limits their products and services. The members of a small credit union, for example, usually insist that the limited pool of savings be allocated to personal loans for housing, college, and cars—not to commercial loans for small businesses. Moreover, even household members find small credit unions wanting because they may lack good back-end office software, online services, or conveniently located ATMs (though credit unions do allow each others' members to use each other's ATMs without penalty fees). Vancity, in contrast, is large enough to provide all the services people expect from their bank, but not so large that its energy, money, and ambitions drift outside the province.

There may be other creative ways for a local bank to achieve this needed regional scale to become an effective pollinator. In Australia, one of the ten largest banks (by assets and deposits) is Bendigo, and like Vancity it has embraced, top to bottom, a triple-bottom-line mission. But unlike Vancity, it is a publicly traded, nonlocal company. In 1998, concerned with the closure of more than a thousand local bank branches over the previous decade, Bendigo deployed a turnkey franchise model to provide banking services to small towns throughout the country. An interested community can get a franchise if it can raise half a million dollars in initial deposits and assemble a representative board to run the branch. Bendigo, in turn, provides software, accounting, and legal support. Each branch has to pay a small fee, but otherwise is guaranteed control of 95 percent of its money. More than 305 communities have bought into this model, reaching more than a million account holders, and this program has become one of the fastest growing parts of Bendigo's business.

The point is that there are many ways a bank or credit union can achieve the necessary scale for offering pollination services. It can grow larger. It can partner with similar-sized institutions. It can grow local roots downward from a much larger bank like Bendigo. Vancity inspires hope

174 | *The Local Economy Solution*

that every community in the world might someday have at least one banking institution that serves as a purse pollinator. But banking is just a small
part of a community's financial picture.

The Great Race

American household savings in banks and credit unions are about a quarter the size of their long-term savings in *securities*, which are financial
instruments that pay holders some kinds of profitable return. And those
long-term savings are roughly 99 percent invested in nonlocal business. So
moving securities from Wall Street to Main Street in the United States is
the holy grail for local economic development.

Fixing today's securities markets will require at least four stages:

• Stage I. We have to make it easier and cheaper for small businesses to
  issue securities to unaccredited local investors.
• Stage II. We have to make it easier and cheaper for those unaccredited
  investors to trade their shares on local stock exchanges.
• Stage III. We have to make it easier and cheaper for unaccredited investors to invest in local investment funds, where financial specialists can
  perform the hard work of choosing and trading local securities.
• Stage IV. We have to make it easier and cheaper for the fiduciaries
  running pensions, trusts, and other funds to place unaccredited clients'
  money into local investment pools.

These four changes must proceed more or less in the order laid out
above. That is, few fiduciaries will begin to invest pension funds locally
when there are so few local investment funds with a track record of profitability. Few such funds will be established until there are local exchanges
that allow the funds to buy and sell securities (illiquid securities are potentially worthless[71]). And no local exchanges in a region will be set up until
there are enough local securities to trade.

This logical sequencing underscores why it's ludicrous to begin with
a Stage IV question like "How can I localize my pension fund?" College
organizers are now pushing for their campuses to divest from fossil

fuel companies responsible for greenhouse-gas emissions and reinvest in community businesses, with little awareness that the infrastructure needed for redirecting those investments barely exists. They need to be patient. We are barely at Stage I. That sounds like bad news, but five years ago we were not even at Stage 0.

Until recently the best option for small businesses looking for capital from unaccredited investors was to do a direct public offering or DPO. Unlike a typical initial public offering (IPO), where the securities might be sold on the NASDAQ or New York Stock Exchange, shares of a DPO are typically sold by a company directly to the public. A DPO can be created by exploiting one of several so-called "exemptions" that the Securities and Exchange Commission (SEC) offers to a full-blown (and incredibly expensive) registration of publicly traded securities. The one that has become the favorite tool for local investors is the "intrastate exemption." Basically, whenever a local company is just looking for local investors within its home state, the SEC leaves it to that state to supervise. Most states give small companies a simplified legal route to raise as much capital as they want (though some set a ceiling of between $1 million and $5 million). It will still cost a company $25,000–$75,000 for the legal work, but once you follow it, you can then freely advertise to potential investors within that state.

The pollinator these days most widely associated with creating DPOs for local business is Jenny Kassan, CEO of Cutting Edge Capital (CEC). Kassan admits that when she was a law student at Yale, she never studied securities law—she didn't even know what it was. Her passion was civil rights and social justice, and she thought that practicing any form of corporate law would be selling out. The jobs available after law school were scarce, so she pursued a masters in city planning at UC Berkeley. She then took a job at the Unity Council in Oakland, California, where she was able to blend her legal and planning skills to organize various community projects in low-income, primarily Latino neighborhoods. That lasted for eleven years.

I had known Kassan throughout this time (she had been an intern of mine in the early 1990s), and I introduced her to an East Bay lawyer I knew named John Katovich, who had been the general counsel for the Pacific Stock Exchange in San Francisco and shared my interest in the concept of local stock markets (a Stage II goal). So when I learned that Katovich was looking for a new lawyer in his small law firm, I connected the two. Katovich's practice was steeped in securities law, and Kassan suddenly got a crash course in the subject.

Kassan, Katovich, and I continued to brainstorm, along with Don Shaffer, then executive director of BALLE, about what exactly a local exchange might look like. Katovich was convinced that it would be easier and faster to piggyback a prototype onto the many millions of dollars of legal work embodied in existing exchanges, rather than create a new exchange from scratch.

Katovich was then offered the job of general counsel for the Boston Stock Exchange, and extracted a promise from his new employer that he could develop a local exchange there. He packed up his family and moved east, leaving Kassan to run the Oakland law firm. Shortly after he arrived, however, NASDAQ bought the Boston Stock Exchange, and expressed zero interest in a local exchange. It took three years for Katovich to extricate himself from Boston.

Even with a local exchange on hold, Kassan decided that the firm, now called Cutting Edge Counsel, should develop a deeper practice in helping companies tap the financial resources of unaccredited investors. In 2008 she and Katovich created a sister company, Cutting Edge Capital (CEC), with the idea that legal work would proceed in the law firm and the consulting work through CEC. To prepare herself to run the new company, Kassan enrolled in an accelerator program run by Village Capital. "It was a tough course," she recalls, "filled with lots of white men with MBAs from Stanford and Haas. But it forced me to get my act together, and gave me the confidence to be the CEO of Cutting Edge Capital."

Kassan decided that she wanted CEC to be the best shop for a small business to obtain an affordable DPO. Over the last three years, Kassan and her colleagues have completed eleven DPOs worth $5 million for clients in multiple states, and more than thirty other DPOs are in the works. CEC typically charges a client $25,000, which is at the low end of what other law firms charge.

Kassan has come up with several ways to lower the $25,000 cost further. She ultimately would like to create a piece of software for clients to fill in the blanks, press a button, and print out a ready-to-file prospectus for their states, but this will require a serious capital investment. For now, she runs "boot camps," where she leads groups of clients through preparing their DPOs, and gets them to improve their filings through peer support. The first two boot camps were in her office in Oakland, and the third one was virtual with clients spread across the country. The class uses an online platform to explain different parts of the DPO prospectus and to guide the students to design their securities offering and write their own prospectus. Attorneys complete the document drafting and assist with the securities compliance process. The price tag is still steep, $12,000, but considering how many attorney hours Kassan provides, it's a steal. And it's the cheapest DPO option available in the United States (short of finding a pro-bono attorney).

To prove her faith in DPOs, Kassan prepared two of them for CEC itself. The first one raised $155,000 from California investors. It was a royalty agreement, promising to pay investors a percentage of gross revenues over five years. If CEC continues along its current business trajectory, investors in this DPO should get about a 3 percent per year rate of return. A second DPO raised $50,000, and CEC uses the funds to underwrite an online tool called CuttingEdgeX.com, which allows unaccredited investors to find current DPOs across the country and invest (through the DPO issuer's website) with a quick credit card transaction.

While Kassan has embraced the DPO option for her clients, she also lobbies for reforms of securities laws, and provided critical support for one reform idea I had. In 2009, I wrote an article for a journal published by the San Francisco branch of the Federal Reserve proposing a $100 exemption in all securities offerings. My argument was that there should be some *de minimis* level of investment below which regulators should let people do whatever they wish. Very few people who invest $100 in a business risk losing their life savings. Sure, a few people will be ripped off, but under the common law they always can take someone to court for fraud to get their money back. And if they lose $100 because of a bad investment, how damaging is it? Public policy lets anyone, irrespective of their wealth or income, enter a casino and gamble away every last penny to their name. Surely we can tolerate letting people take up to $100 of risk to support their community's well-being.

Kassan worked with the nonprofit Sustainable Economies Law Center to assemble a team to write a rulemaking petition to the SEC on behalf of the proposed $100 exemption. Hundreds of letters poured into the SEC in support, pointing out that the severity of the nation's economic downturn required extraordinary action. This led to more proposals coming before the SEC arguing for investment crowdfunding, where large numbers of people place small amounts of money into companies. So what did the SEC do with these proposals? Nothing.

Somewhere around May of 2011, I sat in on a hearing of the congressional Government Operations Committee discussing several different securities law reforms, including investment crowdfunding. For me, the highlight of the day was the cross-examination of Mary Schapiro, then chair of the SEC. A Tea Party Republican asked her whatever came of the $100 exemption proposal and similar reforms (at this point, our petition was two years old). Her response, dripping with condescension, was that we get these silly proposals all the time, and maybe she would assemble a group within the SEC to review them next year. Maybe? Next year? Was she aware that unemployment in the county was currently 9 percent? Did she realize that she basically was saying that the SEC doesn't care about financing small business, the only enterprises truly capable of generating new jobs?

The Committee proceeded to vote—unanimously—for a bill drafted by Representative Patrick McHenry of North Carolina that legislated, not a $100 exemption, but a $10,000 exemption. It was one of the few times during that Congress where Tea Party Republicans and Occupy Wall Street Democrats agreed on anything. The vote in the House was 390 to 23. The bill went to the Senate, where it stalled for several months. Democrats who worried about fraud whittled down the exemption to $2,000, and insisted that all crowdfunding transactions proceed on Internet portals licensed by the SEC. It ultimately passed the Senate 73 to 26.

By the time President Obama signed the so-called Jumpstart Our Business Startups (JOBS) Act in April 2012, many of us felt it was a good step forward but not quite the great leap we had originally envisioned. Remember, we had wanted to permit unaccredited investors to invest small dollar amounts in local companies with no legal paperwork. The JOBS Act allows larger investments, but with new mountains of paperwork. It also introduces more potential for fraud. By focusing on small dollar amounts, our proposal would have been practically useless for financial schemers, and instead would have been used primarily by neighbors to support local businesses they knew, trusted, and loved. By allowing longer-distance transactions among strangers, the JOBS Act makes it more likely that investors will put more money into businesses they have no relationship to whatsoever—and then get snookered. Our proposal also envisioned local transactions occurring at a co-op meeting or via a handshake at the local coffeehouse, the kinds of grassroots financial relationships critical to stimulating a stagnating community economy. The JOBS Act, in contrast, insists that the transactions occur through an elaborate portal licensed by the SEC.

It's now impossible to assess whether, from a local business's perspective, the price tag for a JOBS Act offering will be greater or less than the $25,000 for a DPO. If your offering is less than $100,000, your board just has to certify the accuracy of your financials. But if your offering is between $100,000 and $500,000, your financials must be reviewed by a CPA, and if it's between $500,000 and $1 million, you have to get a full-blown third-party audit, which can easily cost $10,000–$15,000. Additionally, you have to pay a portal a fee to review your company, which could be another few thousand dollars. And a portal might also charge a success fee, perhaps 5–10 percent of the total raised. Whether the total fee for a DPO will be higher than $25,000 might depend on the size of your raise and the exact charges by the portal you are using.

Kassan is convinced that conventional DPOs will remain more attractive than JOBS Act offerings for several reasons. The JOBS Act demands that a company disclose its financials to the public as long as it has outside investors. The requirement that a portal serve as an intermediary also bans direct conversations between a local company and potential investors, whereas these are fine under most state DPO laws. The JOBS Act also, unlike DPOs, allows investors to back out until the entire offering closes. And with DPOs, there is generally no cap on the amount each investor can invest.

Still, it seems that many companies could find the JOBS Act route attractive. If you are raising less than $100,000, the up-front costs would clearly be lower than a DPO. Even if you have to pay a somewhat higher success fee at the end of the raise, you at least have the money then to pay it. Plus, the JOBS Act automatically allows you to raise funds from a broader universe of potential investors, both local and nonlocal, so you have a greater chance of securing the money you need.

Many entrepreneurs apparently share this judgment, because within a year after the JOBS Act passed, hundreds of new portals appeared on the scene. Most were local or sector-specific knockoffs of Kickstarter or Indiegogo, allowing any user to donate money to a project, cause, or business for a token reward. Some had local-friendly names like Community Funded. They anticipated a date in the near future when crowdfunding could include not just donations but also loans and small stock investments. The JOBS Act mandated the SEC issue final rules by December 2012, so it seemed like just a short wait before donation portals could morph into true investment portals.

Offering up variations of "the dog ate my homework," the SEC now seems incapable of complying with the law. It issued draft rules in December 2013, one year late. Everyone has been waiting for finalization ever since. As I write, we are more than two years past the deadline. Some believe that the agency is overwhelmed with other priorities, like implementing Dodd-Frank. Others believe that the securities regulators who saw the act as an affront to the SEC in the first place are just dragging their feet until they can figure out how to repeal it. My view is that the next time Congress passes a law like this, it should eliminate SEC discretion altogether.

Whatever the explanation, the consequences of the delay have been horrendous. The vast majority of the portals that opened up are discovering that they can't make ends meet just facilitating donations. And their start-up capital, accumulated mostly for the expected heyday of investment portals, is running out. Absent new leadership at the SEC, most of these portals will die soon. Perhaps that was the SEC's plan all along: Suffocate the infant industry before it makes us irrelevant.

During this time of great uncertainty, I started to assist an aspiring portal company called Mission Markets. Long before the JOBS Act was ever contemplated, the founder of Mission Markets, Michael Van Patten, envisioned deploying "community portals" across the country where securities could be bought and sold by local investors. The company invested in lawyers (Kassan and Katovich, among them) to figure out the fine print concerning how unaccredited investors could participate in these transactions. The JOBS Act offered a much simpler path forward. Unlike many of its competitors, however, Mission Markets had several business models—and the unprofitable world of donation crowdfunding was not one of them. Instead, it is using its portal technology now to connect accredited investors with socially responsible companies. If the JOBS Act gets implemented, Mission Markets still hopes to offer community portals.

Meanwhile, those who believe DPOs are too expensive and who have lost patience waiting for the JOBS Act have pursued a third option—reforming state laws governing intrastate investment. A number of states, such as Alabama, Georgia, Kansas, Oregon, and Wisconsin, have essentially implemented their own versions of the JOBS Act. Vermont now allows local companies to advertise freely to potential investors living in the state. Colorado increased its DPO maximum from $1 million to $5 million. And most remarkably, my home state of Maryland passed the $100 exemption (unanimously in both houses)—no lawyers or portals needed—for in-state companies borrowing as much as $100,000 from other residents of the Bay State. In all, nearly half the states either have passed a significant reform bill or are close to doing so.

Many of these state reforms fail to define clearly whether these offerings have to be done on in-state portals, how the portals would be licensed, whether they could be run by grassroots groups (instead of expensive broker-dealers), and whether they could charge a success fee (which might be critical to the success of a portal as a business). So in the coming years, there will be a bunch of amendments, experiments, and new legislative frameworks. The fine print of these state laws and minute rules issued by state securities regulators will determine what the ultimate costs of investment crowdfunding in these states will be.

So the Great Race is on! Some purse pollinators, like Mission Markets, are placing their bets on the JOBS Act being implemented. Others, like CEC, will continue to offer DPOs through boot camps and new software packages. And still others will simply continue rewriting their state laws and create portals or other business models to fit them. No one knows which approach will yield the cheapest and best pathway for a local business to accept capital from unaccredited investors. The answer may ultimately depend on the state in which a small business operates.

What's undeniable is that no matter which pollinator wins, the loser will be investment apartheid. Stage I of the local investment revolution is proceeding apace, and we're already beginning to enter Stage II. It's just a matter of time before portals ask for permission to shift from initial offerings of local stock to reselling. The state of Michigan has just passed a bill to create a statewide platform for secondary trading. The SEC could argue that under the original Exchange Act of 1934 states have no right to create their own exchanges, even for purely intrastate transactions. Or it could issue a "no action letter" granting permission to the states to experiment in this area. A breathtaking battle over federalism looms.

Pools for Farmers

Stage III of the local investment revolution also faces formidable challenges in the United States. Any fund that is designated an "investment company" must pay steep legal fees to get started and more each year to comply with SEC regulations. Local investors have therefore sought to create funds that fit within one of the exemptions of the Investment Company Act of 1940. These exemptions include funds with fewer than one hundred participants (what most "hedge funds" are), investment clubs, and nonprofit funds. But even if your fund fits into these exemptions, you still have to comply with complex federal and state regulations, especially if you want any unaccredited investors to participate. Consequently there are only about a dozen loan funds in the entire United States that specialize in assisting small business and also allow unaccredited investors to participate, such as the New Hampshire Community Loan Fund, the Mountain Bizworks in North Carolina, and the Economic Development Institute Funds in Columbus, Ohio.

But if the right legal reforms are implemented, this number could grow substantially. Americans can get a glimpse of the possibilities by visiting the small Canadian province of Nova Scotia. In 1998 legislators there enacted the Community Economic Development Investment Funds (CEDIF) Act, which laid out a simple process by which unaccredited investors can pool money and provide loans to local businesses. The funds must be for-profit, and must have at least six directors elected from the community. Residents of Nova Scotia are allowed to place their tax-deferred retirement savings into these funds, provided they keep them there for at least five years, and then they receive a handsome tax credit. Since then, this province of a million people has witnessed the birth of nearly sixty funds that have raised over $63 million from six thousand investors. All of them support some form of local economic development, and several of them focus on helping farmers and local food businesses. If Americans had as many funds per capita, we would have more than twenty-one thousand such community funds operating nationwide!

One of the reasons Nova Scotia passed the CEDIF law was the awareness that conventional investing was sucking money out of the province. For example, Nova Scotians invest over $600 million every year in RRSPs, the Canadian equivalent of Individual Retirement Accounts (IRAs), and only about 2 percent of that money was historically being invested in Nova Scotia.

One of the more sophisticated grassroots funds in Nova Scotia is called FarmWorks, founded by Linda Best. Growing up on a farm in the Annapolis Valley and spending much of her childhood in 4H programs, Best's roots in agriculture run deep. "Back in the 1960s," she recalls, "we had twelve thousand farms in Nova Scotia, and 60–70 percent of our food was being produced here. Now we have fewer than four thousand farms, and apart from supply-managed dairy, chickens, and eggs, we're probably only producing 10 percent of our food—maybe 20 percent if you count the milk, chicken, and eggs. We need to start rebuilding that food-producing infrastructure. A huge amount of our produce comes from Mexico, South America, and California, and how long can we rely on them?"

The growing conditions in Nova Scotia, however, are not exactly like those of California, or even Kansas. How far can such a frigid region really go in achieving food self-reliance? "Hey, we fed ourselves in the past," points out Best. "Season extension is possible with greenhouses, and we certainly raise excellent animals. We could and should be making agriculture a much larger part of our economy."

As a young adult, Best was a medical microbiologist, studying the bacteria that cause ulcers. She wound up serving on the board of Capital Health, the largest health authority in the province. "I came to realize that if we're going to change our sad health outcomes, the only thing we have a lot of control over is what we eat," she says. "And given socio-economic problems in the province, we should grow more of our food and employment here. Not all farming jobs are high-paying jobs, but they're good jobs with many benefits."

A decade ago Best moved back to the Annapolis Valley, and started talking with farmers about what kind of support they needed. "Being a researcher, I discovered the CEDIF program. I brought together a number of people at my house, and over a period of a few months we incorporated FarmWorks in 2011."

The directors never considered forming FarmWorks as a nonprofit. "Nonprofits do good work," says Best. "But my personal philosophy is if you're in a for-profit business, you should be sufficiently well-informed and confident and prepared to put your own money into it. You should be able to grow your business, without 'free money' being part of the equation."

With a nine-member board in place (which has since expanded to fourteen), a long list of advisers, and a slick brochure, Best and her colleagues hit the road to solicit investors. "We had twenty-two meetings in various locations around the province. People believed in our vision right from the get-go. And to think that even without any product of our own, other than our vision of 'healthy farms, healthy food,' we raised $224,200!"

The next year, FarmWorks raised another $225,000, and then another $271,500. By the time FarmWorks was three years old, it had given thirty loans and was just a few months from breaking even. "The 6 percent we charge for interest will allow us to pay all of the office costs and all the administrative costs of running the operation. At that point we'll have our fourth offer open, and the success of our clients provides a fabulous sales pitch. At the five-year point we will be able to give people probably a 2 percent dividend."

Many of FarmWorks's investors are not looking for a high rate of return. "Some people gave us money because they believed in the broader concept of helping to grow the food production economy. They wanted their money to be safe—they didn't want to lose that money. The fact that we can show them there's going to be a dividend is confirmation that the model is successful. That should pull in more money."

Asked which businesses supported by FarmWorks are success stories, Best responds, "Just about all of them!" She cites the young couple who own the Field Guide restaurant in Halifax: "They have a lot of employees, and it's one of the go-to places in the city." And Big Spruce Brewing in Cape Breton: "It has grown very quickly. They are making wonderful organic beers, are helping to pull tourism, and are providing employment." And then there's The Port Grocer in Port Medway: "The people who owned it had been trying to sell it, and it was in imminent danger of being closed down. Now it's rallied the community, it's growing, it has become the center of that area. When we've been there since, several people have said thank you, because if it hadn't been for FarmWorks's $25,000, they wouldn't have had the equity to look for the rest of the capital they needed."

FarmsWorks typically lends a maximum of $25,000 per business, and only higher amounts for reapplications. The board members do all the due diligence. "We visit all our applicants, we have many conversations, and if necessary we help them with their business plan and their financial statements. And then at least three board members do a comprehensive review, which is sent out to the full board for our vote. It's pretty intensive."

The back-and-forth with borrowers gets even more intensive after they have borrowed the money. "I have a pretty holistic world view, partly from my experiences and my research, that encourages people to discuss their businesses in detail with me."

That diligence has paid off. Thus far, FarmWorks has not had any losses, though Best points to one restaurant that did not succeed. "The chef was fabulous, but the location was an issue. When the restaurant closed, we shifted our repayment terms, and he now does private catering so he can pay us back. His business has changed focus, but it's not a loss."

The directors plan to raise additional capital for the fund. They want to move more of the due diligence to paid staff. "We're hoping to get other groups of people together to start building similar CEDIFs for other sectors such as craft beers and wineries. The hope is that several CEDIFs could rely on one loan officer, who would take over some of the work we're currently doing that is unpaid." They also want to expand the size of loans. "We hear so many stories about businesses that need $100,000. Once we get a lot more money under management, then we'll be able to get to the point where up to $100,000 could be loaned. That would take everything to the next level."

Best's instinct is to expand slowly. "We've been fairly low-key, because when you're so young there's always the potential to suffer losses."

Nova Scotia is a small enough province that it's easy for practitioners and regulators to meet regularly. Best believes the Nova Scotia Securities Commission should create training programs on "good governance" for the boards of all the CEDIFs. And she'd like to see more CEDIFs maintain diversified loans to reduce risk.

Like the architects of the CEDIF law, Best sees herself as a pollinator. "Nova Scotians have a tremendous amount of money invested outside the province. The CEDIFs allow people to bring some of their money back into the province, where it means something, where we can achieve the multiplier effects of local investment and local purchasing. I think it's absolutely critical for the future of our economy."

Street Cred

We have entered a historic period of incredible experimentation and innovation, where methods of finance that no one dreamed of ten years ago are becoming commonplace. Some of these methods are not quite banking, not quite securities, yet still provide critical capital to local businesses. Falling into this nebulous space is our fourth example of a purse pollinator, Credibles. The name Credibles is derived from "edible credits." It is the second pollinator creation of Arno Hesse and Guillaume Lebleu, whose Bernal Bucks in San Francisco were discussed in chapter 3.

Generally speaking, the sale of goods before delivery is not a security, even though a "presale" far enough in advance effectively gives a company capital to invest. We now have coffee shops like Awaken Café in Oakland, California, where the proceeds from the prepurchase of coffee are used to invest in a new retail space. We have authors who presell their books before they write them. We have bands that presell albums. Some US states put restrictions on presales, but the majority do not.

"Credibles allows any food business, anywhere, to grow with up-front payments from customers," says Hesse. "We are building liquidity around a resource that businesses can control, which is credit for their own goods and services and for their customers' loyalty. This is a self-empowerment tool for local economies."

Credibles offers a website and app for users to support their favorite food businesses through prepurchasing. Essentially, it allows businesses to take out a line of credit with their customer base, instead of going to the bank. "You pay the businesses up front and you may get some edible interest," says Hesse. "It's the baker's dozen principle. Buy a dozen bagels, and she'll toss an extra bagel into the bag."

As Hesse was getting involved with Slow Money, he and a half dozen other Bay Area investors visited a local pastured chicken farm as part of their due diligence for extending a loan. The proprietor suggested paying back the loan in cash but the interest in eggs. Hesse didn't take the proposal seriously. But in the days that followed, he wondered if perhaps there could be a business in trading credits for eggs and other food products. Hesse changed his mind, and wound up loving the deal. "They were really good eggs!"

The logic for borrowers to do this seemed powerful to Hesse: "To most business owners, it's pretty obvious that paying back with product is easier than paying back with cash. It just costs them what it takes to produce the eggs, grow the fruit, or cook the meal—and that's something they have more control over than their cash flow."

That was the beginning of Credibles. Hesse hired Jenny Kassan to advise the team on the legal fine print. They determined that Credibles are effectively gift certificates, and the law around these certificates varies from state to state. Since California is relatively restrictive, it was a good place to develop operational rules that could apply nationally. One limitation is that gift certificates cannot be sold by start-ups before they are open for business. "We had new restaurants using Credibles, because they were already cooking for customers," says Hesse, "but that was a boundary case."

Hesse ran a few trials with restaurants and vendors in California and New York, and then unveiled the program at the April 2013 Slow Money conference in Boulder, Colorado. Over the next year, he and his colleagues raised about $600,000 to support its initial development.

Deals are promoted on a website, and change regularly. On any given day, I may be able to prepurchase granola from Nana Joes in San Francisco and get 5 percent more cereal. Or buy in advance humanely raised, grass-fed meat from Open Book Farm, in Myersville, Maryland, and get 10 percent more meat. A prepurchase from The Coffee Stop in East Palestine, Ohio, could get me 20 percent more food and drink. By early 2015, Credibles had listed more than one hundred local businesses across the country. Whole Foods in northern California now accepts Credibles as payment for products of Credibles-listed food makers sold in its stores. "We are literally moving money up the food chain," says Hesse.

Credibles doesn't automatically allow any company to list. "We look for sustainable business practices, anchoring in local community, and transparent sourcing. We count on the community itself to apply these criteria rigorously. It's 'community underwriting' in action. Prepayments move customers from transactions to relationships. People ask more questions, and the companies are held more accountable."

A participating company can design its own rewards. "We give them guidance on what has worked for other businesses." Many use their reward to nurture long-term ties with customers or offer gift cards. Flying Fish in Portland rewards large prepurchases of its smoked salmon with an invitation to customers to join them on their albacore finishing trips. A coffee shop has thrown a big party for all its prepurchasers. A grocery store in San Francisco needed an emergency power generator, and was able to turn to its prepurchasers for help. Some companies listing on Credibles report that prepurchasers then increase their normal purchasing rates 50–100 percent.

The prepaid gift certificates never expire. But what happens if a company that sold a deal goes out of business? So far, only one Credibles lister, a sushi business, has shut down. Then the prepurchase could be a loss—unless the owner chooses to pay the customer back. "But people who worry about their outstanding credits," argues Hesse, "also become evangelists for the businesses, and can help push for more customers and more revenue. Credibles users have a stake in the success of a business."

For the moment the basic business model is to charge 5 percent to process payments. Hesse concedes that he and his team are "still fine-tuning. Initially we had paper coupons. Now users have a mobile app." Revenues are currently covering the cost of paying Hesse and three other staff.

Credibles has received requests to expand beyond the United States into Europe and elsewhere. "When I look at Kickstarter and Kiva, I see hundreds of millions of transactions per year. Every transaction proves that people want to pick projects and businesses to support with their money. That encourages us!"

The next stage is to make Credibles transferable from one business to another. "If you put $200 into the baker, and the baker gives you $220 of credit, perhaps you can use $200 at the bakery and $20 elsewhere. Add everything we've learned recently about the sharing economy on top of that. And once you see that you can use Credibles in many places, you might see that they compare very favorably to the paltry interest your bank is paying on your savings. Instead, you might decide to use some of your money to provide working capital to your community."

The Coming Financial Industry

A new industry of purse pollinators is being born. Every community might soon have its own local bank or credit union, a specialized legal company like Cutting Edge Capital creating small stock issues, and a half-dozen local investment funds. Every region might have its own stock exchange. And every pension and mutual fund might provide investors with local options.

The examples in this chapter suggest that we know how to deploy viable pollinators for each of these financial activities. Sure, some require new technology or new legal frameworks, but the success of the early prototypes described here should inspire confidence that these changes are practical. More challenging will be training a new generation of financial service professionals who, in Arno Hesse's words, strive "to make a living, not a killing." That's where emerging people pollinators can help.

The only industry that appears obsolete is the securities bar. The attorneys who are now protecting their jobs policing investment apartheid may be able to hold off some change for a few years. But as Martin Luther King Jr. might have noted, the arc of history is long but bends in the direction of pollinator justice.

CHAPTER 7

Possibilities

A Million Wishes

*I*n his portrayal of the lovable Genie in Disney's *Aladdin*, the late Robin
Williams tells "Al" he can have any three wishes—except, he hastily
adds, like a good attorney, none of them can be for more wishes! But
suppose he could have more wishes—a hundred, a thousand, a million?
That's the promise of pollinator businesses. Rather than create one business at a time, as economic development does today at ridiculous public
expense, pollinators can steadily grow a multitude of local businesses at
zero cost. Like a healthy ecosystem that has many different kinds of pollinators that fertilize many different kinds of plants, a healthy entrepreneurial
ecosystem will have all five types of business pollinators thriving as well.

Some might conclude that the pollinator models discussed thus far are
interesting but all one of a kind. Supportland, for example, offers a great
loyalty card for eighty thousand Portlandia residents, but how likely is it
to catch on in the other thirty-six thousand communities in the United
States? Fledge, the self-financing social enterprise accelerator in Seattle,
invites fourteen businesses a year for intensive incubation—but how can
it possibly serve America's estimated thirty million home-based entrepreneurs? Credibles reaches more than one hundred food businesses across
the country, bringing them alive through presales finance—but what
about the dozens of other sectors of the economy?

There is no shortage of ways to trivialize these models. They are too
new, too small, too isolated, too specialized, too dependent on unique

entrepreneurs, and too idealistic for an unforgiving marketplace. And as I warned in the Introduction, almost all the pollinator models are unproven or at best only tentatively proven. If perfection is the benchmark, then, yes, everything I've shared with you is irrelevant for economic development. Go ahead and keep wasting tens of billions of dollars of public money on useless corporate attractions.

But I believe the stories here stand for something bigger—the emergence of new kinds of businesses that are not going away anytime soon. Even if some of the pollinators you've read about do not survive, there will be copycats, successors, tinkerers, and innovators who will take their place. The proverbial genie is out of the bottle.

As communities soberly weigh the alternatives for job and wealth creation, I believe the virtues of pollinators will become obvious. Attract-and-retain economic development as usual has been with us for a generation, and there's no ambiguity about its dismal performance. *The New York Times* recently estimated that states and localities in the United States are spending more than $80 billion per year on attract-and-retain incentives that rarely work.[72] And that estimate is almost certainly too low.[73] The diligent researcher can dig up information about subsidies in the form of grants, loans, and capital improvements (especially thanks to a database recently assembled by the nonprofit Good Jobs First), but there's remarkably little recordkeeping on which companies have taken advantage of available tax breaks. What information exists is further distorted by companies easily moving expenses and income from place to place, perhaps to the Cayman Islands or Lichtenstein, to minimize global tax liability. Nor does the $80 billion estimate include the losses of natural capital or fair wages that communities may regard as the regrettable but necessary price for making themselves business friendly.

But contrary to official declarations of TINA economic developers, there is an alternative.

Clown Alley

Just before I spoke at an Eat Local Week event recently in Florida, I was handed a copy of the previous day's Sarasota *Herald-Tribune*.[74] Sarasota

County is a warm, sunny enclave with 380,000 residents south of Tampa Bay on the west coast of Florida. In the city of Sarasota, one of the largest population centers in the county, Ringling Boulevard commemorates the home base of the Ringling Brothers Circus and its famous school for Big Top performers. But the front page of the paper made clear that a very different kind of circus was happening in Sarasota County's Economic Development Corporation (EDC).

Over the previous year, the investigative report explained, the EDC office had spent "eight months working almost exclusively" to lure Xellia Pharmaceuticals from Denmark. The *Herald-Tribune* traced how the economic developers got wind of the company's plans to come to America and build a plant for manufacturing a new generation of antibiotics, how it made repeated trips to Denmark to plead its case, how it shrouded the negotiation in secrecy (the code name was "Project Yellow"), how it treated Danish executives to the finest Sarasotan hotels and restaurants when they visited, how they were able to mobilize a huge incentive package of $137 million, and ultimately how an even more obscene incentive package from North Carolina left them losers.

How many jobs was this elephantine deal going to bring to Sarasota? Ten thousand? Twenty-five hundred? Exactly 191. Put another way, the economic-development department was prepared to spend $717,000 of public money for every new job, many of which would go to outside professionals moving into the community. To appreciate the absurdity of this, consider that if the same $137 million were put into bonds yielding 5 percent per year, 191 Sarasotans could receive $38,000 per year in perpetuity, without ever needing to risk the intermediary of an unreliable outside corporation.

Please understand that I have nothing against the Danes. I love Legos, Tivoli Gardens, Greenland, and all kinds of unhealthy breakfast pastries. And if Sarasotans really loved the Danes as much as I do, they might use the same money to invite 137,000 (about 2.5 percent of the Danish population) to come to Sarasota County as tourists and give each of them $1,000 of spending money. I'm confident that I could prove, using the kabuki of economic modeling, that the economic multipliers of the local direct spending by tourists would be greater than the small fraction of the $137 million that ever would have been spent locally by Xellia.

"The prize was so great," insisted Mark Huey, head of the nine-person EDC. "That's why the EDC exists, to go after opportunities like this. It's what we are paid to do."[75]

One can appreciate the lure of climbing Mount Everest "because it's there," or the aesthetic appeal of visiting the seven wonders of the world. There's a Captain Ahab in all of us that's willing to risk it all to catch the ocean's greatest whale. But do Sarasotans really need to spend $137 million just because "the prize" of 191 jobs was "so great"? To me, this borders on insanity, or at least public insubordination. When your economic-development officials start speaking like this, it's time to fire every last one of them and start over.

A smarter Sarasotan EDC would renounce this kind of folly once and for all, and focus exclusively on locally owned businesses. A newly hired EDC staff might look to many different national networks for guidance on what strategies to deploy. They could bring in economic gardeners, who would help them identify promising locally owned "gazelles," those coveted fast-growing businesses that are fabulous job creators. Main Street practitioners could help them transform downtown blocks into lively destinations. AMIBA-minded developers could show them how to fortify local retailers with buy-local campaigns. BALLE-affiliated developers could highlight local food or energy businesses with high triple-bottom-line standards.

For all the virtues of this kind of shift in economic-development strategy, however, it would still be problematic. Yes, a local business framework generates better results at a lower cost, but most of the strategies above still depend on ongoing allocations of money from the government, foundations, and other sources. Working on one business at a time inherently yields results that are too slow, plodding, and limited.

The smarter strategy for a new Sarasota economic-development department would be to populate its economy with all five species of pollinators. Its staff could mobilize planning pollinators like Guy Bazzani to restore dead parts of the town and Main Street Genome to improve the performance of every local business. They could deploy purchasing pollinators, such as loyalty cards and web directories, to pump up sales for local businesses. They could make sure the city has all the available people pollinators—courses, entrepreneurship schools, incubators, coworking spaces, and maker places.

They could spread partner pollinators like local business alliances, direct delivery services, and public markets. They could maximize the sources of local capital available to local businesses through local banks, local stock issuers, local stock exchanges, and local investment funds.

The question remains: How would the newly constituted Sarasota EDC facilitate the spread of pollinators? Should it just continue to use the old tools of attraction—subsidies, tax breaks, land gifts, capital improvements—to convince outside pollinators to move to Florida? Perhaps, but the rationale for favoring homegrown business generally—more money respent, more jobs and income, more entrepreneurship, greater community resilience—suggests favoring locally owned pollinators. Which is not to say that local proprietors starting pollinators need to go it alone. As we've seen, most of the existing pollinators prefer spreading their services through licensing or franchising agreements. It therefore makes more sense to work with interested local entrepreneurs and transform them into leaders of *local versions* of each pollinator design.

Once all five kinds of pollinators are in place, economic developers also could help connect local businesses with the appropriate local pollinators. In some ways, a traditional economic-development department does this already. Need a site for a new building? Call these local realtors. Need help on your taxes? These local attorneys are great. Want to write a business plan? Here's the phone number of the Small Business Development Center. Why not start introducing local businesses to the expanding ranks of local pollinators? In this new world an economic developer becomes not a recruiter but a convener, not a briber but a persuader.

An EDC committed to pollinators could perform an annual inventory of how well the different functions of economic development were being carried out by local pollinators. Sarasota might find that it had ample loan funds but no community portal for the buying and selling of local equities. Its next step, then, might be to help develop a portal licensed from Mission Markets. Or it could discover that it had a healthy variety of purse pollinators but no purchasing pollinators—so it could reach out to Colin Pape's ShopCity.

It's hard to know for sure what will happen when a community has great working models of all five kinds of pollinators. Even communities regarded as entrepreneurship dynamos today, like Austin, New Orleans, or San Francisco, only have one or two pollinators. Here's my prediction: The economic-development department as we know it will cease to exist. Just as the spread of solar panels and neighborhood wind machines will someday render utilities largely irrelevant, the spread of business pollinators will relegate the work of economic development largely to the private marketplace. If businesses want or need assistance, they will pay for it. Ditto for local consumers and local investors. There still may be a role for one or two city staff to gather and spread information about who's doing what and to monitor the local indicators of success. But the era of a county like Sarasota having a nine-person economic-development department chasing companies all over the world and coming up with crazy schemes for wasting millions in taxpayer money will be over.

Local economic development has the potential to privatize itself. Pollinators performing one function tend to stimulate or attract other pollinators. Purchasing pollinators promoting local debit, gift, and loyalty cards naturally embrace partnership pollinators. People pollinators with incubators and coworking spaces will want planning pollinators that incorporate these spaces in their place-making efforts. And every pollinator species ultimately needs start-up finance from purse pollinators. A healthy ecosystem of pollinators is naturally self-renewing and self-regenerating.

Any economic-development strategy that focuses on pollinators will increase the rate of job creation at a significantly lower cost. This simple fact underscores why pollinators are the future of economic development. Provided, of course, that the ecosystem is healthy and free of invasive species.

No-Brainer Public Policies

That's where public policy—the sixth *P* for local economic development—comes in. The rules, standards, practices, and laws that make up public policy determine the healthfulness of a local economic ecosystem. Dumb public policies waste taxpayer money on flashy big businesses that grab headlines but do little for the local economy—except make resident businesses less competitive. Smart public policies facilitate a thriving, competitive marketplace at as little cost to the taxpayer as possible.

Modern politicians can be relied upon to dream up an infinite number of ways to spend public money, and often dress up pet projects in economic-development clothing. So my challenge to them is this: How can you spur the creation and spread of local businesses *at no cost to the public whatsoever?*

Conservative policymakers instinctively rise to this challenge by proposing to cut taxes. That's the position of the Chamber of Commerce, the National Federation of Independent Businesses, and dozens of other business groups representing retailers, manufacturers, farmers, and so forth. While I'm sympathetic to some of these proposals—I would like to see, for example, the elimination of corporate taxation in exchange for more progressive taxation of corporate shareholders (but that's another book)—an honest assessment also must concede that tax cuts alone usually mean cutting schools and essential services like police, fire-fighting, and street repairs. So let me sharpen my question for politicians: Can you spur the creation and spread of local businesses at *no cost*, financial or otherwise, to other members of the community? Can we put forward sensible policies that would be embraced by a supermajority of the left, right, and center?

We've already seen in this book many examples of public policies that accomplish this. For example, the reforms of federal and state securities law reviewed in the previous chapter reduce the costs and difficulty for every citizen to invest locally, without imposing new costs on anyone else. Nova Scotia's law allowing grassroots groups the ability to create their own investment funds penalized nobody in the province. Changes in zoning laws that allowed Guy Bazzani to build green roofs in Grand Rapids and Gilbert Rochecouste to enliven the alleyways of Melbourne did not impose new costs or problems on other residents. To me, these kinds of public policies—simple, transparent, cost-effective, and consensus-building—ought to be the basis for a new era of local economic development.

Let me give another example of the kind of zero-cost, no-brainer policy change that every local authority can implement: Move the city's money into a local bank or credit union. If we know that a dollar deposited in a local financial institution is two to three times more likely to be lent to a local business than a dollar deposited in a branch of a global financial institution, then there's no good reason a city should not bank local.

This is the logic that motivated the state of North Dakota to set up the first and only state-owned bank in the United States in 1919. Rather than allow the roughly $6 billion of state tax collections and federal transfer payments it now receives annually to be deposited in, say, Chase Bank, where the money might support robust economic development in Singapore, North Dakota places the money in its own public bank, which then redeposits the funds in local banks and credit unions throughout the state. Consequently, the state has the highest number of local banks per capita and the lowest level of unemployment. (These trends, by the way, manifested long before the recent oil boom.) The bank currently has $6.8 billion in assets, and earned the state $94 million in 2013.

A populist movement for creating public banks in other states has been gathering steam around the country. But activists have encountered fierce opposition by large banks, even in very progressive states like Oregon and Vermont. An initiative that might move public capital back into local financial institutions, of course, poses a huge threat to the bottom line of big bankasaurs. For the moment, therefore, reformers have decided that a more achievable goal than creating public banks is for simpatico municipalities to switch their banking. And one of their prime success stories comes from the land of Barry Goldwater.

In July 2012, the city of Phoenix announced plans to invest $50 million in local banks and credit unions—and since has placed about $49.1 million of it. The trickiest part, according to the city's treasurer Randy Piotrowski, was to ensure that every deposit received insurance from the Federal Deposit Insurance Corporation, and that limit is set at about $250,000 per year.

"Initially," says Piotrowski, "we sent out and contacted every local bank with fiscal presence in Maricopa County to solicit their offers for certificates of deposit. We received over twenty responses back that met certain qualifications." Besides insisting that participating banks have a physical presence in Phoenix, the city also needed a rate of return equal to a two-year treasury note. "But that still left us with $40 million to place."

The solution was to place the $40 million in the Certificate of Deposit Account Registry Service (CDARS), which spreads the money through a network of local banks nationwide to ensure that every dollar is covered by federal insurance. The system encourages reciprocity, so for every $250,000 placed on deposit in, say, Bangor Savings Bank in Maine, Bangor Savings makes a $250,000 deposit in a Phoenix bank. "This way," says Piotrowski, "the city of Phoenix is protected, and all of the deposits are spread across the network with each of the banks in the network only getting up to $250,000."

What were the costs of setting up this program? "None," according to Piotrowski. "It's at market rate, so we're not losing any money. And recently when we reached the two-year mark, we ended up rolling over most of the maturing CDs. The only real cost is internal, but we have an investment manager already on board, so it's no additional work for him." The program was supported by the mayor, the city council, and civil servants. Even skeptics lauded the fact that it was a zero-cost economic-development initiative. "It helped our local banking community," says Piotrowski, "and provided them with liquidity to lend to local businesses and the public in general."

The same logic compelled nearby Tucson to launch its own "Community Banking Program." A grassroots group, Arizonans for a New Economy, supported by Local First Arizona and the national advocacy group Move Your Money, identified three community banks operating in the city, and invited them to make proposals on how they might reinvest city funds moved into their institutions. Only one bank, Alliance Bank, with branches statewide, responded. The city council reviewed and accepted Alliance's proposal that the city move $5 million into its CDs, which it would then protect with federal insurance using the same CDARS program as Phoenix did. Within seven months, the bank was able to leverage the deposits into $36 million of new loans to sixteen Tucson businesses. It loaned $2.9 million to a local spin-off enterprise from the University of Arizona that helps ensure patients receive the right medications. Two million dollars went to a church-based nonprofit to build a facility providing medical care and vocational training for distressed individuals. The city council was so pleased with the results that it has since doubled its money on deposit.

In most communities the biggest employer is the municipal government (especially if you count public schools), so mobilizing that "business" as a pollinator is a critical lever to moving local economic development in the right direction. For example, municipal bonds can be floated to support local business expansion, which is why Massachusetts State Treasurer Steve Grossman issued "Green Bonds" to help underwrite local companies retrofitting houses and commercial properties with energy and water efficiency technologies. Municipal land can be leased at a discount to promising local businesses or local developers (this was one of the carrots Sarasota was providing to Xellia Pharmaceuticals). As the local investment revolution matures, municipal pension funds might be directed to local investment funds—or might offer local investment options to municipal employees. Municipal contracts can be targeted at local business, not by awarding across-the-board local preferences (which are hard to defend legally or economically), but by taking into account the tax consequences of various contract bids, which, as we saw from the Local First Arizona study on state procurement in chapter 5, can be enormous. Because nonlocal contractors generate less local tax revenue, a fair and economically rational procurement system would incorporate these different tax levels into "full-cost accounting" of *all* the costs of different bids to the municipality before awarding a contract.

But municipal government is just one of the many local institutions that a smart local economic-development strategy can mobilize. The full range of institutions that can and should be recruited to assist in pollination is suggested by a recent initiative in northern Ohio.

A Laboratory of Applied Hope

David Orr is not your typical professor. In 1979 he founded and ran a 1,500-acre farm in rural Arkansas called the Meadowcreek Center that spawned dozens of projects around environmental restoration, crop diversification, energy conservation, water efficiency, and sustainable living. He added an 18,000-square-foot conference center, two dorms, seven houses, a restored barn, and a wood products shop, and over the following decade brought more than a thousand students to learn, hands on, about sustainable living. (I was one of many guest lecturers he involved in the program.) Orr then was appointed Distinguished Professor of Environmental Studies and Politics at Oberlin College, a highly selective liberal arts school about an hour's drive from Cleveland. He recruited noted architect William McDonough to design the Adam Joseph Lewis Center for Environmental Studies, which, when it opened in January 2000, was one of the greenest buildings in the United States. The Lewis Center remains an architectural marvel, supplying 140 percent of its energy needs and purifying its wastewater on site in a "Living Machine" designed by the eminent biologist, John Todd. It houses large indoor gardens and tilapia-growing ponds, and its surrounding land includes a restored wetland as well as orchards and gardens, all of which facilitate environmental education. Since 2009, Orr has focused his ambitions on what he calls the Oberlin Project, which aims to combine the power of the university and the surrounding city into creating a model sustainable city that is as self-reliant as possible when it comes to basics like food, energy, and water.

"Here's the deal," explains Orr. "The connecting thread for all these projects is to think and act like *systems* are important." By systems, he means the intersection of ecology, economy, and community. "Meadowcreek was designed to be its own curriculum. In effect, we drew a line around the 1,500 acres so that we could transform the agriculture, forests, the woodshop, the sawmill, and the community into an educational system. The Lewis Center at Oberlin was designed to the same end—to see a building as a system instead of a haphazard set of unrelated parts. The intention was to optimize that system, and achieve superior performance at a reduced cost. The next step is to apply that model to a city of ten thousand. That's the Oberlin Project.

"The goal is to see if we can get to carbon neutrality," he continues, "but to do so in a way that builds a prosperous, efficient, and fair economy. We're interested in promoting local business with local ownership, developing local supply chains, and keeping money in the community. We'll get to carbon neutrality by tapping local sunlight and wind. We'll grow a local food economy within, say, a 15-mile radius. In fact, we've got so much vacant land in this town, we could have a small economy just growing fruits and vegetables, and make it year-round with season-extending greenhouses."

The centerpiece of the Oberlin project, already under way, is the redevelopment of a 13-acre "green arts district" with a new, entirely solar-powered and LEED-platinum hotel, conference center, and commercial space, all close to a famous art gallery, a music conservatory, and a performing arts center. The hotel also will contain a culinary school linked to Cuyahoga Community College in Cleveland, featuring public art by Ohio native Maya Lin, who designed the Vietnam Veterans Memorial in Washington. "The Gateway building will be a driver for a more prosperous and sustainable local economy," argues Orr. "It will be a buyer for local foods, a seller of local arts and crafts, and an economic force right smack on Main Street. It provides a model for completely solar-powered and (possibly) zero-discharge buildings, which is exactly the world we are trying to create."

More than $100 million has been committed for the Oberlin Project from the university, the city, foundations, and other supporters, and Orr aims to raise at least $100 million more from every other source of finance he can squeeze, including federal New Markets Tax Credits. When I interviewed Orr, the ground had just been broken for a zero-carbon-emission home, the first of dozens of carbon-neutral housing units planned for low-income residents in the area. "Coming out of this we will be trying to put together a new local housing company."

Orr wants the Oberlin Project to expand its work to the larger deindustrialized heartland that includes Cleveland, Youngstown, Toledo, Detroit, and Flint. "We want to take the buying and investment power of the region, starting with universities and colleges, and shift it to local food, renewable energy, and smart-growth urban redevelopment. We plan to bring in the sports teams. And then the hospital and health facilities. There are three huge ones in Cleveland—the Cleveland Clinic, University Hospitals, and Metro Health Hospital. These are among the biggest pools of buying and investment power in the region."

This is not just a wish list. Orr has just taken a half-time position at the Cleveland Foundation—the biggest philanthropic institution in northern Ohio—to help create an alliance of foundations that will reach out to anchor universities, medical centers, and sports teams. "Our main request to universities is to send their chief financial officers (CFOs), the people who make the investment and purchasing decisions. We want to change the rules for money management, coordinate purchasing and investment, and seek out those opportunities where 2 + 2 equals 22, not just 4. We have assembled a group of high-powered investment advisors to help in the transaction. The goal is to change the addresses on their invoices.

"It's Jane Jacobs 101," explains Orr, his academic roots finally beginning to show. The late Jane Jacobs was a prolific writer whose books expounded many of the principles of local economic development. "If you grow it, make it, process it, or service it locally, then you should buy it locally. Import substitution is a strategy for economic development that keeps money in the local economy longer.

"The beauty of this is that we are not asking anybody to do anything that they don't otherwise do. This is money already in play. All the organizations already buy food, buy energy, and pay for urban infrastructure. All we are asking them to do is three easy things. Extend your payback horizon a little bit further—invest in long-term things like municipal infrastructure. Do this as a collaboration, so that the institutional CFOs in the region begin to talk with one another about their investment and purchasing decisions. And help us identify all those big investment and purchasing opportunities with high synergies."

But why shouldn't Oberlin just focus on educating its students? "Oberlin has a responsibility to lead in this," Orr insists. "We're a typical Rust Belt city with a poverty rate of 27–28 percent. An institution with an endowment of $750 million can and should play a major role—and there are plenty of collateral benefits. The Lewis Center brought Oberlin lots of good publicity, many students interested in ecological design, a remarkable building for faculty and students, and a great deal of new money. The result is a visible and powerful model of education—a laboratory of applied hope." This is the logic that convinced the college to invest $18 million in the Gateway district project.

Despite the presence of considerable public and philanthropic money (more about that in a moment), Orr is thinking like a pollinator. "The Oberlin Project itself is temporary. At the end of five years or so, we go out of business. In the meantime, we catalyze as much activity as we can, and show what economic development should be all about." And when you look under the hood, the Oberlin Project actually will be leaving in place all five species of pollinators:

- For planning and purchasing, there will be the network of anchor institutions—universities, foundations, hospitals, and sports teams—working together.
- For people, Oberlin College has a program on entrepreneurship under-written by the Kauffmann Foundation of Kansas City. (Graduates of the Lewis Center also have gone on to form ten successful environ-mental-service companies.)
- For partnerships, the Oberlin Project is creating collaborative networks of local entrepreneurs around local food, renewable energy, affordable housing, and infrastructure redevelopment.
- For purse, Orr plans to create a $10 million revolving loan fund in the short term and, again, in the long term aims to redirect the portfolios of the region's anchor institutions.

The Oberlin Project reminds us that pollinators can come in unexpected forms. When a major institution begins a local purchasing program, mindfully trying to stimulate other local businesses in the region, it is acting as much as a pollinator as, say, Supportland. Indeed, what could possibly be better for a community than to have its biggest institutions taking on the functions of economic development, and prodding other major businesses in the region to do the same?

Not a Way of Life

A theme running throughout this book is that entrepreneurship is better than charity. If an economic-development program has two paths forward, one of which requires raising $1 million from foundations and the other of which requires the beneficiaries to pay $1 million, I strongly counsel the latter. As I argued in the Introduction, the process of begging the wealthy or public authorities for grants is too unreliable, too limited, and too corrupting. Better to preserve your independence and integrity, and ground your work in a valuable product or service that people in the real world genuinely want. And if you must raise money through charity, be sure to use it, as the Oberlin Project does, to leave self-financing activities in place.

"Welfare should be a second chance," President Bill Clinton used to say, "not a way of life." That should be our view on corporate welfare, too. I appreciate that there are important causes in life for which business models are difficult to imagine or counterproductive. As I write, for example, the Ebola virus is ravaging West Africa with no easy treatment and no proven vaccine. Even if an Ebola vaccine existed, very few Africans could afford it, and that reality has meant that few drug companies have been willing to embark on the long, expensive journey to create a vaccine. Yet the need for Ebola prevention is critical. This is a crystal clear case for government or philanthropic intervention—to create an effective vaccine and to administer it to millions of people halfway around the world that we will never know.

But if you had to identify a category of human activity least in need of special dispensations, it would be economic development. Economic development is about expanding private business and strengthening commercial markets. If it's working, if the benefits truly exceed the costs, then the beneficiary businesses should be able to pay some combination of fees, taxes, royalties, dividends, and ownership shares to compensate the economic developers for the costs of the programs. Pollinator models should be the norm of economic development, not the exception.

Wait a minute—what about the disadvantaged? Doesn't economic development for poor communities, low-income individuals, discriminated-against women and minorities, and long pilloried immigrants justify charitable intervention? Isn't this a legitimate expenditure for federal grant programs like New Markets Tax Credits and community-development financial institutions?

I'm sympathetic to this argument, but I also worry that it really just perpetuates discredited stereotypes. For years, mainstream banks refused to provide loans for the poor because they were supposedly "unbankable." But then the Grameen Bank in Bangladesh proved that lending to low-income women who were microentrepreneurs, fortified by peer support circles, could generate a repayment rate of about 97 percent. My own experiences working in inner-city and rural communities have reinforced my conviction that adversity doesn't thwart entrepreneurship, it deepens it. There may be a role for targeted programs to educate the poor about how to approach financial institutions and to educate financial institutions about working with the poor—sure, let foundations pay for some of those programs—but wholesale assumptions that the poor cannot run successful businesses are repulsive.

Even if you disagree with me on this fine point, remember that assistance to the poor is not what TINA is about. That $80 billion in state and local incentives is going to the most powerful businesses in the world, not the weakest. And a compelling reason to insist that we not waste government or foundation money on corporate welfare is so that we can use our limited philanthropic dollars for those causes for which business models won't work. Every dollar not put into an economic-development boondoggle is a dollar that can be used for that elusive Ebola vaccine—or anything else.

Acting Globally

Pollinator businesses have as much to offer internationally as they do domestically. Arguments about international development today often get bogged down in dead-end debates about what's better for impoverished nations—aid or trade. The traditional model of international aid, everything from disaster relief led by the Red Cross to famine relief by Save the Children, seeks to mobilize immediate assistance in the form of food, shelter, clothing, and medicine. Critics recite the platitude—don't feed a hungry man a fish, give him a fishing pole and teach him how to fish. And the best way to do so, many then argue, is to open up international trade so that wealthy countries of the North can help struggling fishermen in the South develop their fishing businesses.

Bill Drayton, the founder of Ashoka, a nonprofit that supports social entrepreneurs worldwide, offers a third viewpoint: "Social entrepreneurs are not content just to give a fish or teach how to fish. They will not rest until they have revolutionized the fishing industry."[76] Pollinator businesses share this perspective. Here's how pollinators might reframe the old fishing saw:

- Let's spread planning pollinators to improve the efficiency of fishing businesses, and to develop in fishing communities more livable, more green neighborhoods.
- Let's spread people pollinators to create more effective, more innovative fisherman, and ensure that more of their value-added processing occurs locally.
- Let's spread partner pollinators so that fishermen in a community can operate more competitively through joint marketing, joint production, and joint procurement.
- Let's spread purchasing pollinators so that more people who live in the fishermen's community can buy more of the local fish.
- Let's spread purse pollinators so that fishermen can own their own boats and equipment and perhaps own their own processing plants through a cooperative or partnership.
- Let's spread public policies that ensure that multinational fishing conglomerates no longer enjoy preferential treatment over the local fishermen.

As is the case domestically, an approach to international development that emphasizes pollinator businesses should increase impact and reduce cost. The role of international developers increasingly becomes studying, convening, replicating, and propagating pollinators globally. This is happening already, below the radar of most of the development community. Several years ago, with support from the Kellogg and Gates Foundations, I collaborated with the Wallace Center for Sustainable Agriculture (an arm of Winrock International) to study twenty-four great local food businesses in a dozen countries. The resulting study, "Community Food Enterprise," showed that local food movements were thriving in six of the seven continents, and that these two dozen businesses were all using similar techniques for beating their global competitors. But the most surprising finding was that almost all the businesses spontaneously were networking and collaborating with businesses worldwide. Farmer cooperatives in Mississippi were visiting and sharing ideas with farmer cooperatives in Zambia. Fair trade producers of chocolate in Africa or coffee in Latin America were working alongside fair trade distributors in the United States and Europe. Two socially minded restaurants, Cabbages and Condoms in Bangkok and the White Dog Café in Philadelphia, bonded themselves together as "sister restaurants." No one organized these relationships, top-down. They were initiated by the managers of each enterprise who understood that they could improve their own competitiveness by studying and partnering with similar businesses abroad.

Following this logic, one project that I've started to design with the Schumacher Center for New Economics is called "Locapedia," an open-source, Internet-based descendent of Wikipedia. The idea is to compile basic knowledge from grassroots contributors about local businesses in every sector of the economy. This could then inform and empower entrepreneurs worldwide. If I wanted to start a small-scale poultry processing plant, I could look up a category like "Manufacturing-Food-Chicken," and read about ten examples of successful small-scale poultry processors worldwide. I then could contact the CEOs of these ten companies for further details. Perhaps we could even create a formal network of chicken producers to jointly procure technology or market their products under a unified brand.

Why would any local business be willing to reveal its secrets to its competitors through an open database on the Internet? The answer is that local business entrepreneurs have a fundamentally different mindset than global entrepreneurs. They are seeking not to build global empires but to succeed in their own regional niche. Like pollinators, they see value in supporting other local businesses in other communities.

By facilitating networks in every business sector, Locapedia could naturally facilitate relationships among pollinator businesses, too. Business accelerators would communicate regularly, as would public market managers, local delivery companies, local investment fund pioneers, and every other pollinator model. Economic developers in any place eager to create this or that pollinator could review these options and see which ones best suit their community. And slowly, gradually, and inexorably communities around the world equipped with these pollinators would see their local businesses grow, their economies diversify, and their wealth expand.

The reinvention of economic development cannot solve all the world's problems. But every community that invests in pollinator businesses can reasonably expect more jobs, income, and prosperity, which provides a strong foundation for thousands of other kinds of initiatives in health, education, housing, energy—you name it.

Just as importantly, a pollinator approach to economic development is empowering. No longer does a community need to look to a distant corporation's decision about where to locate a factory or a distant bureaucrat's decision about where to spend public money. Nor does it need to cloak its initiatives in secrecy. Pollinators invite the participation of every local business, every local consumer, and every local investor, and it's all out in the open.

Perhaps what excites me most about the pollinator approach to economic development is how it scrambles old political divisions and opens space for new kinds of community action. It provides conservatives with an approach that's market-driven, entrepreneurial, business-oriented, and highly decentralized, and progressives with proven tools that expand participation, shrink poverty, and promote diversity.

In chapter 6, I suggested that the ultimate goal of purse pollinators was to end investment apartheid, which separates 99 percent of the public ("unaccredited" investors) from the 99 percent of firms that are locally owned. The current TINA obsession with "attract and retain" amounts to economic apartheid; it guarantees that less than 1 percent of the world's elite is showered with local subsidies, while the 99 percent foots the bill and waits for the elusive benefits. Populists of all political stripes can agree that the walls holding up this apartheid regime should be torn down. The emergence of the pollinator models outlined in this book suggests how wrong TINA is and how much more is possible. "It always seems impossible," Nelson Mandela once said about ending apartheid in South Africa, "until it's done." Now that we know that every kind of pollinator can succeed somewhere, it's time to help all of them flourish everywhere. The rest is up to you.

APPENDIX

28 Models of Pollinator Enterprises

A "pollinator" is a self-financing enterprise committed to boosting local business. Some pollinators are for-profit businesses, some are nonprofits, but all allow a community to undertake one or more of five key economic-development functions—planning, purchasing, people, partnerships, and purse—with far greater efficacy and at a substantially lower cost than typical, taxpayer-funded programs. All of the following models deploy business frameworks that ultimately aim to avoid dependency on government grants or charitable contributions. Each is described in detail in the preceding chapters, but outlined here for quick reference.

Planning Pollinators

Definition: Planning means both "spatial" planning undertaken by urban planners and "business" planning undertaken by consultants.

Key Challenge: What are the most plausible opportunities for new or expanded local businesses to meet local needs?

Development Tools. The Business Alliance for Local Living Economies (BALLE) has developed a tool that helps communities easily measure "economic leakage"—the dollars currently leaving a community—to assess opportunities for more jobs and income from new or expanded local businesses. *www.michaelhshuman.com*

Business Efficiency. The Main Street Genome Project analyzes data from local businesses to help them identify weak spots and remedy them by, for example, getting better prices from suppliers and sharing the savings with clients. *www.mainstreetgenome.com*

Green Design. Bazzani Associates brings old buildings back to life with green designs, and has revitalized several neighborhoods in Grand Rapids, Michigan. *www.bazzani.com*

Placemaking. The Village Well, based in Melbourne, is hired by public and private property owners to help stakeholders set in motion a plan to revitalize a place with many new kinds of work and play. *www.villagewell.org*

Purchasing Pollinators

Definition: Purchasing refers to buying by nearby consumers, businesses, and government agencies.

Key Challenge: How can the community help its businesses flourish with concerted buy-local or "Local First" efforts?

Coupon Books. The Chinook Book, active in a half dozen cities, enables consumers to buy a book of coupons worth thousands of dollars of savings at local businesses. *www.chinookbook.net*

Local Business Magazines. Edible Communities is a magazine, currently licensed in 85 cities across North America, that raises consumer awareness of local farmers and local food businesses and is underwritten primarily by local advertising. *www.ediblecommunities.com*

Local Web Marketplaces. ShopCity licenses a web platform to three dozen American and Canadian cities that draws consumers to great local goods and services. *www.shopcity.com*

Local Debit Cards. Bernal Bucks in San Francisco has partnered with its local credit union to issue a debit card that rewards local business purchases. *www.bernalbucks.org*

Local Gift Cards. Tucson Originals provides foodies an easy "stocking stuffer" to buy for friends and relatives that ultimately can be redeemed at local restaurants. *www.tucsonoriginals.instagift.com*

Local Loyalty Cards. Supportland has 80,000 users in Portland, Oregon, who receive gifts and discounts for loyally making purchases at local stores and service providers. *www.supportland.com*

People Pollinators

Definition: People are the human factor in enterprise development, including entrepreneurs, employees, and economic developers.

Key Challenge: How can existing and new generations be trained for new and expanding local business opportunities?

Enterprise Facilitators. The Sirolli Institute, based in Sacramento, has helped 300 communities worldwide deploy "enterprise facilitators" that transform local entrepreneurs with great ideas into successful businesspeople. *www.sirolli.com*

Local Economic Developer Training. Simon Fraser University in Vancouver runs a successful "adult education" course that teaches development professionals how to do *local* economic development. *www.sfu.ca/cscd /professional-programs/community-economic-development.html*

Youth Entrepreneurship Schools. Fundación Paraguaya now runs three high schools in Paraguay that pay all their expenses through the revenues generated by student-run enterprises, and is working with another organization based in the United Kingdom, Teach a Man to Fish, to spread this model worldwide. *www.teachamantofish.org.uk*

Short Entrepreneurship Courses. ZingTrain, part of the Zingerman's Community of Businesses in Ann Arbor, Michigan, provides training through two- or three-day courses to more than one thousand entrepreneurs each year. *www.zingtrain.com*

Maker Spaces. Maker Works, also in Ann Arbor, educates its members on how to use advanced industrial tools to make cutting-edge products. *www.maker-works.com*

Co-Working Spaces. The Impact Hub represents a worldwide network of 63 spaces where social entrepreneurs can work and cross-pollinate shoulder-to-shoulder with like-minded people. *www.impacthub.net*

Incubators. The Northwest Regional Planning Commission in rural Wisconsin runs a network of ten small business incubators over an area of 11,000 square miles, with "circuit riders" who move from site to site and provide various forms of technical assistance. *www.nwrpc.com*

Accelerators. Each year the Seattle-based Fledge leads three cohorts of promising local entrepreneurs through intensive trainings, and pays for its work through modest royalty payments from its graduates. *www.fledge.co*

Partnership Pollinators

Definition: Partnerships means collaborations of, by, and for local businesses.

Key Challenge: How can local businesses improve their competitiveness by working together as a team?

Joint Support. Local First Arizona has grown to be the largest BALLE network in the United States (with 2,600 businesses) by providing members with technical assistance, peer support, and effective buy-local campaigns. *www.localfirstaz.com*

Joint Advertising. The Calgary-based organization REAP (standing for Respect the Earth and All People) mobilizes consumers to local ethical businesses through ads and an online directory and finances its work by positioning itself as a one-stop marketing firm for its 120 business members. *www.reapcalgary.com*

Joint Purchasing. Tucson Originals (noted above) negotiates discounts from "preferred" local suppliers that all its food-business members can enjoy.

Joint Delivery. Small Potatoes Urban Delivery directly delivers the products from small farmers and local food processors to locavore households in six metro areas in North America. *www.spud.com*

Joint Selling. The Reading Terminal Market is one of a growing number of permanent "public markets" that are effectively shopping malls for local food providers, local artisans, and other local businesses. *www.readingterminalmarket.org*

Purse Pollinators

Definition: Purse means capital for local business, including debt and equity, short- and long-term, in small and large amounts.

Key Challenge: How can local capital be mobilized to finance new or expanding local businesses?

Local Banking. Vancity is a pioneering locally owned credit union that serves 500,000 members in metro Vancouver and has staff who support 38,000 local business members with credit, partnerships, and technical assistance. *www.vancity.com*

Local Securities Creation. Cutting Edge Capital, based in Oakland, teaches local small businesses how to jump through the legal hoops necessary to mobilize investment from non-wealthy, "retail" investors in their communities. *www.cuttingedgecapital.com*

Local Securities Trading. Mission Markets is one of a growing number of companies that licenses to communities trading platforms that connect local businesses with local investors. *www.missionmarkets.com*

Local Investment Funds. FarmWorks is one of sixty investment funds that Nova Scotia permits grassroots groups to organize and through which locals can reinvest tax-deferred retirement savings into local food enterprises. *www.farmworks.ca*

Local Prepurchasing. Credibles, based in San Francisco, provides a platform for local food businesses to raise capital from their customers—without legal paperwork—through preselling. *www.credibles.co*

Notes

1. Jenna Johnson, "'House of Cards' Threatens to Leave If Maryland Comes Up Short on Tax Credits," *The Washington Post*, February 20, 2014.
2. Joseph Henchman, "Kevin Spacey at Annapolis Bar Tonight to Lobby Legislators for Subsidies," Tax Foundation Blog, March 21, 2014, www.taxfoundation.org.
3. Liz Malm, "Maryland Film Tax Credits: A House of Cards," Tax Foundation Blog, February 21, 2014, www.taxfoundation.org.
4. Stephanie Condon, "'House of Cards' Gets More Tax Credits to Keep Filming in Maryland," *CBS News*, April 28, 2014.
5. Howard Gleckman, "Oscar Nominees Cash In on State Tax Subsidies," Forbes Blog, January 21, 2014.
6. Johnson, "'House of Cards'."
7. Jenna Johnson, "How Did 'House of Cards' Get Millions in Maryland Tax Credits?" *The Washington Post*, February 21, 2014.
8. Transcript for *This American Life*, Show #435, "How to Create a Job," originally aired May 13, 2011.
9. Foreign companies are more likely than domestic companies to buy inputs from outside the United States (which lowers the economic-development benefits for Americans), and their corporate leaders, many thousands of miles away, are less likely to let their operational decisions be influenced by pesky U.S. local officials.
10. Scholars like David Harvey have argued that this competition helps global companies achieve "spatial efficiencies," and there's no doubt that globe-trotting companies are moving because they are finding comparative advantages in wages, markets, workforce, productivity, and so on. But what's good for General Motors is not necessarily what's good for the United States. Moreover, the critique here is not of companies

relocating—it's of companies that insist on having the public pay for their relocations. Why is helping a small number of already well-off companies become more productive worthy of public subsidies, when it effectively disadvantages other companies from becoming more productive?

11. Robert Tannenwald, "State Film Subsidies: Not Much Bang for Too Many Bucks," Center for Budget and Policy Priorities, updated version, December 9, 2010, p. 1.

12. Ibid., 2.

13. Ibid., 8.

14. Gleckman, "Oscar Nominees Cash In," citing a 2012 study by the Louisiana Budget Project.

15. What I mean by "entrepreneurship" here is the ability to create private enterprise in a free market. By a broader definition of the term, of course, the hustling and begging in economic development are certainly "entrepreneurial" as well.

16. Christina Romer, "What Do We Know About the Effects of Fiscal Policy: Separating Evidence from Ideology," Speech to Hamilton College, November 7, 2011.

17. Approximately fourteen million Americans were unemployed in 2008–2009. An army of Lou Steins could have gotten them back to work for $7 billion. A counterargument in defense of at least the public works portions of the stimulus package is that they bestowed on the US public valuable benefits besides jobs—namely roads, bridges, airports, and the like that Uncle Sam would have had to buy sooner or later anyway. In other words, targeting "public goods" rather than private companies might be an inherently better kind of economic development. But if that's the case, then the stimulus package was sold to the American public under false pretenses. What the public wanted, and needed, during the financial crisis was jobs—not more public infrastructure.

18. It's worth noting, however, that this website, and the Dun & Bradstreet data it uses, defines "local" as a business with a headquarters within the same state.

19. The data in this paragraph come from Heidi Pickman and Claudia Viek, "Do-It-Yourself Economic Growth," *Economic Development Journal* 13, no. 1 (2014): 19–26.

20. Ibid., 21.

21. Michael H. Shuman, *The Small-Mart Revolution: How Local Businesses Are Beating the Global Competition* (San Francisco: Berrett-Koehler, 2006), 40–42.

22. Pillowtex itself also was the victim of poor management and a huge debt caused by a series of leveraged buyouts. It filed for Chapter 7 bankruptcy protection in 2003.

23. See, e.g., Timothy Bartik, "Who Benefits from Local Job Growth, Migrants or the Original Residents?" *Regional Studies*, 27, no. 4 (1993), pp. 297–311.

24. Shuman, *The Small-Mart Revolution*, pp. 47–48.

25. Ann Markusen and Katherine Ness, *Reining In the Competition for Capital* (Kalamazoo, MI: W.E. Upjohn Institute for Employment Research, 2007).

26. Ibid., 1.

27. Michael Greenstone and Enrico Moretti, "Bidding for Industrial Plants: Does Winning a 'Million Dollar Plant' Increase Welfare?," NBER Working Paper 9844, National Bureau of Economic Research, 2003.

28. Peter Fisher, "The Fiscal Consequences of Competition for Capital," in Markusen and Ness, *Reining In the Competition*, 62–65.

29. Some siting decisions, of course, are more flexible than others. If a film can be made in any downtown setting, every state has a shot at the deal. In reality, however, even films must comport with a story line that makes some places more plausible than others. No subsidy level from New York City will be compelling to a production company making a Western.

30. Markusen and Ness, *Reining In the Competition*, 3.

31. Ibid., 27.

32. Timothy Bartik, "Solving the Problems of Economic Development Incentives," in Markusen and Ness, *Reining In the Competition*, 114.

33. Robert B. Reich, *The Wealth of Nations* (New York: Vintage, 1991).

34. A striking example of this can be found in a study of the Environmental Protection Agency that found that the average amount of toxins released by absentee-owned facilities or those with out-of-state headquarters is nearly three times more than plants with in-state headquarters and fifteen times more than single-location enterprises. Don Grant, et al., "Are Subsidiaries More Prone to Pollute?," *Social Science Quarterly*, 84, no. 1 (2003), pp. 162-73.

35. See, for example, Michael H. Shuman, *Local Dollars, Local Sense: How to Shift Your Money from Wall Street to Main Street and Achieve Real Prosperity* (White River Junction, VT: Chelsea Green, 2012), 17–25. Also see Stacy Mitchell, *The Big Box Swindle: The True Cost of Mega-Retailers and the Fight for America's Independent Businesses* (Boston: Beacon Press, 2006).

36. Ibid.

37. Edward L. Glaeser and William R. Kerr, "The Secret to Job Growth: Think Small," *Harvard Business Review*, July-August 2010.

38. Anil Rupesingha, "Locally Owned: Do Local Business Ownership and Size Matter for Local Economic Well-Being?," monograph, August 2013. For further empirical support on this point, see David A. Fleming and Stephan J. Goetz,"Does Local Firm Ownership Matter," *Economic Development Quarterly*, August 2011, pp. 277-81.

39. Richard Florida, *The Rise of the Creative Class* (New York: Basic Books, 2002).

40. Amartya Sen, *Development as Freedom* (New York: Anchor Books, 1999).

41. Robert Putnam, *Bowling Alone: The Collapse and Revival of American Community* (New York: Touchstone, 2001).

42. Statistics Canada, "Firm Dynamics: Variation in Profitability Across Canadian Firms of Different Sizes, 2000–2009," Publication 11-622-M, No. 26.

43. Jane Jacobs, *Systems of Survival* (New York: Vintage, 1994).

44. Michael H. Shuman and Kate Poole, "Growing Local Living Economies: A Grassroots Approach to Economic Development" (BALLE, 2012), available at www.michaelhshuman.com.

45. See, for example, the SBA Office of Advocacy, "Frequently Asked Questions," March 2014, www.sba.gov/sites/default/files/advocacy/FAQ _March_2014_0.pdf.

46. The savings are split until the customer decides to stop purchasing from Main Street Genome's network vendors. "That's part of our secret sauce," explains Koester, "Typically, when a restarant switches to a new vendor, it initially gets good prices, but then those prices gradually creep up. Our solution helps make sure that those savings are locked in."

47. A recent issue of United Airlines' monthly magazine for travelers agrees: "In Melbourne, this sense of wonder is best represented by the city's apparently endless maze of alleys (or laneways), which would be seamy and uninviting were they not bursting with art, eateries, retailers and a theatrical lust for life." Jacqueline Detwiler, "Three Perfect Days: Melbourne," *Hemispheres*, October 2014, p. 78.

48. F. A. Hayek, *The Road to Serfdom* (Chicago: University of Chicago Press, 1947).

49. Matt Cunningham and Dan Houston, "Independent BC: Small Business and the British Columbia Economy," February 2013 (available from Civic Economics in Austin, Texas).

50. American Booksellers Association and Civic Economics, "The Indie City Index 2011: Executive Summary," American Booksellers Association and Civic Economics, 2011, www.independentwestand.org/wp-content/uploads /Indie_City_Index.pdf.

51. "2014 Ten Best Downtowns: 8 Bellingham, WA" Livability Blog, March 17, 2014, livability.com/best-places/top-10/ downtowns/10-best-downtowns/2014/bellingham.

52. Officially, the state has designated the Port of Bellingham as the "Associate Development Organization."

53. In full disclosure, I spent one day working on contract for Groupon to help them improve their offerings to locally owned businesses.

54. A few regions put a cover price on the magazine.

55. E. F. Schumacher, *Small Is Beautiful: Economics As If People Mattered* (New York: Harper & Row, 1973), 53.

56. Ibid., 54–55.

57. Bridget Lair and Dinah Adkins, *Best Practices in Rural Business Incubation: Successful Programs in Small Communities* (Athens, OH: National Business Incubation Association, 2013), 73.

58. Ernesto Sirolli, *Ripples from the Zambezi: Passion, Entrepreneurship, and the Rebirth of Local Economies* (Gabriola Island, BC: New Society, 1999), 43.

59. Ibid., 3.

60. Ibid., 8.

61. Ibid., 9.

62. Ibid., 11.

63. Ibid., 27.

64. Thanks to Mary Liz Keller, the US representative of Fundación Paraguaya, for providing helpful updates about the spread of this work in recent years.

65. Although REAP is a nonprofit, it is not a registered charity that can receive tax-deductible donations.

66. Sometimes "producer cooperatives" that primarily undertake bulk purchasing are called "purchasing cooperatives."

67. Edward O. Wilson, *The Social Conquest of Earth* (New York: Liveright, 2013).

68. Shuman, *Local Dollars, Local Sense.*

69. Depending on one's perspective, these fees are absolutely necessary to fully apprise unaccredited investors of the risks they are assuming, or they are unnecessarily enriching securities attorneys with frivolous paperwork that no unaccredited investor ever seriously reads.

70. Jenny Kassan, whom we will meet shortly, suggests that even investment clubs could be viable businesses, as long as the paid principal serves as an administrator rather than a decision-maker.

71. Well-designed illiquid securities nevertheless can provide assured streams of value. Bonds and loans, for example, can provide a steady stream of payments to the security holder. Preferred stock might guarantee an annual dividend.

72. Louise Story, "As Companies Seek Tax Deals, Governments Pay High Price," *The New York Times*, December 1, 2012.

73. *The New York Times* agrees: "The cost of the awards is certainly far higher. A full accounting, *The Times* discovered, is not possible because the incentives are granted by thousands of government agencies and officials, and many do not know the value of all their awards. Nor do they know if the money was worth it because they rarely track how many jobs are created. Even where officials do track incentives, they acknowledge that it is impossible to know whether the jobs would have been created without the aid." Ibid.

74. Josh Salman, "$137 Million Deal Got Away," *Herald-Tribune*, October 28, 2014, 1A.

75. Ibid., 4A.

76. The quote appears at www.ashoka.org/node/4047.

Index

ABOUT THE AUTHOR

MICHAEL H. SHUMAN is an economist, attorney, author, and entrepreneur, and a globally recognized expert on community economics. He is one of the architects of the crowdfunding JOBS Act signed into law by President Obama in April 2012. He's a fellow at Cutting Edge Capital and Post Carbon Institute and a founding board member of the Business Alliance for Local Living Economies (BALLE). He teaches economic development at Simon Fraser University in Vancouver. He has authored or coauthored nine books, including *Local Dollars, Local Sense; The Small Mart Revolution;* and *Going Local.* Shuman has performed leakage analyses and related economic-development planning in more than ten states and has analyzed opportunities for food localization for several states, cities, counties, and regions across the nation. He has given an average of more than one invited talk per week, mostly to local governments and universities, for thirty years—in forty-seven states and eight countries. He has appeared on numerous television and radio shows, such as *The NewsHour with Jim Lehrer* and NPR's *Talk of the Nation* and *All Things Considered*, and has written nearly one hundred articles for such periodicals as *The New York Times, The Washington Post, The Nation, The Weekly Standard, Foreign Policy, Parade Magazine,* and *The Chronicle of Philanthropy.* Previously, he was a W.K. Kellogg National Leadership fellow. He is also a member of both the State Bar of California and the District of Columbia Bar, and he lives in Silver Spring, Maryland, with his two children.

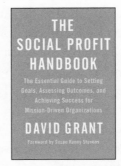